DR ANNIE I

MBBS MRC

Opening the door
to the worlds

A handbook for the future

An introduction to the Basidian
And through their words,
To the wisdom and knowledge of the universe

BASIDIAN
PUBLISHERS

First published in Great Britain in 2009
by Basidian Limited

A CIP Catalogue of this book is available from
the British Library

ISBN 978-0-9562290-0-7

Cover Picture: NASA photo – courtesy SpaceImages.
Companion website: www.cosmicdoc.com

Cover design and typeset by Chandler Book Design,
www.chandlerbookdesign.co.uk

Printed in Great Britain by the
MPG Books Group, Bodmin and King's Lynn

This book is printed on paper responsibly
manufactured from sustainable forestry.

© **Mixed Sources**

Product group from well-managed
forests, controlled sources and
recycled wood or fiber
www.fsc.org Cert no. TT-COC-002303
© 1996 Forest Stewardship Council

FSC

C o n t e n t s

Part 5. The Evolution and Development of the Soul

For Gus, with love, for he is the future

And also for Dorothy, with love and gratitude,
for without her, it would not
have been possible

*"Do this from your heart.
For your heart is the voice of your soul.
And your soul is my friend."*

Basidian

Foreword

Most of the early information in this book has come from conversation with the spirits through the medium, which I have transcribed from recordings. Latterly, more has come directly to me and I have written down what they said. The language and grammar of the spirits are considerably more elegant than mine. I have confirmed the subjects and the more startling pronouncements in conversation with them, through the medium. Although the spirits are operating as a collective, there are different authors of these pieces and the flavour of their transmissions is different, as are the subjects. The transmissions about the nature of the universe and the coming Earth changes come from Uncle Theo. My father sent the ones about the nature of love and the problems of emotion. Many of these were personal to me, but are included because I'm far from unique. The simple pieces of practical advice come astonishingly from the Venusians, whose spokesman is "Orta," which means "the speaker." They commented, sadly, that they can only send me very simple information because my scientific knowledge is so poor. They are right in that! Some of the loveliest messages have not been verbal at all. The albatross that takes me flying seldom says anything, but allows me to experience the world through his senses. He is physically a solitary creature, so most of his communication is telepathic, and he has retained the ability to see past, present and future.

The information that appears as conversation came as speech via the medium, and the blocks initialled in the script (𝓑.) in writing, directly to me.

B. *(or 𝓑.) Indicates the Basidian collective.*
T. *Is Uncle Theo.*
P. *Is my father.*
A. *Is me.*

Many of the transmissions have been reduced in length, but I have tried to keep the words as they were given, where possible.

The section on the Basidian healing methods is only intended as an introduction. There will be an operator's manual available for those who need it as an adjunct to their study.

The sections on The Earth and its Turbulence, The Nature of the Universe and The Evolution and Development of the Soul were as much a surprise to me as they may be to you. What I have written is what the spirits told me and much of it cannot yet be proven.

This information does not come from me, but through me. I am not as wise as this. Much of this information was new to me, although some has been around for years. Man's effect on the environment was not one of my preoccupations. Neither was radiating peace and love my personality style. I was a combative little mixer with a low flash-point! The peace I now feel may have always been within me, but it was extremely well hidden!

Be that as it may, I offer it to you as it was offered to me – with love.

Annie Paxton, 2009.

Part One

A Little About Me

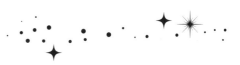

I

How I got from there to here

"Oh, I have slipped the surly bonds of earth
And danced the skies on laughter-silvered wings
Sunward I've climbed and joined the tumbling mirth
Of sunsplit clouds – and done a hundred things
You have not dreamed of – wheeled and soared and swung
High in the sunlit silence"

Magee

B. "I have great power here. I have great power not just of my making – there is great power for you to anchor. This we agreed; we agreed that you would be the anchor for me for this power. The power to heal, to heal the mind.

You have within your grasp now, and with your background knowledge, the understanding of the connection of the energy between the cells and how the energy between the cells and the cells make up the body. That energy can be changed. This you will be working with. This you will be teaching. This we will teach through you. We will be the power, as you are our instrument – teamwork.

Where there is disease within a body, it is created in the energy between the cells. The energy between the cells can be changed. It is possible to reverse, it is possible to bring wellbeing back to the cells, so that they regenerate in a healthy way... You have the healing power, to heal this..."

This was the Basidian's first message to me, on 29th April 2003, through the medium Dorothy Chitty. I had enlisted her help, because I was worried that I was failing to hear my intuitive prompting. Ten minutes into the reading, she said that she was being taken over by a powerful energy and went into trance. The information and instructions that followed left me open mouthed.

The message was from the Basidian, who are a highly developed, highly specialised group of teachers from Sirius. Sirius is the star system of healing and this was what they were teaching. They said that they were giving me a new system of medicine that was effected through manipulation of energy alone. All healers work in this way, but this, they said, was from a higher level of vibration and was therefore more powerful.

I did not immediately understand the enormous significance of this transmission, but over the next few years, I gradually found that my life was changed. There is much that I still do not comprehend, but the journey they have taken me on since then has been the most rewarding, fulfilling and fascinating part of my life so far. At the time that I received this message, I had been completely retired from the NHS for two years and partially retired for thirteen.

Back to the beginning.

After medical school and a certain amount of casting about for direction, the choices I made found me training to be a haematologist. I enjoyed all my medical training, but being a consultant was another thing altogether. Somewhere along my medical journey, I got lost. I was clever, but immature, and during my early years as a consultant, I started to unravel. I disliked my job and my life had no meaning, but I hid that from myself by working too hard and drinking too much. Having always worked to the point of exhaustion, or until opening time, I had no existence outside my work and this led to a series of episodes of depression, laced liberally with anxiety, during which I barely functioned.

I used to call the feeling the "anxious aching emptiness" and it wasn't until very much later that I realised this feeling was the truth about my life, which I was no longer able to hide from myself. I had reacted to the various hurts along the way by shutting down the part that gave me pain, until there was very little of me still operating. It took four of these episodes before I worked out what the problem was, because I was programmed to endure but not to change.

I left my teaching hospital consultant job and moved out of London, but the post I took next bored me almost to extinction. I was used to having bright intelligent minds around me at work, but here I was single-handed and saw few people during the day. After three years of this I was almost suicidal with boredom and frustration and usually drunk by 9 pm. However, the universe has its own ways of resolving problems...

Although my intuitive faculty had been partially crushed by my education, I had throughout my adult life been intermittently aware of a presence standing behind one shoulder. This presence would comment "I wouldn't do that if I were you," as I contemplated some course of medical action. Sometimes he was ruder than that: "Take the pulse, you bloody fool." I always listened to this voice and he was always right. There has been many a patient with chest pain of doubtful cause that I have admitted from Casualty on his advice. Inevitably, the next few hours brought an event that made me very grateful that I had. Presumably he intervened when my decisions were about to interfere with another soul's life path.

This voice started when I was a medical student and lasted throughout my career. The last time the presence spoke to me at work, it was so plain that I turned towards him and answered out loud. Fortunately, although I was in a hospital corridor, I was alone at the time! You don't actually get locked up any more, but the medical profession still holds pretty definite views on people with inner voices! The information on that occasion was as accurate and useful as usual and the patient survived against the odds.

Once I realised that my drinking was out of control, in great anguish, I finally took a grip on myself and stopped. On the same day, I gave up using the nicotine chewing gum that had replaced the cigarettes. It was an interesting week!

The night before I stopped, the presence spoke again: "You will do this and you will get through and you will be fine" was what he said. I was so accustomed to this voice giving good advice that I was much comforted and, indeed, that is exactly what happened.

The gradual reawakening of my brain and reconnection to life was wonderful and extraordinary and changed everything. I started questioning all my opinions and changing everything about my life that I didn't like, starting with clothes, hairstyle and car and progressing to my career. With the loss of my tranquillising props, I went up in a sheet of blue flame every time anyone spoke to me, so my colleagues largely left me alone, and I was able to focus on myself for the first time in my adult life. Although the job I was doing was dull, it was well within my capabilities, so I had both mental and physical freedom.

After a few years, I could see where I had gone wrong but not why, so I enlisted professional help – and discovered the problem had its roots in my relationship with my mother! I found it most unwelcome to be so predictable! But there it was, waiting to be dealt with, a process that bored me almost as much as it must have bored the analyst! However, the process was successful enough for me to take back my power and start thinking how I might want to live my life.

(Ironically, the mother in question, who was also a doctor, would have absolutely loved the professional life that I could no longer see the point of. At the time that she studied medicine, training to be a hospital specialist required a private income, and this she did not have.)

The kick in the pants from the universe to help me give up my career came from the usual unexpected direction and I grabbed it with both hands in case it ran away. The mechanisms regulating the supply of doctors have no fine controls and there are always far too many or far too few. At this time, there were far too many fully trained specialists for the number of consultant jobs available, and the older and stroppier among us were invited to apply for early retirement. They didn't have to ask me more than once, but since I was only forty-nine, the universe had to supply a little extra to oil the wheels!

When we replaced our laboratory electronic cell counter, we also bought a computer package to help us run the laboratory. For this, we used largely NHS money, but we didn't actually tell anybody what we were doing. I'm not sure that anybody would ever have noticed if I hadn't asked for a new phone line for the modem link. If I thought at all about the hospital administration, it was to think that this was none of their business! Their sense of outrage reached higher and higher levels until I was formally ticked off at head office, in the company of a nice lady from the Medical Defence Union and a new red jacket.

Since the phone line wasn't allowed until after the disciplining and no-one was in any hurry to undertake that, I was in the habit of phoning the senior administrator once a week, implying that it was pitiful that he couldn't even organise a ticking off. When I asked him a little later if my name could go on the early retirement list, he could hardly contain his joy! Because of my age, he would never have allowed this if I hadn't been a severe embarrassment, mostly because nobody had noticed what we were doing!

Looking back, it is just as well they let me go. By that time, I was taking back all the unpaid overtime that I had done in my youth, and I could scarcely get myself to go into the hospital in the morning, I hated it so much. Every day in the car park, I turned into an unpleasant short-tempered bitch on arrival, and back into me on my way home. My technicians said my tongue stunned at a hundred paces and was lethal at fifty! I said that the only people in the department with any balls were me and my secretary! Time to go, I think! So at the age of fifty, I retired into my garden with my pension and a pile of books and there I stayed all summer.

Almost the last significant event of my career happened in Outpatients about six months before I left. At my clinic, I regularly saw an elderly man with myelofibrosis. This is an untreatable chronic condition in which the bone marrow (which makes the blood cells) gradually silts up, leaving less and less room for blood-forming tissues. The spleen and liver also enlarge and become heavy and uncomfortable. This poor man felt unwell and tired all the time and there was very little I could do for him except allow him to whinge, which he did regularly every couple of months.

Over the course of my last six months, I noticed that the whingeing had gradually stopped and he was becoming almost cheerful. His physical condition was not changed. Finally, I asked him what had happened and he shuffled his feet and looked at the floor and admitted that he had been seeing a healer who had made him feel much more comfortable. I was rather shocked. This healer had done what I could not do. She did not alter his physical condition, but she had altered how he felt and the benefits to him had been enormous. It was this episode that informed the choice of books I took into my garden and opened a door for me to something new.

For the next ten years, I went on a journey through complementary medicine and learnt a number of new languages. The Latin-based jargon of the medical world has always annoyed the rest, but at least we all speak the same language. In the complementary world, I discovered that everyone's language is different. After I had been unable to understand the first healer that I talked with, I went to healer school. This proved enormously illuminating, but I remained unable to understand this healer, because she spoke her own private language! In this world, language was not always a method of communication!

Many of the people operating in these fields used only their right brains and were unable to explain in words what they were doing. Nevertheless, I learnt much along the way. In particular, I learnt what sort of conditions and patients most benefited from these approaches. It was the chronic sick, for whom orthodox medicine could offer very little, who obtained the most relief. Part of the effect could be explained by the time and care that they received from the practitioners, but it was more than that.

The other group that did well were those with acute minor conditions such as colds, bee stings and headaches. These would have got better anyway, but the treatment often accelerated their recovery.

After listening for some years to the practitioners, I realised that they were all doing the same thing in their different ways and with their different explanations. They were all using planetary energy to improve and realign the energies of the patient in ways that they believed to be beneficial. I discovered it made them very upset if I said this. They all felt that what they were doing was unique. I was also very amused to find that many of these people were at least as bigoted, inflexible and narrow-minded as the medical profession, at which these charges are often levied!

However they saw things, I began to realise that neither orthodox nor complementary medicine had all the answers, though they were both effective at the bits that they did well. So I was driven on to investigate newer principles with more general application.

The first of these was the use of light. This is used extensively in Russian medicine, but is considered highly toxic in the West – this is because we use such high doses. The Russians were using a thirty-times smaller dose than we were and were irradiating a small sample of the patient's blood with light and reinjecting it back into the patient. This they used for diseases from pneumonia to alcoholism. The Russian scientist whom I heard discussing her methods wondered why we were not using it for our cows with BSE, which was a problem at the time. Here in the West, we use it only as part of a chemotherapy regime for serious skin conditions and, at a much lower dose, to help premature babies convert their excess bilirubin into a form that does not damage brain tissue.

The research project on the therapeutic effects of light refused at the hurdle of the four-inch deep pile of paperwork required before there was any hope of NHS funding. But shortly after this, another Russian invention appeared in the West.

In the late 1990s, a British doctor was using an electromagnetic device, developed for Russian space medicine as a pain-relieving tool. (Russian medicine has much less dependence on pharmaceuticals than the West and has used more in the way of physical methods to treat its people.) Once the Russian space programme ended, the inventors continued to develop their device for commercial gain. They quickly realised that it did a lot more than relieve pain, at which it was very effective. (This it did by persuading the body to release its own supply of endorphins.) After considerable experimentation, they discovered that it was in effect an accelerator of normal healing. They tried it out on a wide range of medical conditions and came to the conclusion that there were few illnesses that could not be helped by it. I was on the first training course in the West, held in 1998. It was held in Russian, through an interpreter, with whom the scientists argued constantly! It lasted four days.

Over the course of time, the treatment programmes with this device became increasingly complex, and many had a mathematical base. This reflected the mind of the neurophysiologist who developed it, rather than medical necessity. I always felt that if you put the electrodes of the device on the part of the patient that hurt, it was just as effective. I believe those still in this field are returning to that point of view now. It worked all right for me.

The device was called the SCENAR, which is an acronym for "self-controlled energetic neuro-adaptive regulation." (The Russians are very fond of acronyms.) Six months into learning how to use this tool, I was convinced that when I used it, there was an energy flowing through me that did not come from me or the device. When cross-questioned, the Russian doctor who taught us admitted that she thought that an energy came from the cosmos and that the device was a transformer rather than a producer of energy. The energy from the cosmos was the "X" factor that could not be measured and it turned out to be of the most extraordinary benefit to the patient and also the operator.

The device itself provides an ever-changing electrical wave that passes easily through human peripheral nerve fibres and is able to set up a "conversation" between itself and the patient's nervous system. The *information thus provided enabled the human system to proceed more rapidly with its own healing. It was certainly information rather than energy: one nine-volt battery used to last about three months even with frequent use.*

The unexpected effect of the energy from the cosmos was to make us more sensitive to psychic influences, and I started to get messages from whom I knew not. Gradually, I understood that there were intelligences out there helping me, and I learnt to follow their instructions. The intelligences were not without a sense of humour. At that time, I jokingly referred to them as "little green men" and, more than once, I saw a tumbling mass of little green leprechauns rush down my arm and into the patient!

At a more ordinary level, the journey of the SCENAR was fraught with falling-out between groups of practitioners. The doctor who had brought the device to the West was determined to hang on to all the credit, and he fell out with other groups who had adopted the method. The Russians, deeply paranoid, fell out with everybody. Meanwhile, the spread of knowledge and use of the device continued on its unspectacular way and reached five continents long before there was ever any advertising promotion – a fine idea whose time had come.

Neither of these methods has yet been generally accepted in orthodox medicine. But I expect they will take their place when the pharmaceutical companies lose their stranglehold on medical practice.

The developments in me that the SCENAR produced eventually started me thinking that this was nice, but what would be really classy would be to have the same effect without needing any machinery. I had no idea how this was going to come about, but I knew I was searching for something at a higher and more effective level than the methods already available.

> *"Man cannot discover new oceans unless he has the courage to lose sight of the shore."*
> A. Gide

At this time, I made my final break from orthodox medicine. This was astonishingly liberating and was underlined by the final disappearance of the stethoscope I had been losing once a month for forty years. The finishing of a way of thinking and working that had lasted so long allowed my mind to range freely and without boundaries. The searching continued until 29th April 2003, after which I gradually realised that I'd found what I was looking for.

While I was still searching, I used to say "Why do we have to have all this stuff? Hospitals, waiting lists, MRSA, Clostridium difficile and government initiatives. Previous civilisations managed the whole thing using nothing but energy. Why can't we?"

And we can.

2

The Basidian

The Basidian are a highly evolved group of teachers from the star system Sirius. They have taught their method of healing to beings on many worlds. They operate entirely as a group and communicate with me through a spokesman. They have evolved beyond the need for physical bodies, so they have no mass, although they can assume form. Like other highly evolved beings, they roam the cosmos; but Sirius is the world that they call home. They have taken me there. The sea is golden and the rocks are soft. Evidently hardness is necessary only to combat the effects of gravity.

Sirius is the world concerned with healing. All souls who are destined to undertake healing in any of its forms either come from there, or pass through to be taught, on their way to whichever world they intend to work in. The Basidian have less experience of humans, especially very sick humans, than of other beings, but they are learning fast. You don't have to tell them anything twice. They have been surprised at how much the negative emotions held in humans' bodies delay the healing process. This is evidently unique to us, so it must be either a design fault or a way of persuading us to examine our emotional baggage.

We have been talking now for six years and they have taught me an immeasurable amount. Because I have recorded our conversations, we have been easily able to clear up most ambiguities and misunderstandings. Considering that they do not use language for themselves and they are teaching medicine to a doctor, using a medium with absolutely no biological or medical knowledge or vocabulary, we have managed very well!

They use English as if they were using a foreign tongue. When guides who had recently been human started to speak to me, they sounded as if they were familiar with the language, but the Basidian as a whole do not. It is not difficult to distinguish between them. It seems to give them pleasure to teach me, and I am certainly delighted and privileged to be taught.

The fundamental principle of their method is the delivery of universal energy to "the spaces in between." This energy is directed by their intention. This is how they described this to me:

B. "We are trying to teach you to communicate with the cells of the body and the cells of the cells, the minutiae, and to feel the energy between, to feel the power. The cells take their power from the energy field. Everything has its own field of energy; we need you to be aware of this energy and to understand it.

There is truly nothing that cannot be helped by this method and it is totally non-invasive. It is the way we heal ourselves in the energy that we inhabit.

As you use the energy, as you see its rays penetrating, it will become clear that you can see the particles of energy in the field between matter. It is that that shapes the mass, that allows the mass to be the shape that it is. It is in livening, or healing, this energy that is in between matter that is the key to full health."

As the Basidian say, their method is to alter the energy between the cells. If that energy is changed and improved, the cells can use the energy to undertake their own healing. In health, the energy between the cells sparkles, but when it becomes affected by an unresolved emotion, it becomes denser and more compact and the cells become crowded.

The energy between the cells is subject to the laws of quantum physics, and changing the energy of the particles in one place can instantly inform others, so that the healing effect spreads as a chain reaction. Each cell and organ has its own intelligence and in health they operate to maintain the whole. The energy between the cells is of course part of the energy between everything, the background energy of the universe. This is what scientists call "dark matter" or "dark energy" and what Lynne McTaggart calls "The Field."

Science is currently nearly at the point of identifying this force, and eventually will discover how to use its power for our physical purposes – heating, lighting and transport – as well as healing. It is an energy source that cannot run out and, when we can harness it, it will supply all our needs without harm to the planet. I have been taken on a journey to near the centre of the Earth to find this energy and my guides commented that it will be freely available for all, with many outlet points on the Earth's surface.

The Basidian can supply us with limitless energy also; but maintaining our bodies, so that we are able to retain the energy, is a matter for us. They are astonished at our lack of care, and how we allow our own energy to drain out of us by exposing ourselves repeatedly to a variety of insults and failing to give ourselves rest and recovery time. In the future, we will come to understand the importance of, and how to maintain, our energy levels. This will reduce the frequency and number of physical illnesses.

My first lessons with the Basidian were very simple, and the images with which they illustrated what we were doing varied from the anatomical to the absurd. One day I would find myself sliding down a sheet of cervical epithelium and the next, was surrounded by dwarfs in hats with leather aprons bristling with tools. The anatomical images were disconcerting because the organ on which we were working appeared hanging in front of me, completely apart from the body it belonged to.

Sometimes the images became surreal. I remember struggling to remove a large wardrobe from somebody's brain, to discover that the easiest way was to liquefy it and pour it out through a funnel! On other occasions, I would see jewellery and gemstones. I discovered that the brilliance of the gems was related to the spiritual development of the patient, and the settings indicated whether that patient had a need for cleansing or not. It was different from the health service!

As I progressed, the images changed to flowing energy lines in complex patterns and areas of light and darkness. The Basidian taught me to interpret these signs and to alter them with my intention and my tools until the pattern was something that I recognised as harmonious energy flow. Although I spent increasing amounts of time working in this way, measurable results were slow to come by. If I had worked on a problem that had not yet manifested in the physical, it was easy, but there was then no physical proof.

At this time, there were numerous exponents of the "everyone can do anything" school of thought. We were exhorted to tune into the divine energy and let the healing flow, and that was all one had to do. The Basidian commented later that a human view of healing was coloured by the work of Jesus. They would not allow that even He could heal instantaneously (except in the matter of restoring sight), and of course He was a much higher and more powerful being than most of the healers operating today. They said that humans expected healing to be quick and complete, without any effort from the patient. I discovered over the next few years that it wasn't just as easy as that. In fact, not only I but the Basidian discovered that it wasn't as easy as that!

The stumbling block to health in humans is our unique habit of storing negative emotions in our bodies. These negative energies work against the positive energies of the healing, and this means that the work takes a great deal longer than it might. The difficulties this human trait presented came as a surprise to the Basidian themselves. They have not worked so much with humans yet, and were not expecting this to be such a problem.

The spirits will help with emotional clearing, but they say that it is necessary for the patient to be willing to help themselves for true progress to be made. Since they can see what is really happening, they cannot be hoodwinked by people's words in the way that humans can. I was astonished to find how few of my patients really wanted to help themselves, whatever they said! When I think of the amount of energy I have poured into patients who had no intention of changing, I wish I had become wiser sooner! (One of the things that has made my journey more difficult was my determination to do everything the hard way! Few of my patients had been ill for less than twenty years and even fewer were ready for the powerful change within themselves that was necessary to achieve permanent healing. I can only assume that my unconscious mind thought that the easy way was effete!)

Modern medicine views the patient as an object, and the patients have lost the habit of trying to help themselves. There is also an enormous fear of change within many patients' minds. Add to all this the fact that most of them had very low energy because of the length of their illness, and you will recognise that I had set myself an uphill task. Many times I despaired, but when I reviewed the patients with the spirits, they pointed out the changes that had occurred that I could not see. I was measuring success in terms of physical changes to the body, and they were able to see the benefits to the mind and the soul.

The Basidian method, they say, is to heal from the inside out and to heal the emotional wounds that led to the illness in the first place. They taught me that all illness is of the mind, and that unresolved emotional trauma is the trigger for each disease, and the site of the physical problem depends on where the negative emotion was stored. They were dismissive of the "connect to the divine energy and let God do the rest" school of healing. They agreed that miraculous changes were possible, but said that this was usually just surface healing and, unless the work was completed, the illness would return.

Despite the difficulties, the journey of exploration that the Basidian took me on was so wonderful and beautiful that it completely altered my way of looking at everything. I have slid down sheets of cells, played among quarks and superstrings, visited planets and stars, and have been surrounded by love, care and support throughout. It beats the NHS by rather a long way in terms of treatment of employees! There have been so many attempts to bring effective healing to people who need it that it took me a long time to believe that this could possibly be it.

In order to help my limited human brain, I was given, bit by bit, an army of symbolic tools to use – which presented themselves as images in my mind. Some of them were for specific tasks and some were more general. The most versatile were the Indigo crystals. They remove negative energy, which they indicated by changing colour. When the crystals were removed, the negative energy went too. The most beautiful were a pair of scissors with gold handles and amethyst blades, which were only to be used for cutting out negative emotion. They were kept for their protection inside a crystal brick. Many were more serviceable. I had a surgical knife, artery forceps and a sucker. For larger jobs, there was a crystal power drill, a vacuum cleaner and a length of industrial-sized corrugated tubing!

Intention

The Basidian tell me that these tools, being symbolic, will not always be necessary, but they are powerful aids for accuracy of intention. They taught me to be very clear in my intention and not to move on until I had seen in my mind's eye that the job was completed as far as possible on that occasion. The healing is initiated by the intention and then carries on until some other intention is applied, or the energy runs out. This intention needs to be quite specific and focused. Directed by our intention, the Basidian are able to channel energy through the healthy human to the patient.

The Basidian need a human conduit to work through to heal other humans and since the patient will, almost by definition, have depleted energy, they need a healthy human. The usual principles of informed consent apply, although there is no paperwork! They can only enter a human body that requires healing at the human's request and by using the intention of a human healer as a channel. This has more effect on the healer than they expected. Although the Basidian give energy to the healer as they work on the patient, the effect on the healer can be very draining of energy, because the vibrational level of the energy they are transmitting is so much higher than the human is used to. This can be rectified, but has serious effects if the healer's body is unhealthy.

Most healers would suggest that the draining effect indicates that the healer was using his own energy, rather than allowing the planetary energy to flow through him. I'm sure this is correct at the planetary level, but the Basidian are using a higher and more powerful level of energy than we are used to. Its effects are more powerful, but the price is higher. They say that our healers use the energy of the magnetic field of the Earth to do their work and the Basidian use the universal magnetic energy, which is of a much higher level and very much more powerful than the magnetic energy around our planet.

With the Basidian method, the combination of intention and universal energy is all that is required. The speed of success depends on how much energy can be safely transmitted by the healer, and how much can be safely received by the patient. Since few of us are working at the level and power of the Christ, this will obviously take some time. The longer the patient's illness has lasted, the lower and more static their energies are, and these must be replenished before healing is possible.

If all patients were receptive to healing and all healers were powerful, that would be that, and indeed it is over most of the universe. However, the patients in this case are human, with their unique ability to store negative emotion in their bodies. This negative emotion works against the healing they are given. The Basidian say that each organ has a mind of its own and many of these minds do not wish to heal at all!

When the Basidian were first working on me, this was precisely what happened. They told me that my heart was extremely unwilling to go back to the emotionally and physically stressed existence that it had led before, and I could hardly blame it! So it initially refused to heal in case it might have to...

Eighteen months into this work, I developed a transient stroke (TIA). Fortunately, the paralysis only lasted about twenty minutes, but for the next six months, my brain felt muzzy and my body very tired. As usual with life's little disasters, it turned out to be a blessing. The event relieved me of my professional responsibilities, both real and imagined, and I was able to look more deeply into things.

A career in medicine does not encourage you to consider your own feelings. Sick people must be attended to, however tired you are. After a few years of this, you lose the habit of considering how you feel, and I had developed the tendency to drive myself until the job was done. Forty years of that had taken a toll on my heart and, together with a genetically poor arterial system and an explosive temperament, I was much sicker than I knew.

Throughout the year after the stroke, my transcripts became peppered with exhortations from the Basidian to do less and rest more. What they meant was do nothing, but I thought that, since I **was** doing so much less than I had ever done before, that I was doing nothing! They likened me to a creature in a spider's web, lunging about and breaking the fine fibres of their healing. Fortunately, they did not have the same intentions toward me as a spider!

At the beginning of 2006, the Basidian decided to repair my aortic valve and thereafter went on to work on my ailing myocardium. The effects of this on my body were extraordinary. Although I rarely felt ill, I was so tired that, at the end of the day, climbing the stairs to bed was a struggle. Once I recovered, they started on my left coronary artery. This has really been difficult for them. For a start, my heart was quite unwilling to let me go back to a state where I could push it so hard; and then there was the stored emotion.

The pivotal part of the emotions in the causation of illness is not yet accepted by the orthodox medical world, although it seems to be strongly suspected by nearly everyone else! I'm not the first person to come from an emotionally repressed family, but it certainly didn't do me any good. The combination of an emotionally distant, busy and ambitious mother, an absent father, public school and medical school left quite a bit of damage. The public school was run exactly as if we were boys, and *at medical school, they were all boys! There were four girls among a hundred men in my year. This last was enormous fun, but professionally we had to be men, otherwise we were told to go home to mother or "Wouldn't you be better in nursing, dear?" This was all in the 1950s and early 60s, long before open male emotion became acceptable.*

All of us misunderstand our instructions as children, but some of us are loved well enough to believe that we are lovable and alright, and some of us are not and believe that we are not worthy of the good things in life. So I worked to clear the suppressed memories, both professional and personal. It went on and on! There was nothing difficult about any of it, although I wept a lot, but the process took time, because of the number of unpleasant memories of one sort or another. The benefits of all this work were enormous. My heart felt freer, lighter and softer and it was much easier and nicer to be me.

> *"A flower has opened in my heart....*
> *What flower is this, what flower of Spring*
> *What simple secret thing?*
> *It is the peace that shines apart,*
> *The peace of daybreak skies that bring*
> *Clear song and wild swift wing."*
>
> *Sassoon*

For those who are worried about their own health if they try to do this work, the Basidian have learned from me and this will not happen again. They can see past and present and future, so they are able to detect coming health problems. They knew I was going to be ill, but they did not anticipate their difficulties in mending me. What they cannot do is interfere with any person's life plan or free will. This is a law of the universe. If there are illnesses or events that a soul must experience for their learning, then these will happen. If physical health is an accepted outcome, then they will give healing. They will give healing anyway, but if the soul's path is towards death, then that is what will happen. The Basidian do not view death of the body as any sort of ending; they view it as the entry into life and joy. They can understand, but do not feel, the fear that humans have of the transition.

"What do you want with a body?" *they said to me once;* "Come home."

For the reasons discussed before, not everyone can be cured, but everyone can be healed. Approaching the death of your physical body with all your relationships resolved, your emotional patterning cleared, and your work done, is a triumph, not a disaster! Such a person can be said to be truly healed. The rest of us have to return to finish the job.

Fortunately for us, the Basidian are very able to heal the emotional problems as well, so long as the patient is willing to work on the subject themselves. This relieves us all of the burden of having to become psychotherapists, a group for which I have a great respect, but whose work is often very long drawn out and painstaking. It is not necessary for our patients to discuss their problems with us at all, so long as they discuss them honestly with themselves and are able to come to a resolution.

Working with the Basidian makes discovering what is at the core of the problem so much easier. If your intuition does not tell you, you can always ask the spirits and they will! So much quicker than psychotherapy! They will also tell you whether the patients are truly working to clear their problems! They consider that a healthy being has a healthy and evolving soul, but not necessarily a fit body.

Despite the fact that they use pure energy in their work, and talk of healing the cells, the Basidian's main focus of healing is directed towards the negative emotions, which are the cause of all the physical conditions. Many of these negative emotions have been stored away many years before the onset of illness and lie dormant until they are triggered by something else, maybe an event, maybe a memory. If the person is energetically depleted, then they can no longer prevent the negative influence from exerting a physical effect and illness eventually follows.

This only applies to emotions that were not resolved at the time. If you watch an animal that has been frightened, you will see that it shakes and trembles for a short time after, and then resumes its normal activity. The effect of the trembling is to release the fear from the body. Healing stuck emotion takes energy, just as healing sick bodies does, and without the healing and clearing of the emotional stuff, long-term physical health is unlikely. The Gospel of Thomas tells us:

"If you give rise to what is within you, what you have within you will save you.
If you do not give rise to what is within you, then what you do not have will destroy you."

and also

"If man knows everything, but does not know himself, he knows nothing."

This is a most unpopular view in today's medicine, which infinitely prefers to see patients as compliant objects who can be repaired by a drug, a ray, or a knife without any input from them. Some of the tools of modern medicine are magnificent, but the price is often very high. The only drug without any side effects is vitamin B12 and this is a normal constituent of the human body.

Man is an ingenious and inventive creature. I shall be glad when he breaks the stranglehold of the pharmaceutical houses and begins to find other ways of practicing medicine. However many ethical and responsible people they employ, industries are driven by money. Were it not so, there would be drugs available for the treatment of AIDS in Africa, and children of the Third World would not die of malaria and bacterial infections. But until there is more money to be made solving these problems, rather than working to have the whole of the Western world with the same cholesterol level and blood pressure, this is how it will continue...

The Basidian do not view health as we do, by the fitness of the body. They say that the soul is what they observe, and what they do is primarily for the health of the soul rather than the body. I think if the body recovers too that is just a bonus! The understanding of the journey of the soul towards perfection, and the parts played by illness and apparently adverse life events in helping the soul to learn and grow, has also transformed how I see man's life. For those of you who are unfamiliar with Paxton's third law, it states that: "Shit is manure, but not yet." Or there is a more respectable version: "Compost happens." However you say it, we only learn from life when things get tough!

There are souls who are unable, at the time, to profit from their lessons. The spirits describe them as lost, and until they find their path themselves, very little can be done to help them. I found out this useful fact the hard way! While I was drinking, no-one could help me and, once I stopped, I found my own way out of the pit I had dug for myself. I have always wanted to "make it better" for people and of course you cannot. This has been a hard lesson for me and I'm still a bit inclined to try and rescue people. This is not to suggest that you cannot help them, but you need to allow them to make of the help what they choose. Every soul takes a different amount of time to learn each particular lesson, and, after all, there is plenty of that – aeons in fact.

The Basidian are always conscious of the life path of each soul and of what experience will most help his soul growth. Although they work to heal the body, their primary focus is the soul, and their initial work on any soul is to help him heal his emotions, so that they do not cause imbalance and stagnation in the body. It is the stagnation that causes illness. When they show me the energetic pattern of a sick person or organ, I often see dark patches without energy flow or jagged disordered patterns of flow. In health, a person consists of harmonious waves of energy flowing smoothly and intermingling without disorder. Disease is static. There is nothing healthy in the universe that is static – even rocks and glaciers flow at their own rate. The whole universe is made up of continually changing waves of light, each influencing the next and harmonising with the whole.

The Basidian are wonderfully versatile. Working with them, I have been shown the problem as if I was on the end of an endoscope, or as if by X-ray, CT scan or microscope. I could see gross pathology, histopathology, stuck emotions, lack of love, bacterial infections, energy flows, the level of spiritual development, the light the patient was emitting, and whether or not they were lying or dying! All of this information comes instantaneously and for free! Not only this, but if one of my patients has surgery, I get a grandstand view of the proceedings. I seem to be sited somewhere between the surgeon's head and his hands, and you can't get a better view than that.

Imagine an NHS that does not need any specialised departments. No X-ray department, no diagnostic pathology services, no psychiatric department, nor most of the diagnostic teams. The Basidian say that there will still be a need for some surgeons for emergency situations and the treatment of accidents, and so there will be a need for nurses to take care of these patients and also the ones who cannot take care of themselves. In this hospital, the rest of the staff will be medical healers, cleaners and people employed purely to be kind to the patients, feed them well and love them a lot. The running costs would be a fraction of the current level and the surroundings could be beautiful and comfortable, a place that would give pleasure as well as healing.

If every medic was his own diagnostic and treatment service and there was no need for equipment except in the surgical department, the hospital could again become a beautiful place. In the distant past, places of healing were places of peace, safety and beauty, with a strong sense of the sacred. Bringing the sacred back into medicine would be wonderful. I remember as a medical student in the wards at night, feeling a sense of holiness that was undetectable in the busyness of the day. It's not a feeling I've often had in a church, but it was freely available in the hospital.

3

The Three Strange Angels

"What is the knocking?
What is the knocking at the door in the night?
It is somebody wants to do us harm.
No, no, it is the three strange angels,
Admit them, admit them."

D.H Lawrence

One day, the Basidian were talking about the way disease manifests in the physical. I commented that the last time I had listened to such a lecture, it had been given by my uncle, who was the Professor of Pathology when I was a student. They astonished me by saying "He is a high being, he is still here." He was the first of the Basidian that I had known in my lifetime to appear in his most recent and familiar personality, in order to comfort me while I was ill.

It took me a while to understand that he, so eminent, in both spiritual and earthly spheres, was there to help, inform and guide me. In life, he had been kindly, austere, eminent and somewhat distant, but freed of his earthly gravitas, he is warm, supportive and very funny. I am learning such a lot from him, particularly now that I can channel him myself. I still call him Uncle Theo. (He was an honorary uncle by virtue of the fact that he and his wife and my parents, had all been at medical school together.)

He roams the cosmos wearing nothing but a robe of light and a bow tie, and retains a little of his professorial nature. I have developed with him the sort of light-hearted banter, bordering on friendly abuse, to which I subjected my favourite bosses when I was young. He never lets me have the last word and he has the ability to come back instantly with a witty retort. I love that! I would have been much too in awe of him to treat him so in life, although I always loved him.

A bit later, I made contact with my father, another Basidian, only to discover that he had been with me all the time also. My father took his own life when I was a child, for reasons that I entirely understand, but he has been protecting me ever since. He too turns out to be a warm and loving soul. He was not quite tough enough for the things that happened to him on Earth. Bloody-mindedness passes down the female line in my family!

So having been fatherless for fifty-six years, I now have two! I feel more loved, supported and cared for than I have ever been in my life. I have my Basidian family, since I come from the same roots, and some of them are men I loved and respected in this life. My path has been largely solitary, but no longer. It is a very joyful feeling.

More recently, I discovered that a third being, whom I had known in life and who left the physical world much more recently, had joined the others in the personalised fraction of my supporting group. He had also been medical. His name was Rory. In fact he once asked me to marry him and I am ashamed to say I roared with laughter and hurt him considerably. Since he had never so much as taken me out for a drink, you can understand my surprise, but I am sorry to have hurt him. He was a nice man and we were fond of one another. He still thinks it might have worked, but, since I was twenty-two and just starting my career and he was thirty-two and looking for a home and children, I have my doubts. Certainly he was the nicest man who ever proposed to me!

So not only am I learning about things I never dreamt of, I am having enormous fun. The teaching is wonderfully varied, ranging from the changes expected in the Earth, through how to create electricity using a drag anchor and tidal water power, to the nature of wisdom. I also have lessons about the nature of the universe, the spiritual development of souls, and the use of methane from pig manure as a fuel! My father specifically instructs me on the emotional problems of life, the nature of love and the journey of the soul. The period when I was unable to do anything much physically, has truly been "a time of gifts," when I stopped giving and at last learnt to receive.

These three spirits have told me a lot about my family background, which has helped in the emotional clearing, and have taken me on journeys to other worlds to see things from different points of view. They have told me about life in the spirit world. Imagine being able to do whatever you choose, for as long as you like, without getting tired and with no deadlines. Add to that, constant feelings of bliss and joy and the complete absence of fear, worry, or "oughts" and "shoulds." Life after death sounds as if it has a great deal going for it. If I had only finished my journey in this incarnation, I would have taken one of my opportunities to leave; but I still have some work to do. It would lack completion to leave now, and be a perfect nuisance for the Basidian, who would have to start from scratch, training somebody else. So here I stay until my information can be passed on, when I will go joyfully to my home in the stars.

There have been those who doubted that I was communicating with these beings and felt I was just connecting to the universal consciousness. Of course when we speak, I am connected to the universal consciousness because those in the spirit world are constantly aware of their connection. The doubters wonder if the three people I say I talk with are just a figment of my imagination. Since our souls evolve in groups, it would be perhaps more surprising if I did not recognise some of my guides.

In fact, the spirits did not reveal their previous personalities until I became ill, and they did so for my comfort and to help me to clear the "stuff" that was delaying my healing. Certainly they have entirely different styles and ways of speaking to me. Uncle Theo is patrician but kindly and funny, my father is loving and warm and always on my side, and Rory joshes me the way he did in life. The medium, through whom they first spoke to me, did not know any of them in their earthly lives, but they instantly adopted their previous personalities, so that I could distinguish them easily.

As for the Basidian as a whole, these are a group who have a specialised purpose, and it is a specialised part of the universal consciousness that they are teaching me about. The information they give me is very pure and also reproducible. They rarely contradict themselves and I can recognise the worlds they take me to when I visit them again.

Any difficulties we have had, occur when they have told me that it is in the pattern of something to happen and then it does not happen. This is sometimes just a matter of timing, but otherwise it is always due to the intervention of human free will. They can predict difficulties with humans if they look, but unless I ask them to, they do not usually bother. What is supremely important to us down here looks very different from the cosmos. If I do ask them to, they will help me with anything, from finding homes for kittens, to helping with the evolution of my soul! But I have to ask. In this universe of intention, it is necessary to put out a clear intention so that the request can be answered. The clearer the request, the easier it is to answer. This is one of our discussions on this subject.

A. *People have doubted that I am speaking to the Basidian. When I am talking to you, why am I not just tapping into the planetary consciousness?*
T. This we understand. We cannot clear their doubts. Humans always doubt what they cannot see. Because we are not widely spoken of, it will present difficulties.
A. *You are a personalised part of the universal consciousness and it is universal, not planetary?*
T. It is universal.
A. *Is all the information that you are giving me available at the planetary level?*
T. Yes, the information that we give you will be available at the

planetary level, but the information we give to you personally would be more refined. You see, the planetary consciousness is part of the universal consciousness. It is as if you are reading a novel or an encyclopaedia. The novel gives you the information that the author chooses you to have, that would be the planetary level, and the encyclopaedia is at the universal level, which would impart a more intelligent view of what is understood at the planetary level. It is all the same knowledge, but the level of understanding of it is different.

A. *It is about the level of understanding, not the knowledge itself, so we are operating at university level as distinct from primary school?*

T. Yes, that is an analogy that all the people would understand.

A. *The next doubt is whether I am communicating directly with three beings that I knew in life or are these just figments of my imagination?*

T. No, they are not. Because each of us chose to come from that particular lifetime to help you. It is a choice we make to go back into the memory of the lifetime, to be that personality, to communicate with you. We do not require to, we could choose to be pure souls.

A. *Just as the rest of the Basidian are, who have backgrounds that I know nothing about?*

T. Exactly so, but we understand the comfort it gives you, as it would other humans, and that is why we would all choose it. It is not just in communication with you, but in communication with others. The people that communicate with them have moved on spiritually, the soul moves on, their soul continues to grow, but they choose a character, a personality that meant something to that soul in order that the soul is comforted.

A. *But that would be one of their own characters – they don't use someone else's?*

T. No, they cannot – it is in their own soul memory.

A. *And it is the choice of the other soul, not the choice of the human?*

T. Correct. They work as a collective, but if there are specifics about your past in your life, that one soul speaks to you.

A. *So when I speak to any of you, exactly the same group of people speak to me and they just take on a bit of the personality that I knew in order to comfort me?*

T. Correct. We work as a collective, but if there are specifics in your mutual past, that one soul speaks to you.

A. *So everybody has guidance from people that they have known in life, because they are part of the same soul group, so it isn't quite so unlikely that you are three people that I knew and loved?*

T. Not at all, it would follow.

A. *Is this a soul group of origin or of choice?*

T. It is a soul group of growth. From the origin, you will all have grown and so in certain phases in your soul's growth, the soul group disperse, but it would be perhaps that the soul, instead of being in the centre, may be moving out to the outer edges of the soul group. They are at that stage stepping into a new soul group for their growth. The groups are not static.

A. *So are these groups of current interests and development levels?*

T. Yes, and it will be their current interests and development also, it will be what they need to move their soul on, to grow.

A. *So that means that my father, who is very near the centre of my soul group now, is not necessarily there for all time?*

T. No, not for all time. He will change his roles many times. People see evolution as one line – it isn't it, grows out. It is like an apple tree, starting off with one stem, and it grows its branches, and then it blossoms, it bears fruit. The fruit then becomes the point where it grows again. Each time it fruits, that is a lifetime. From one beginning, it bears fruit towards others and, of course, each one of you souls touches many others, and that would be the analogy of the fruit tree.

A. *You took me to meet someone you said was my soulmate. Is that a longer term thing?*

T. It is. It is for all the lifetimes that you can remember.

A. *And how many of those would you have?*

T. One true soulmate. It is the evolution of the soul, that's what matters. Humans see it as of the evolution of humans, yet it is the soul. Humans cannot see the soul – they speak of it, they say they understand it, but they do not. The soul is a library of memories, everything that happens in any lifetime and every lifetime is stored within the soul. When the body dies, the soul lives on of course. The soul then will cleanse itself of the unnecessary baggage and just retain what is necessary for the future.

A. *I remember you telling me that you kept the medical stuff because you knew you were going to need it.*

T. Yes. This will help you in your explanation to others, so that they will be able to understand more. Of course, some you speak to will not want to understand, and some will need more explanation. You need to let them understand about the physics of life, the physics of the universe. In physics, where does the first equation come from? Who created that equation? They need to look back into science and understand how it began with two souls believing in what they had captured, what they had understood, and then trying to convince others. They convinced those who were prepared to be convinced, and then it stopped for a while, and then began to grow again. Just as there are some scientists and physicists on your planet now, who are coming up with answers which would not have been listened to ten years ago. They also need to understand "where was the original thought?"

A. *That is a good question. Where did the original thought come from?*

T. From the Source. It is not as a thought from the Source, the only way we can describe this is as a Source of information. The Source is not of thought.

A. *It is a well of information containing everything that could ever be thought?*

T. Yes, it is, it is thought beforehand. It would be difficult to explain for you to fully understand, even we do not fully understand.

I am sure now that they are who they say they are. For you, it is up to you to decide for yourselves. They have often said to me:

"You do not have to convince anyone that we exist. We are."

My family of spirits comes from Sirius, but the star from where I started my soul's journey is on the far side of the galaxy and does not have a human name. The Basidian call it icicle star, but commented that the name would sound very much better in Latin! So I have called it Astra Stiria, which would give any Latin teacher conniptions, but it sounds alright to me and the Basidian approved. I have visited both these stars on a number of occasions. They are both beautiful in different ways and, on both, I get a feeling of being loved and cared for.

My journey has been so extraordinary and I am so grateful to have been chosen. Even the periods of illness have been rewarding. I used to be such a busy little person and the ill-health has taught me about patience, calm and peacefulness. Here, I am ahead of Uncle Theo, who said that patience always eluded him! My three strange Angels discuss the faults of their previous personalities with abandon and it troubles them not at all that they were not perfect humans! This I find very comforting! However it is, it is fun, and I have the feeling of fulfilling my destiny.

> *"Crying; What I do is me: for that I came."*
> *G.M. Hopkins*

That is all that is necessary to say about me.

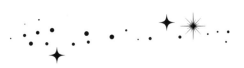

Part Two

The Basidian System: Medicine for the 21st Century

4

Healing with Intention

"The day will come when after harnessing space,
The winds, the tides and gravitation.
We shall harness for God the energies of love,
And on that day, for the second time in the history of the world,
We shall have discovered fire."

Teilhard de Chardin

The Basidian have been my constant companions and teachers of the past six years. They are showing me a new system of medicine, to join the many new ways of living and being that we are finding all around us. I am sure that it is not the only system. The universe never created just one of anything; but it is one that we can use until we have evolved far enough to avoid illness altogether. It works entirely on energy transfer and uses a higher – more powerful and more refined – energy vibration than has been available to us in the past.

This system is a gift to our world from the Basidian and the universe. It works on the cause of illness rather than its effects, although it can relieve unpleasant symptoms such as pain, along the way. Unlike Western medicine, the approach is entirely individual and the methods used depend on direct observation of the energies of a sick person and not on a diagnosis. It is not about curing disease, it is about replenishing energies in an intelligent way, to allow a return to health. The Basidian say that they work from the inside out rather than the outside in. This way, they can heal the soul as well as the body.

The Basidian are a group of advanced spirits whose home is Sirius, although they are able to roam freely throughout the cosmos. The group that I work with have specialised in the teaching of healing, and this section is about what they taught me.

*This is the whole of their initial conversation with me on 29*th *April 2003. I understand considerably more of it now than I did then:*

B. "I have great power here. I have great power not just of my making – there is great power for you to anchor. This we agreed; we agreed that you would be the anchor for this power. The power to heal, to heal the mind.

You have within your grasp now, and with your background knowledge, the understanding of the connection of the energy between the cells and how the energy between the cells and the cells make up the body. That energy can be changed. This you will be working with. This you will be teaching. This we will teach through you. We will be the power, as you are our instrument – teamwork.

Where there is disease within a body, it is created in the energy between the cells. The energy between the cells can be changed. It is possible to reverse, it is possible to bring wellbeing back to the cells, so that they regenerate in a healthy way... You have the healing power, to heal this...

We need you to understand the teaching of calm that has helped you to keep your thoughts away, to use your mind in the most positive healing manner. Allow us to teach. We will teach you the method, you will teach others this method, and others will listen. We need you to help those who come in contact with you for healing. You need to have them look at their minds, their mind talk, for they fulfil what they think of. The universe answers the call of the mind. It answers the desire whether it be positive or negative. It is not enough that they just speak positively; it only works when they truly know and believe, not in us, but in themselves.

We are teaching you in your sleeping hours. We are teaching

you at a higher vibrational level when you rest. The knowledge that you have learned but may not be aware of yet will come forth at the appropriate times and with the appropriate people. It is our desire to bring wellness to humans. Unfortunately humans seem to seek unwellness, albeit through the mind.

Firstly, they must look at what is reflecting to them. We understand you all have issues. If these are not addressed, the energy between the cells becomes dense. It holds memory; every space holds memory; you are made up of memory. Understand that the energy of who you are is made up of memory. It is an energy of lifetimes past, of patterns learned, and it is a memory of both good and bad; you have a choice of which path to follow. Of course, you ask for your lessons on planet Earth.

The power of Sirius comes through me to you. You have been asking from whence we came. My source is beyond your knowing as a human, but in your total understanding, you know. My source is not different from yours, but my choices are."

A. *Is there a name I can call you?*
B. We are of pure light, we know each other of vibration. We understand your need for a label. I reach back to the ancients. The name "Basidian" feels at one with me. When I come closer to you, you will be aware of a lighter brighter feeling. You have done much work in your slumber time; we are at one with you at that time. You are being taught from a vibration that not all understand. There are those also around you who do. Recognise your fellow souls of many lives together. It matters not from whence you teach this, from whence you practise. It matters greatly about the purity of the teaching and the practice.

You were brought into the sphere of learning in preparation for this work, even though we recognised your disappointment in your earlier years. To stand on the pinnacle that you have now, to understand fully the pattern that your life has taken is to bless it, is to thank all that has gone, and now to understand. All that has gone before has not always been good, but all that has gone before has been part of your teaching.

Then they asked me to look at the heart of a friend.

B. You will start to look at the arteries that are going to and from his heart. We would like you to look at the structure in your mind's eye. Look at the cellular structure and keep looking till you can see the density between the cells. When you arrive at this point, we would then ask you to remove your mind from any medical matter; look at it and just be with it. Be with the energy that is between the cells. It may be many or just one that is shown to you, but understand the feeling and the vision of the energy that is shown to you. We will do this with colour and light to start with. We will do this in this way to help you to see the sense of its changing, the reversal of the energy to bring wellness. Once you work with one cell connecting to another cell and then another, then a chain reaction is set up.

You need to sit in the same room as him in total quiet and absolute peace, and come from your heart. He is to have no expectations, just to be at one with the moment. The only way to heal is in the moment. You cannot heal in the past or the future; be in the moment. Thus, you will understand our need of your quiet in your resting time.

You have souls that come from Sirius. We always answer the calls of those to who we are connected, always. The only time we can't is if it were to interfere with the life pattern.

A. *At the moment I have no idea what you want me to do, but I expect I will find out when I get there — is that right?*

B. You will be instructed at the time; there will be a sense of knowing. We are in the process of reminding you how to. Worry not. If you worry, you cannot do this work. Accessibility is through the mind clearing; it is just easier for us to work through a calm mind. Have no desire for the outcome while you are working. Do not put an end result before you start. Know that you are capable of reversing the energy between cells; what we need from you is the desire to do it. The desire to do it will create a greater energy field from you that we can work through. Do not see yourself as "The Healer." You are indeed a healer, but if you think of yourself as being "The Healer" to change the energy between the cells, you have got your mind in the way.

You need the *intention* to do what is right for the soul, intention for changing the energy between the cells to clear and positive. Once you are in the work, we require you to look at what you are seeing. Just look at it, do not think about it, just allow it to come. It was spoken of that you are in this time of waiting. This is the state that you almost need to be in. Your energy is to observe, not to change the energy yourself. This we will show you and you will see how effective this is, you will see a change. The ageing of the cells can be reversed. This has always been known. We use this here all of the time, even to the point of someone who has been told they have just a short time to live.

First you must change the energy of the mind. Then you must change the energy between the cells. Look at the energy between the cells of the mind. This work is vast; it is new in the way in which you can do it, for you do not touch the patient. It is required that you do not. Leave it for at least fifty breaths after completion. It is changing the energy between the cells that is important, and once you have changed one bit, it starts a chain reaction which can communicate with the next and so on.

A. *Is it working by the quantum effect? Everything is connected to everything else, so if you change one part, the rest will know and change.*

B. That is correct, and it is helping the body to understand this and recognise the experience of wellness and youth. Remember we wish this work to be taught, once you feel proficient and comfortable. We call you, as you requested, at this time in your evolution. We call you to bear witness of your ability.

A. *I will do my best.*

B. You will do more than that. This we all know. Remember, have no expectations of yourself. Do this from your heart. Your heart is the voice of your soul and your soul is my friend. For we have been friends my friend. Now look forwards without restlessness, without agitation and find that calmness within you. Let go of the "must do" and just be. The energy of who you are is strong in the healing of the patient. The patient must take their responsibility; do not take it on for them.

A. *This is very exciting. Will everyone be able to work this way in the end? If you can change the energy between the cells, you don't need to do anything else?*

B. Many will. Eventually all will. Many are stuck in their patterns... For people who work with mind healing, this is very good. This will change the energy in the mind. This is an easier way and this is what we choose for you; it has always been known in our world. It has had to wait for man's evolution.

So I found my destiny after very many years of searching. This is what I have to write of and teach. It took me some time to get to grips with these beings and their methods. I am really glad I did, because not only am I going the right way, but they give me love, care, healing and information in enormous quantities. They have told me about the fate of the Earth, the nature of the universe, and the evolution of souls, as well as their healing. These make up the later sections of this book.

I asked about the name they had given me and this is what they said:

A. *You gave me the name "Basidian" to call you and you said it was an ancient name, but I can find nothing about it at all.*
B. It is more ancient than your world. There will be others who have heard this word, it will be familiar to them. That is when you visited this place that we are from. It does mean healing. It means many things – a collective word. It is teaching, healing, love. There is much more to it. If we were to tell you all the meanings, we would have you here much longer. Who we are and what we are – we have our basis in love and healing and teaching. We are at the very highest level of teaching.

From the healing perspective, it is best to allow the Basidian to tell you what they do and how they do it.

B. "Our central ethos is healing and the teaching of healing. This is the part of the work that we have specialised for. We are particularly concerned with the healing of emotional wounds. These are the cause of all illness and must be healed before there can be a full return to health.

Humans store emotional wounds in their bodies, which makes them uniquely challenging to heal. This is why we have been so interested to work with you, dear one, who was so severely damaged by these wounds. We have learned immeasurably from healing you and from the many challenging patients that you brought us.

We would like to summarise our work for your writings.

We start our work with the replenishment of energy. A wounded soul has low energy which must be replenished before healing can occur. The energy that we instil works on the "energy between," in the spaces in between the cells. Once this energy has been restored, it becomes sparkling and can transmit its own energy to the cells themselves. In this way, healing is effected, for everything is energy and what we do is to replenish and restore energy.

In physically less complex beings, this is all that is necessary, but the stored negativity in human bodies works against our energy, and undoes what we do. So we work with the negative emotions and stored memories, releasing and transmuting them until they are no longer damaging. After this is done, then physical healing can take place. We can restore damaged cells to health and we do, but cells that are completely dead we cannot heal, because there is no energy left in them. Dormant cells we can awake with our energy, but not dead.

The energy that we use to effect this healing is the energy of love, but it comes from the universe, not from the energy around your planet, and it is of a higher level and greater magnitude than has been available on Earth before. This energy is too powerful for most sick humans and so we need to transform it to make it safe.

We need a human healer to work with and this is why the human healer must be healthy. If he is not, then the energy can be too much for his system and we can make him ill. This is what happened to you, because, although we knew you were ill, we did not realise the effect our energy would have on your body. We will scan the healers in the future to ensure their fitness to work with us. At this time, we can only work with healers who are sufficiently evolved for us to be able to reach them.

We are not from the human world. Our home is on the star Sirius, although we travel freely in the cosmos. Sirius is the star of healing, and healers of all types will pass through on their soul journeys. We have been so happy to work with you, our sister, on your Earth. You are one of many who are making our work available to planet Earth. There will be a time on planet Earth when illness will cease to happen as it does now, and eventually each human will be able to heal himself. This time is not yet, and meanwhile, you need help with your many physical problems. We give this freely, and freely it is for you to receive.

When sitting still, seemingly alone, we will take you deeper into the cells and, as you fall deeper into it, we would ask you to look around you, enjoy the ride in, enjoy the journey. Once you are in, look at the energy. Be the observer, not the judge. The mind is just too active here. On doing this, ask to be taken to the core of the problem. That's all you need the mind for at this stage. It will help you get back on course on any one particular journey.

We are trying to teach you to communicate with the cells of the body and the cells of the cells, the minutiae, and to feel the energy between, to feel the power. The cells take their power from the energy field. Everything has its own field of energy. In part, you understand this, but not in the depth to which you are being taken. The analytical part of your brain can be used at a later stage, once you are out of the journey.

In order to help you heal a being, we need you to be aware of this energy and to communicate with this energy and to understand it. It will take a few journeys till this truly happens. This, for you, is not a fast-track way of learning. It is so basic to us, as it will be to you in the near human future. You will have within you, now that it has been awakened, a greater capacity for diagnosis, born of understanding, born of feeling, born of your senses. Can you see the picture we are speaking you through? We will take you deeper each time. We wish for you to experience the journey throughout the body. We will take you through the eyes also.

There is truly nothing that cannot be helped with this method – it is totally non-invasive. It is the way in which we heal ourselves in the energy that we live. As man advances, man will understand how to heal himself. You are going to be one of those teachers.
Blessings to you all."

The Basidian use the energy of intention to direct the universal healing power of love, from which all is created. This power they direct to "the energy between the cells." Once "the energy between" is fully replenished, the cells and thus the organs can use this energy to heal themselves. The cause of human illness is our unique habit of storing unresolved negative emotions in the body. The influence of this negativity causes the space between the cells to lose energy, become dense and contract, causing collapse of the energetic shape. Eventually, illness ensues in the part of the human in which the emotion is stored.

They say that anything can be healed, although not everything will be healed. For a lasting healing to occur, the human must participate in the clearing of the unresolved emotion, or the illness will recur or healing be incomplete. This is because an illness is part of human learning, and the lesson must be learnt for soul evolution to progress.

They are not permitted by universal law to interfere with another being's life path, so if bodily death is the predetermined outcome, then that is what will happen. This they do not view in the same way that we do. The primary concern of the Basidian is to heal the soul and the emotions. The body is a secondary consideration. They consider that death of the body, with all the emotional conflicts resolved and all relationships healed, is a triumph rather than a disaster, viewed from the perspective of the soul.

A. *You say the primary concern in your healing is to heal the soul, so can the soul get sick?*
T. No, but the soul becomes scarred by the emotions and memories, and it is far easier to heal the soul while it is in a human container than when it comes here. When it comes here, that scar remains deeper and that is why many of you humans come back with old patterns, because the scar has gone deeper. Even though the souls are healed on the surface, it contains that memory still, and that is how you all remember past lives that are perhaps not pleasant.
A. *And that's why we have to come back and deal with it – because it is easier to do this when we are incarnate?*

T. Correct. That is why we are looking to heal souls whilst they are in a human body.

This is one of the reasons for children with disabilities or fatal illness in childhood. They have brought the problem in with them. Although it seems very hard to make a child suffer, it is important to remember that they themselves chose to deal with whatever problem they brought in. Their souls made that decision before they came. Many of the children with serious illness are souls with a high degree of evolvement, who have chosen that illness to teach those around them, as well as to learn a particular lesson of their own. I have often been struck by the wisdom of a child with leukaemia and how they try to protect their families from the knowledge that they are going to die. Hard though it may be, all souls have to have experience of all types of life, and childhood illness with early death is one of them.

5

Intuitive Thought

The Basidian have taught me many methods for healing different types of illness, but the principles do not vary. I have included a few of these below, but this book is an introduction to these spirits, rather than a textbook of methodology. What is important to understand is that the spirits are bringing us a higher level of energy than we have been able to use before.

The healing energy that is currently in general use on Earth is of the planetary magnetic force, whereas the energy the Basidian bring us is universal magnetic energy. Planetary energy and knowledge are available to all of us, as we are now, without effort. Universal energy and knowledge are also available to us, but at this time, accessing it takes soul development and conscious effort. The information carried by these energies is the same, but the quality is different. Working with the Basidian is possible for us if we use our intuition, our inner knowing and our inner eyes to see what they are showing us. They tell me that intuition is merely the ability to tap into the planetary consciousness and to make use of the much greater field of information. This is not difficult, but the voice of the inner self speaks quietly, and to hear, there must be inner stillness.

Each person has guides around them who are fully connected with both universal and planetary consciousness. The guides are not allowed to interfere with another soul's life until that soul requests it, but they are a rich source of information. One of the tasks these spirits undertake is to guide me, but they do many other things and their message is for everyone.

Once the vibrational level of human consciousness has risen enough, we will all be in conscious connection one with another and with the universe, and then all of this will be easy. This time is coming, but has not yet arrived. We have been fitted with mechanisms that tell us whether what we are doing is in our soul's best interest. Indeed, we have everything we need both to heal and guide us, within our beings. The information comes in through the heart rather than the head, and this is the way that the spirits think.

B. We are without the thinking mind. There is the intelligence within the soul which communicates to us.
A. *Do you think through what would be your heart, if you had one?*
B. This is correct, the rhythm maker.
A. *So you don't think through what would be your brain, if you had one?*
B. We are, as you would understand, all brain. All parts are intelligent.

The intuitive "knowing mechanism" is accompanied by a set of feelings that indicate to us whether our actions serve or impede us. The positive feeling, the "sweet right feeling," is unmistakable once felt. So is what I call the "cold hard feeling," which indicates a mistaken action. At the point of any decision or happening, there is an added indicator, in that there is a sudden, momentary lift or fall of the spirits. It is almost a physical feeling within the heart. This cannot be faked and is therefore very useful if the head is arguing on another, apparently more sensible, course of action. Since I have learned to follow these feelings implicitly, my life has become ever smoother and more rewarding. I am told that this is because these feelings help us to stay on our soul path. So often, we smother our misgivings and assure ourselves that it will be alright! Left-brain logic has very little part in keeping us on our soul paths. (This has been a great comfort to me, as I appear to be intellectually challenged in the matter of logic!)

There are very many spirits from very many worlds helping this planet as we approach our time of turbulence. The Basidian are one group of these. They have not worked so much with humans as with beings from other worlds, and they have found this much more time-consuming than they expected. Our habit of storing our negative emotions in our bodies and the way we treat these bodies are the reasons. Throughout the rest of the universe, beings will always take care of their energies and replenish themselves when necessary. In the human world, as we all know, we disregard signals of tiredness from our bodies and carry on until we have completed what we intended to do, or until we are forced by exhaustion to stop.

The best description I have found of the effects of depleting our energies was given by a man with the wonderful name of Garnet Dupuis and is valid for any life form on this planet. This is my understanding of what he said:

The Effects of Stress on Biological Systems

An organism's first intention is survival.

When an organism is stressed or damaged, its energies are diverted to healing the damage, to ensure its survival.

If there is no further stress, the healing will be completed.

If further damage occurs, the organism will concentrate its energies on whichever problem threatens its survival and put the other one on the back burner.

Thus an organism is likely to collect incompletely healed stresses which require energetic input to keep them at bay.

Eventually the organism will be using all its available energies servicing existing problems, and the next stress will cause illness.

(This is believed to be the mechanism by which a relatively minor

condition can deliver the coup de grace to an elderly or sick person.)

Most of us in the Western world do not think of giving ourselves healing time, in the race to do whatever it was that we set ourselves to do, and it is small wonder that we become ill.

The Basidian say that maintenance of our energies are a human's own concern and not one they will interfere with. This is what they said:

B. "It is not meant for you to be solely giving and not receiving. For in that way, we will stand beside you and watch you drain. We will not stop it, for it is you as a human who is required to stop it. We can protect you in any other way, but we cannot protect your energy."

So a human has the free will to drain his energies if he wants to, and what he so often forgets is that if he does, there are consequences that will inevitably follow. The spirit world cannot interfere in our free will unless asked. I used to see an image of my guardian angel sobbing into his spare pair of wings, as I foolishly pushed myself harder and harder!

"The Energy Between"

"The energy between" is a key concept in understanding how the Basidian work. "The energy between" is the energy between everything, from cells to planets. The energy between planets also contains magnetic energy, but the energy between cells is of a purer form, and is the energy of love, of which the universe consists and from which all is created.

This energy obeys quantum laws (which are among those that the human race has got right) and so, when the energy between is replenished, one molecule passes the message to another and a chain reaction of energising is set up. "The energy between" is known on Earth as "dark energy or matter." It is only dark because we have not discovered yet how to see or measure it, but it is perceptible to spiritual eyes. Spiritual eyes can see a great deal that is not within the limited wavelengths of physical sight. (There is a description of a journey into the Earth to look at dark matter in the section on The Nature of Earth.)

This energy is of enormous importance to our lives as, in the future, we will learn how to use it for our energy needs, instead of oil and coal and so on. It has the advantages of being inexhaustible and free.

A. *It is the energy which is in the space between anything of any size at all and not only the cells?*
T. Between the cells, it is between any matter. It is a matter all of its own, that energy, but it is not a matter that can be seen by the physical eye, but it does have a physical weight, it is physical. Man has not learned yet how to weigh this.
A. *It is of too high a vibration for us to be able to perceive it under normal circumstances?*
T. Exactly so.
A. *So it is part of the physical?*
T. It is, and it is required in order to hold the physical together. You think of it as the skin that holds it together, but it is the energy that surrounds it also. It is the level of energy and the shape of energy that creates the shape of the human. Also, when you have disfigured organs, it is because the energy is disfigured, so that the energy would be either too much or too little in a particular area, and it is that that causes the problem in any particular area and that produces cell damage.
A. *So is that the energy of the etheric that is damaged?*
T. No it is not, the etheric is a different thing, the etheric is just a memory. It is similar in that it has a memory of what shape each organ should be, and what shape each cell should be. In a way, it is as the etheric, although we do not understand it to be such. The energy we speak of is the single most important thing in a human physical body. That energy, if it is not used wisely, the physical body breaks down from the inside. Every molecule has energy around to support it, so that the light of its own energy is allowed to grow and continue. The energy that is around every part within a human is supportive energy which allows it to survive. When a surgeon cuts through the energy fields and cuts into the physical body, the energy between is bleeding and so it is lost. That energy is very good at replenishing itself, but with some humans who have a lower vibration, the energy will become slightly distorted, and so, what is inside would be slightly distorted and complete healing would not occur.

A. *And by lower vibration, you mean less evolved, do you?*

T. Less-evolved people and also people who are harbouring a great deal of negative emotion – fear and anger, for instance.

A. *And that is what makes them ill. There is a reason for everything!*

T. There is, and we can match our energy field to your human way of thinking, because of course your thoughts are the energy. Your thoughts fuel the energy of the organs.

A. *Does your thought act as an intention?*

T. It does. It is an intention, but humans have not discovered yet the power of these thoughts.

The Basidian showed me what the energy looked and felt like by showing me the energy running between the medium they were speaking through and me.

T. Perhaps you would like to just take a look at the power of the energy that we speak of. We will put it in front of you. You are looking at the power of the energy between the two of you and the power of the energy that holds everything together, even what is on your physical table.

A. *I have a feeling of a force between the two of us which I could probably touch more easily than I can see, but I know it is there. It is a powerful force, but it is not visible.*

T. It is. Look into it, go into the power of the energy. Feel it – is it warm or cold?

A. *It is warm, it is not dark, and it is not light either. It is like heat – there is more to feel than to see.*

T. Correct. Go into this? It may have its own pattern, it may not.

A. *I'm getting bright gold chains.*

T. Yes, they are links, the energy is linked. It links itself to its own energy to create a vastness. It is not as a cell will link up to another cell to create a line or a shape. This is about that vastness.

A. *I've got an impression of an enormously fat gold shape made out of tiny little links.*

T. Yes, now you are seeing the energy that is in between. Touch it – what is the energy like?

A. *It is warm and quite soft and it is loving.*

T. Yes, all the energy in the universe is made of love. When humans put themselves in a dangerous situation, with anger and perhaps death to ensue, that heat becomes so intense that it begins to destroy itself. Humans must not overheat and if they overheat, it destroys itself, and there would be penetration into the physical and emotional, because they become then entwined. What is the weight of this energy?

A. *It is heavy.*

T. Yes, and why is it heavy? Consider how you are both feeling.

A. *Do you mean that it is heavy because we are both feeling heavy?*

T. Yes, it is the tiredness in you, and so it is heavy, and so you will be able to tell what the body feels like, and not just your own. When you go in and it is heavy, it means that the organs need a rest for whatever reason and healing will be given for that purpose and to create rest. Energy will work in whichever way it is required. It has, as you would understand, a mind of its own.

A. *This energy will always do what is needed first, whatever you say to it?*

T. It will not do what you say, it will do what it feels is right. When you are completely negative and there is depression, it becomes cloying. The energy changes its substance.

A. *Is that what makes depressed people so difficult to be with?*

T. It is.

They also showed me how to tap into the magnetic meridians of the universe.

B. "Now, our way of you learning to identify these power sources will be to be very still, just as you do when you are observing your breath. Go into that place and call on the power to show itself, and you will see coloured lines. Where the lines cross, there will be a power surge and you then will tap into that power surge and a new colour will come out of it. It looks a little bit like crossed wires. Do you remember the cat's cradle that we used to do as children? A little like that. Now each time human souls use their energy for healing, they have tapped into this in a lesser way.

Because of the level of your healing, you need to tap into the universal meridians and not just the Earth meridians. The healers among you use the Earth meridians. Because of the magnetic field, they are able to heal a human who is within the magnetic field. We are calling upon the energy that is outside of the Earth's magnetic field. By using the universal energy, the power of healing is one hundredfold."

6

How the Basidian Work

When the Basidian are healing us, they work always in a similar order: replenishment of energy, emotional healing, and then the restoration of energy between the cells.

Replenishment of Energy

The first thing that must happen is the replenishment of the overall energy. This may be very depleted if the patient has been ill for a long time. Many of my early patients had been ill for twenty years or more and the Basidian repeatedly warned me to protect myself properly. This is how they warned me about one patient:

B. "Your energy level is not at the level we would prefer for you to work with him. He takes a great deal from you. He is like a dry sponge soaking up the moisture, and it is important you remember you become very quickly depleted by him. In order to do justice to him, it would be good not to treat another patient after."

Emotional Healing

Once the overall energies are restored, the Basidian turn their attention to the emotion that caused the problem. For this to be successfully cleared, the patient must do part of the work himself, by going into the emotion and healing as much as he can. This he must do for his own learning. Illness is not a random event.

People have become accustomed, in Western medicine, to being passive receivers, and no longer remember that the outcome of their illness depends on themselves. It is the patient's spirit, mind and body that do the work, whatever method is used. All the healer/doctor/surgeon can do is to create circumstances in which it is possible for healing to occur. If the patient fails to do the emotional work, then the Basidian say that health cannot be permanently restored.

At the beginning, I struggled with many patients who had no intention of looking into their own problems. It is unbelievably difficult to persuade most people to deal with their emotional stuff.

> *"We would rather be ruined than changed.*
> *We would rather die in our dread,*
> *Than climb the cross of the moment*
> *And see our illusions die."*
>
> *W. H. Auden*

It is a fear of the pain they believe they will find, and the fear of unleashing uncontrollable rage or grief, that stops people. However, most of these emotions were laid down in a much earlier part of life and feel more like memories than current events. Even where they are initially painful, the pain is transitory and the healing process highly releasing and satisfying to the person concerned. It is subconscious buried memories that cause the damage. Once the memory is in full consciousness, it is often seen differently and feels much less powerful than when it was buried.

Because we are beings in physical bodies, it is necessary for the human to make positive physical efforts to clear and heal their negative emotions. It is necessary to go right into the emotion and feel what it is about. Once the subject is known, then the emotion must be spoken, written or, according to inclination, painted out (see below). This was what the Basidian said about one patient, who was an artist.

A. *So she needs to acknowledge her fear and then find her way of expressing it, but not by distracting herself.*

T. To distract yourself from your fear is not dealing with it. In dealing with fear, all humans work differently. This soul has the ability at her fingertips that she could use.

A. *Just to paint her fear until she really understands it and finds the anger behind it.*

T. Yes, she will find the anger at the base of it. She must not allow herself to lead the painting, she must allow the painting to lead her, just as the writing leads you.

A. *Yes, we often do something rather controlled at the beginning.*

T. It needs a starting point.

A. *And this is a useful technique for any form of negative emotion that we need to get rid of? The person just needs to find the right way of getting it out of themselves.*

T. They need to be able to find the right space in their mind; rather than they ought to do it, that they want to do it. They need to say "I need to do this now."

A. *What about people who have none of these communicating skills – can they just go and split logs?*

T. Yes, some people run, some people will need to do something very physical. Rather than hit someone, they hit something. They need to think about it positively while they do it. Just using the physical is distraction, so you need to use the physical positively with intention. There has to be an action, it is cause and effect. The cause is the fear, so they have to do something to have an effect. It needs to be physical with humans, rather than passive, and they will then get an effect.

A. *And writing and painting are physical?*

T. Physical yes, it does not have to be muscular.

The method must be active and the mind needs to stay on the problem and not just be sidetracked or anaesthetised by the activity. The method I use is to write a heading "Why I am really so angry about, or miserable about..." and then just keep writing until there is not one more thought left in me. The initial writings are often rather trivial until the conscious mind uncovers the hidden thoughts; but perseverance shows the true nature of the problem. Once all the thoughts are on paper, it is best to take a break before reading them. Once read, and if there are no more thoughts arising (if there are more, these must be added), then the next stage is to crumple the paper (not tear it) and burn it. If possible, it should then be buried in the earth, but the burning stage is essential or the problem eventually returns. With deep-seated problems, it may be necessary to do this a number of times, but the emotion will gradually lose its power and hold.

Artists prefer to paint their stuff out, but it is important that they do not try to compose the picture of their emotion, just allow it to happen. Musicians can work with their instruments, but the same provisos apply.

These techniques are particularly useful if you are anxious about what might come up about a partner or other close person. It is one thing to find your hidden emotion, but it is better not to allow it to take an axe to your loved ones! I have always been aware of the "mad axeman" within me, but it does come as a surprise to many, especially if they have been very successful at burying their hurt.

> "Give sorrow words. The grief that does not speak,
> whispers the o'er fraught heart and bids it break."
> Macbeth

Speaking out the emotion is just as effective, but needs a listener who is not emotionally involved. This is the basis of the psychotherapeutic process, and sometimes the listener can help you discover why you got into such a muddle. Other people's problems are always easier to understand!

All these techniques depend for success on getting all the hidden thoughts into full consciousness. Only then it is it possible to see whether these thoughts are still valid or whether they are outdated and limiting. These methods work for any emotion old or new and work just as well for fixed thought patterns that are born of a long-past emotion.

Much of what we suppress is laid down in childhood. I have found it useful to go into the being of the hurting child within and comfort it by whatever means appear at the time. Being female, I always give my sad child a new dress at the end of the process, which is a most effective way to convert tears to laughter! All of the hurt children that I have found in my inner being have just wanted to be loved and heard and are no more difficult to deal with than any other child.

While the Basidian were healing me, they repeatedly asked me to release my unshed tears, and I became accustomed to little painless fits of weeping that just occurred, apparently for no reason. The effect of this was to allow my coronary arteries to heal to some degree, which they had been unable to do while affected by the negative energy of the unexpressed grief. The Basidian tell me that they see a human's distress as like a hedgehog's spines and say that each spine represents another facet of the emotion. Examining each facet is a most worthwhile exercise and it is really surprising how many there are to each problem.

B. "Today our subject is war – the war within the heart. The war within the heart must be fought and won before the soul can live at peace and at one with himself. The weapons to fight this war are not guns and explosives, but honesty and self-examination, and cleansing of the heart.

Each human has come to Earth to learn about complex emotions and it is these that must be examined and cleansed. There is no alternative to this process if the soul is to be able to evolve to its perfection.

If every hurt is examined, then understanding of why it happened and why it was painful will arrive, and with this arrival comes peace. Peace cannot come without understanding. It is not so hard to achieve, but the rewards are great. Inner peacefulness is the reward and this is a pearl beyond price."

None of this is difficult, but it must be done for lasting health to be possible. Unless the patient is willing to change the mental and emotional patterns that caused the illness, then long-term health is unlikely. The Basidian will help and indeed have the power to release it all, but what would we learn from that? They will not do anything to interfere with our true soul journey.

Often the basic problem is a feeling of worthlessness: "I'm no good." This has always been laid down in childhood and can be dealt with accordingly. It is important to replace thoughts like these with positive encouragement: "Look how good you are at......, you are amazing!" Human life is really difficult, and we need all the help we can get!

It is not possible in a human life to rid ourselves of all negative emotion – we apparently need a little for the balance. The emotions that need shifting are those that are causing us problems, be they conscious or unconscious. Here is what the Basidian said to me one day when I was having an emotional down:

A. *Why have I been so miserable?*
T. You are disappointed within yourself. It is time to dismiss this feeling. Understand, in a human, it is virtually impossible to heal all negative emotions. It is only possible to clear the most negative emotions. Those who would write that you can clear all and that you must be able to do this, clearly do not understand themselves. We do not have negative emotions here, but we do not request that humans clear every negative emotion, for without the negative emotions in small amounts, there is not the balance. Humans need it. Do not treat yourself so harshly! For one with such deep feeling and such high intelligence, I wonder my dear!

Which highlights one human problem, that of forgiveness. All of us have people and things to forgive and usually the most difficult is ourselves. Many of us treat ourselves very much more harshly than we would our partners and friends. There is no virtue in refusing to forgive yourself. In fact, forgiveness is one of the main healings that needs to be carried out for emotional health and lightness.

"O my beloved fill the cup that clears
Today of past regrets and future fears."
Omar Khayyam

The negative thoughts and feelings remain damaging if not resolved.
The Basidian showed me the power of positive and negative thoughts in
an early lesson:

A. *What about the positive and negative thoughts?*
B. Look around and we ask that you put the intention out for something positive. Good. Now look at the energy of it.
A. *It is almost exploding and full of energy, like fireworks.*
B. That light attracts us, and not just us, but beings from other worlds also. If you were to go within the energy of that light, you would then hear the request. When you come up here, you will be able to hear requests and understand how you will be able to fulfil them. As much as it grieves us, we now ask you to look at a negative thought.
A. *That just imploded and is the reverse of energetic.*
B. Yes, it is – and the colour?
A. *Black, dark anyway.*
B. It may not be completely black. Can you see how a negative force might be attracted to that? Look at the magnetism in it.
A. *So negative beings and thoughts will join this implosion?*
B. Yes, and it will grow to become like a growth, because of the intention. So the greater the intention of anything negative, the stronger it will become. It will grow faster than the positive. In your bodies, you can create cancers. If you look at this, it looks very similar.
A. *Now how do you deal with negative thought? Putting it out of your conscious mind does not mean it has gone, does it?*
B. Absolutely not. We need you to look at the matter of it, its configuration, to understand how you go to heal that with your crystals and your colours. You can change that energy.
A. *So if I have a negative thought, I can take my crystals to it; how wonderful!*
B. You can, and you will see it changing form and colour.
A. *And this will work for persistent negative thought?*

B. This is correct.

Restoration of "Energy Between the Cells"

When the emotions have been cleared, they stop exerting the repeated negative effects on the physical body and at that point, the restoration of the energy between the cells allows healing to occur. This, each cell in the body knows how to do, by virtue of its own inbuilt intelligence. Each organ also has intelligence, as well as its etheric pattern to refer to, and all of them know how they are designed to be, just as a tree knows what shape to grow. If there is energetic damage to the pattern, say to a limb, then eventually deformity of, or damage to, that limb will occur. The same occurs in the internal organs.

The Basidian see all this in terms of energies rather than structures. I do not think that they concern themselves very much with structure, although they will examine it if they are asked to do so. All the healing work that I have done with them has been about changing energies, and images about energy are what they usually show me. They have a fine and varied line in images, be they symbolic, anatomical or surreal, to help humans understand what they are doing. I have come to trust that they will show me whatever I need to understand the problem, in a way that makes sense. I have even been woken at four in the morning to look at an X-ray. Just like being on the house!

Energy patterns

The energies of which we are composed are, in health, a continuous, flowing, harmonious series of patterns, and the nature of any disturbance of the flow gives information about the nature of the disturbance of the body. Positive energy is light and sparkling and flows in wavy lines with smooth edges. Negative energy shows a variety of patterns. It may be dull or dark and the energy flows appear different depending on the problem. Negative emotions show jagged energy lines. Blocked energy either looks confused, like a tangle of wool, or goes round in circles. In the presence of disease, the energy lines are interrupted, like a series of dashes. There may be no apparent energy flow at all in a dead or *dormant organ or cell, and there are a variety of disturbed flow patterns which give clues to the cause of the problem. All these energies have an emotion within them that identifies the unresolved problem.*

Examining the waves of energy themselves also gives information. A thin line of energy indicates a soul who will "tell you one thing and believe another." A wider line will happen in a person who is comfortable in themselves and lives "as far as it is possible in a human life, according to their truth." A jagged flow of energy waves will show a person who "wishes to and has caused harm."

There is nothing the Basidian can do about a cell or an organ that is dead, but if these structures are merely dormant, they can be re-energised and awakened. When I inquired about the raising of Lazarus, I was given to understand that he "wasn't as dead as all that." This is a well-known, if uncommon, phenomenon which is particularly upsetting to mortuary staff!

The factors that limit successful physical healing are: first, the soul's intention for death of the physical body; second, the patient's unwillingness to clear the emotional cause of the problem; and third, the limited capability of the healer. The healing energy is always successfully delivered, but physical healing cannot be instantaneous because it takes time to be translated from the energy into the structures of the body.

The Basidian say that they work from the inside out, not the outside in. The speed and completeness of physical healing depend on how long the patient has been ill and how much energy must be replenished first. They have enough energy to replace it all instantly, but if they did this, the physical of the patient would be unable to cope with the energy and another part would break down.

Entrenched memories are difficult to shift and the negativity that these memories have induced in the organs has also to be overcome. The organs, having their own intelligence, do not always wish to heal and have a tendency, until the negativity is removed, of undoing the healing that is given. (Negative and positive energy cannot exist in the same space – one must overcome the other.)

When all this has been achieved, then the strength of the patient must also be built up gradually before full physical health is achieved. The Basidian have had less experience of working with humans than with other beings who do not have either our biological complexity or our bad habits with negative emotions. They were surprised at how long it took to restore a chronically ill human to health, but they have learned much from those whom they have worked on and are developing methods suitable for use on our refractory bodies.

When they started on my coronary arteries, they expect to be finished within weeks, but it was more than six months before they had succeeded in coating the insides of these vessels with spiritual "non-stick Teflon" in such a way that it would stay put. There were a number of setbacks because, as they finished with one part, another battered vessel or section of myocardium would threaten to give out. On the whole, my cardiovascular system was pretty much worn out and my heart muscle unwilling to return to the high-pressure life of earlier years.

This is the record of a rather ungrateful conversation I had with the spirits while they were healing me. They were wonderfully patient and I can only say in my defence that I had to learn all this from the sharp end, and sometimes I got a bit fed-up!

A. *I can quite see why I can't heal people quickly, because I can't take the charge, but why is it taking so long for you to heal me? You have all the power you can use.*
B. In the process of your healing, there have been many fractions to be dealt with. The initial area in your brain was healed. The effects of the illness remained with you. What we continued to do was to work with your energy levels. Now, in the human frame, the energy seeps out very quickly, so we continued to heal you. As you become stronger, the energy stays put longer. Only when you work or exercise does the energy start to seep away again. We have plugged some leakage points with you. There has been a weakness in the vessels around your brain; as one was healed, sometime later another would weaken and show itself, and so we would heal that.

We do not carry out blanket healing. We heal individual areas, so to speak. The wellbeing of the soul we heal, but the frailty of the physical body after an illness shows itself up by degrees. We have healed whatever has shown itself.

A. *So there is a worn-out system and things keep going wrong, so why can't you rejuvenate all that at once?*

B. If we were to do all that at once, you would be bedridden – the surge of energy would be too much for you to control. Those people that speak of healing the complete do not do so in actuality They think they do, but they do not. They heal a specific area that holds on to energy, so the person will feel stronger. You have felt strong in different ways at different times.

After dealing with your brain, we looked into your heart. There was the beginning of a ballooning at the end of an artery. This was dealt with very quickly while you slept. From that there has been heart disease. Parts of it do not want to renew, but a greater part of it does want to. We cannot go against the body's wishes. Understand that every tiny fraction of energy that you have has its own will.

A. *I do understand that. Is that something that I could help to change?*

B. This would be good. The will power within a soul is one of the strongest things to work with, and against. We can do so much, but we cannot do all of it. We have the ability to heal you completely.

A. *I know, but not very quickly.*

B. It has been quick, but other parts of your body have shown themselves to be weakened. We would say that your system has worn thin to the point when you were ill, of overload. That was all going to happen. You really did need that to happen, even though you as a human would not wish it.

A. *It was a blessing, but very heavily disguised, as they often are! Is it then possible to take a worn person like myself, but a stronger one, and heal them quickly, or is it always going to be like this?*

B. The stronger a person is, the quicker the healing would be. Understand that once we leave that soul after a request for healing, the healing is then continued, for as the body continues to renew itself, it also continues to wear itself out. In order that you can have an active life, continuous healing for the rest of your life is necessary.

And on another occasion:

B. We are pleased that you understand that we cannot send too much energy to you at any one time. It would zap you, which is not our intention.

A. *Yes. Is it the same for any patient?*

B. It does depend on the patient and the illness.

A. *But if they were as weak in the body as I am, there would be the same difficulties?*

B. There would not be difficulties. We would use caution, so it would take longer.

A. *So you would have to give the energy in smaller fractions?*

B. The amount of energy we can put into a human is dependent on their physical and emotional strength.

Sometimes they put it more pithily:

B. It would be our wish to heal you at a stroke, but if we did that, then you would have a stroke!

When I worked when I was tired and sick, my energy sometimes drained alarmingly and for a long time. I did not understand the depth and seriousness of the damage to my heart and felt that I "ought" to be working. I look now in astonishment, both at my stupidity and the Basidian's patience.

The following happened after I had failed to detach myself properly from an "energy sucker":

B. We also needed you to understand the state that your heart has been in.

A. *I found it discouraging how ill I felt, so quickly after treating that patient.*

B. Understand about the energy systems. We will teach you about these and show you what they look like. You need occasionally to have something like this to happen to you. We speak with you. You take it seemingly on board, but you do not always equate it with you personally – it is for others. When we speak with you, we understand completely which part that that information goes to.

A. *It doesn't always touch me personally, I agree. I need these little* *shocks to remind me that my body is mortal. How did that happen, what did I do wrong?*

B. Firstly you were tired. You did not heed the tiredness. Your need to heal overcame your need to look after yourself. Recognise this in the future. You were not resting as much as you were normally. You need to rest to a regular pattern. All human systems need a regular pattern. When they are out of their regular pattern, the system becomes unbalanced. It is then very easy (no matter how well protected) for the energy to seep out of them, and your energy, when you are healing a soul, flows through you very quickly.

A. *What was specific about this woman?*

B. She was put there for you as a test.

A. *Which I failed!*

B. This you did, but you would not fail that test again. This is the main way that we teach you. Unfortunately it has to affect your health in a way that frightens you. We would wish now that we do not need to do this with you. We did not cause it, we just allowed it. We were not going to let you come over here. You were not about to die. Your heart does need more work. If we were to heal your heart too quickly, it would overload your brain.

When it is spoken of about speed of healing, it needs to be in the context of what is being healed. A broken bone can be healed far quicker, a tumour can be cut out and dispersed. Anything that grows is easier to heal than what is wearing out, because the tissues become thin. The energy there has dispersed.

When we take you in next, we will show you the energy of this dispersion, what it looks like so that you can fully understand. The heart is very tired. We are working diligently at the patching. We are concerned of the sacking around the heart at this time. There is a weak spot and then another one. We need to seal both of these spots. We have sealed others. There has been a seeping, and as such, we heal as it occurs.

You would ask why do we not heal before it occurs. We are not here to pre-empt what the body needs to do energetically. We are here on hand to observe and step in to heal. We start with it as the problem starts to arise.

It is difficult sometimes to contact the human to say "slow down, we need to complete the healing here." Sometimes you are in your vehicle, or walking, and so we help that the energy does not dissipate completely, and we keep you ticking over until you can have an energy surge in your body. This happens as you sleep.

There are leakage points for your energy, and they will also absorb negative energy. Being round needy or angry people, you absorb. They break through your energy fields.

Now that it is your wish to heal completely, we will speed up as much as we dare. We do not quite understand the feeling of being in a human body.

There is a platitude about "the gift of illness," which like many, turns out to be true. For the first time in my life, I had time and I was unable to rush about. The learning that I was able to absorb during this period is worth several myocardial infarcts, and I finally learnt to look after me. Not that this insight was immediate. There are records of any number of conversations with the Basidian trying to persuade me to do less! However, I got it in the end!

They have often told me that low-energy degenerative diseases are harder to deal with than high-energy conditions such as cancer. The other difficulty with humans is the multiplicity and diversity of our organ systems, which means that they can only heal them part by part. Evidently most more advanced races, who consist entirely of energy, can use the energy given throughout their systems immediately. All in all, it is not surprising that healing the human body takes time.

A. *Could you explain why you heal the part rather than using blanket healing?*
B. When we heal, it seems to you as a human that we heal singularly, but we do not. We ask you to look at the energy surrounding and within a particular organ. It will have a chain effect on the rest of the body. Blanket healing will blanket and not disclose elements of the illness that are waiting to arise.
A. *So it is too general to be useful?*
B. It is useful, but it is too general. Healing within the physical body, once completed, looks for other organs that need healing.

You are healing from within, the outer is taken care of from within, and generates outwards. The healing will generate through the bloodstream, the nervous system, the energetic system.

They commented once that humans expected healing to be instantaneous and complete, because of the stories of Christ's healing in the Bible.

A. *Why can't we have instant healing, like Christ did?*
B. This is an intelligent question. Instant healing is never completely innocent of the soul doing the healing. Understand that the one we know as Christ (who truly was an exceptional healer) gave more healing than was told. His healing was not instantaneous, but his healing created a positivity within the subject for them to feel so, and with their positivity, the healing process was speeded up. There are souls with this level of healing on your planet Earth, who can do what would seem like instant healing. He was calling upon the greatest power. We all work with this power, but we are not all quite of the level.
A. *So there aren't many people on Earth capable of transmitting a high enough power. Will that always be or will there be more who can in the future?*
B. As humans open up to the greater universe, there will be more people that will be able to heal vastly more quickly. It requires an immense amount of power to flow through you, and if the souls we are flowing through with this energy are not at full power themselves, they drain of energy very quickly.

When I asked why, if they can see past, present and future, they did not heal the illnesses before they arrived in the physical, they pointed out that the experience was part of the person's learning and that they could not interfere with that. The pattern of the illness can be present in the body for years before physical manifestation. Some of the illnesses can be avoided by the person and some cannot. The Basidian say that, if the illness cannot be avoided, the healer will not be able to find the causative emotional wound. This argues that the rest can at least be modified.

A. *If you can easily see past, present and future, why do you always heal the present?*

T. Because the present can change the future. That is important. We do not necessarily need to heal the past. You can do that.

A. *No, but what about the future if you can see something is coming?*

T. That is always part of the lesson the humans need to learn.

A. *So in other words, you can stop it happening, but the human needs at least some of the experience in order to learn.*

T. The particular human would have chosen that for their life path, for their learning.

A. *Then you must not interfere with that, that I understand, but if there is something coming along that they don't have to experience, you can heal that in advance.*

T. Correct.

A. *So you do in fact heal in the future.*

T. We do, but only if we are requested. We assist more in helping them understand what they are going through. They would get greater learning from the understanding of the illness.

7

Basidian Healing Procedure

I don't think the Basidian method can be taught from a book. I learnt by working on a patient and the Basidian, channelled by a medium, gave me a series of images and instructions as to how to proceed. The Basidian can teach you perfectly well on their own, but you need to be able to dialogue freely with them. Unless you can do this, you need a human teacher who can see energies well enough to know whether you are off track or using your own mind. Using your own mind, or worrying about what you are doing, blocks the connection with the spirits. (For those who are studying with the Basidian, there will be an operator's workbook.)

The patient's permission must be obtained before working with the Basidian. It is a universal law that one type of being should not interfere in another's life path without their permission. Apart from just good manners, this ensures that the patient will be cooperating with the spirits. It is also necessary to ask the spirits to help on each healing occasion. This is more than just good manners, as the energy of the request opens the energetic connection.

In principle, the healer is required to go up through several levels of energy to meet the spirits and then follow their instructions. In order to do this safely, the healer must first surround themselves with spiritual protection, then make sure they are centred. The chakras must then be opened one by one, starting at the base, to allow the healer's spirit to rise to the level of the Basidian. It is much less effective to attempt this work while at ground level, so to speak.

Once the healer has put his intention to work on a particular part of a particular person, this opens the channel of connection. Once the intention has been made, it is not necessary for it to be held, but it is necessary for it to be done without emotion or wishes for the outcome.

After this, the stages of healing are more about allowing than intending, and this part of the procedure is entirely driven by the Basidian. It is the human healer's job to ascertain, from the images and feelings that they send to him, what they want him to do. The images will usually arrive immediately, but may not be visual. They also use spoken word, feelings and intuitive knowing to indicate what is required. If visual images are provided, they may be anatomical, symbolic, cartoon-like or frankly surreal, depending on the knowledge and understanding of the healer.

Once the healer has observed what the Basidian want him to see, and has identified the emotion held in that part of the patient's energy, he will be shown tools for directing and replenishing the energy, so that it is healthier and flows more smoothly. The tools appear crystalline and are merely symbolic aids.

At each step, he will have to answer the Basidian's questions and make decisions about the next appropriate action, before the healing is allowed to move on. Eventually, the energies will be altered in the optimal way for that moment, and the healing for that part will have been accomplished as far as it can be at that time.

Once the intention and the right tools have been deployed, and the energy is being changed, the atmosphere is astonishingly like any other operating theatre. Discussions about almost any subject may occur until it is time for the next phase. (It makes me homesick for the places where I spent so much time when I was young. The repeated disappearance of the anaesthetist for coffee and the bursts of ribald laughter are all that are missing! The spirits even supply sounds such as the noise of the sucker or the diathermy!)

Once the procedure is complete, the healer seals the path he has taken, as he leaves the body. He can then return to his own level, remembering to close down his chakras as he does so. This last step is particularly necessary for the ordinary world, as with the chakras open, we are vulnerable to any other soul that might care to help itself to our energy. Any form of energy work is tiring to the physical body, as the energies of the healer are reaching up to a higher frequency. If the chakras are not closed and the patient helps himself, then complete exhaustion follows very quickly! The other good reason for closing down before rejoining the mundane world is that the healer will find himself much too sensitive if he does not. Try visiting a supermarket with chakras open, to find out what I mean.

B. "Each time you contact us, you reach higher; each time you reach out to heal someone, you go higher. That is why the tiredness will sweep upon you – for it is a different energy level to the one you normally frequent. We are in the process of working with humans so that they can stay in the higher frequency for a great deal longer. The one through whom we speak has worked for a longer time at higher frequencies; even so, she tires also. There is ageing of the heart vessels in the one through whom we speak, as there is in yours. We match these two similarities, but that is why the lethargy that your heart pump suddenly feels is felt by both of you, usually at the end of the session."

If the problem that has had healing directed towards it has not yet manifested in the physical, then this energy work may deal with it. If there is a physical problem, it will take very much longer. I have been astonished to discover how long the energy of an illness precedes its physical manifestation, often by many years. There are often warning signals given that all is not well, which are nearly as often ignored. Truly we do create what happens to us.

I wondered why the Basidian needed to work with a human healer, since they can patently harness the power to do the whole job themselves. They say that they need a human, firstly to gain permission from the patient, secondly and most importantly, they need our intention to heal, possibly as a sort of spiritual guide wire, and thirdly they need us to earth the energy that they send. They also feel that it must be a partnership between them, healer and patient.

This is one of our conversations on the subject. I am not sure it completely satisfies me, but that is possibly because it is like attempting to reduce a four-dimensional matter to two.

A. *Can I ask you again about why you need a human to participate in this healing? Why can't you just use your own power?*
T. Yes, we do, because we need the interaction of the human. Remember we are also dealing with free will – it is not just free will of the mind, it is the free will of the soul and we need the interaction of a human being for all their frailties. We can understand a human being a great deal more through healing in this way. Because of the energy, we need to interact with the energy of a human being.
A. *And you can't do that on your own?*
T. We can, but it is part of our learning also that we work with a human being. Understand that we need the participation of a human being, in order that the human also grows from this healing. When we give healing to a human being, they also grow. When you use our healing from a distance, you gain permission before you work. We also gain permission from humans. Before we worked with you, we did not. We learned that we needed to get permission, not from that person, but from their physical body. Before we worked with you for the very first time, we needed to establish that, without permission, it would not clear as quickly – that is part of the universal law.
A. *You need us to earth the healing, but it is you that steps down the power, not us?*
T. We judge how much is needed and this also we have learned through you. If we use too much, it wears out the vessel, the body. The human is needed to bring it down, if you like, to earth it, to ground it. We need the humans in the physical in order that they use their brains and physical limbs in order to give the healing, to

use their ability of sight, all of their physical abilities — sight, hearing, sound. We need those. Once they are aware of their deeper senses that match those, they are able to heal "the energy between" and the energy that holds matter together.

A. *You use the universal energy, you are channelling it down from the universe, and the human is intending the healing and earthing the energy.*

T. It is; we use the human as interpreter.

A. *And of course he is looking at the body, whereas you are not, so we are all cooperating at our different levels to achieve healing of whatever sort.*

T. Exactly so and that is what drains the human of energy, because they are connected with a higher energy, which, yes, is energy as well, but to stay in that state for too long is draining we have discovered for humans, whether they be fit physical beings or not. Anything to do with energy work is draining.

The healing part of each session is quite short, not more than fifteen or twenty minutes. But because they are so tiring, I have found it impossible to work with more than two patients in one period. The Basidian are insistent that we do not work when we are tired. It drains our energies and does not benefit the patient. They finally got this through to me with the following comment:

B. "It would not be good for you to send the energy that you are feeling now to another soul."

8

Methods

Most of the Basidian's techniques are described in another volume (the operator's workbook), but I have included those for grounding, centring and protecting here, because I think they are generally useful. I have also included transcripts of a few of my sessions with the Basidian to demonstrate the way that they taught me.

Grounding

The healer has difficulty receiving the images if not properly grounded. The technique I use is simple:

- *Connect the soul to something on the surface of the Earth – I use a rose.*

- *Connect the soul to the Earth.*

- *Connect the soul to the central core of the Earth.*

Protection

I learnt about protection while I was still working in the NHS. It abolishes the problem of the energy sucker. I used to sometimes find myself with my head on my desk, saying that I would have a nervous breakdown if I could raise the energy! A good protective technique is the answer to this problem, whether working with the Basidian or in Outpatients.

An effective method is to imagine a skein of light wrapping itself spirally round you starting below the feet and finishing above the head. The openings at top and bottom should be closed to seal one's being within the protection.

Once I learnt this, I usually finished Outpatients relatively unscathed!

Centring

When the protection is complete, the next necessity is for the healer to centre himself. All of us with busy lives get scattered by the multiple demands made on us. The technique for this is very simple:

- *Cup your hands slightly apart in front of your chest and imagine a candle flame between them.*

- *Very slowly move your hands further apart and watch the flame become larger.*

- *When it fills the space between your hands, become the flame, for it is you, it is your essence.*

Tools

The Basidian have shown me a number of tools that I use repeatedly. But for specialist jobs, the right implement always appears! Most of the tools that appear when I am working look crystalline, and some, like the Indigo crystals, are very versatile.

B. We will give you pictorial teaching also, so that your teaching is twofold. We would like you to go into the cluster of diamonds. One will stand out to you, its form matters not. Go through the vortex. Now follow the line of the vortex, this energy. Be aware of the energy, the colours of the energy, about you. Some may sparkle and some may have geometric shape. Speak them and we will identify it for you.

A. *All the lines of the vortex are different colours and, when I came* *through the end of that, I could see little black diamonds, not sparkling very brightly.*

B. These are an alteration in energy. The colour is not so much black as what you would call indigo. These indicate where a healing needs to take place. You are going to use these as an energy source; you will use these to disperse their energy. You will go in as if to implant and disperse their energy. In your language they are a vacuum, they will absorb negative energy. That is why they are the colour they are, they can absorb it and transform it. When they have absorbed the negative energy, it must then be taken through another vortex, out of the body, to transform.

A. *I am putting the crystal on her vocal cord.*

B. Now intention it to go within the cord. Now observe. What is around it? Speak what you observe and what you sense.

A. *I don't know what I am seeing – it is a muddle of pink and yellow without much form, rather woolly.*

B. This is the energy that is inside.

A. *Is this useful energy?*

B. It is useful when it is flowing; at the moment it is going back on itself. This creates congestion in an area, so when you see forms like that, not flowing, it has been blocked. The crystal will absorb this and it will become a clearer colour.

A. *I saw it change not so much colour as shape. It turned into flowing lines of energy. That has changed completely. Does the crystal change in appearance? It looks paler.*

B. That is good. Yes, it has absorbed. To do both sides would be good. Use another crystal, and you need to put this in a holding place so that it will not leak. It can leach out back into that energy form, if you do not remove it. Don't go in with expectation; just wait to see what happens.

A. *Yes, this isn't quite the same. It is as if it is going over and over like a breaking wave.*

B. This is its rhythm, the rhythm of the energy going through. Now, how would be the best way for the energy to come through – smooth or like a breaking wave?

A. *Smooth.*

B. Correct. Now use your crystal to disperse.

A. *The crystal is going paler and milkier and the energy is flowing now, not in a straight line. It is wavy, but it is going in a direction now.*

B. Good. Now take out the crystal and put it in the bubble with the other, and go back to the cords and insert whatever comes to you, an energy to protect.

A. *Little pink crystals with a yellowish tinge. I've just had a vision of the cords looking comfortable.*

B. Good. We put the pictures there for you. It is for you to accept the pictures, for it will help you. We have discussed amongst ourselves the way forward with your healing; there are many ways. This one is less strain upon your thinking brain. That was the consensus of opinion among us.

This session was typical of many and gave me my most versatile tools, the Indigo crystals, which absorb negative energy. Like everything else, they have innate intelligence and if I have intentioned an action that has not helped, then I can ask them to do whatever would be best at this time, and they do! I was also given a "bag of diamonds," which I was able to sprinkle over the malfunctioning energy and leave to do their work.

B. "As you use your diamond healing, as you see its rays penetrating, it will become clear that you can see the particles, the energy, in the fields between matter, and you will understand how a ray of light, of energy, can help change the mass of non-energy that is the energy between matter. We call it non-energy because humans do not see it as full energy yet; because it is that that shapes the mass, that allows the mass to be the shape that it is. It is in livening or healing this energy that is in between matter that is the key to full health for humans. It is how we keep ourselves in health – there is no illness here.

We do require that you learn to see – allow yourself to see the energy that is in between, to see and feel its form so that you can describe what this energy is. This to us seems like the basics and, as you move on, you will understand why we are teaching you in the way that we are. We can only give you one slice of your cake at a time. It is a big cake."

Early on, the Basidian taught me how to use my intention.

B. We wish to show you now how to use your own energy to drill through a calcified plaque with your crystals. It is a rocklike mass that forms gradually on the inside wall of arteries. It is not rock, of course. We would now require you to choose your tool.

A. *I have a crystal chisel and a little crystal hammer.*

B. This would be good. There is also an easier way for you. There is also a crystal drill that has firm and yet soft edges to it, that you can take through the artery. It is important that when the particles fall away, that they are turned to dust and then to liquid. You need to transport them from the area they are in to take them out.

A. *Can we transport them in a vortex?*

B. This would be excellent. If you dropped the dust into the vortex, and we would ask that you take it outside the body.

A. *This crystal drill seems to have a little spade on the end, rather than a point – a flat cutting knife.*

B. Now move through the artery gently – you will see the drill's flexibility also.

A. *Now I am having difficulty in detaching it at one point.*

B. Determine that it will. You are the surgeon.

A. *I was just wondering if I needed another instrument.*

B. If that is your choice, then do so.

A. *I am going to cut that off with some crystal scissors. I don't think the surface is in any way smooth yet. Do I carry on with the same instrument?*

B. Once you have cleared away all that you wish to at this time, then we would use particles that will liquefy to smooth it.

A. *That is better – a gel over the surface to remove the rough edges. Oh, that is interesting. There were some resistant bits and I just said "remove yourselves" and they went.*

B. You have taken control. A surgeon must always be in control. A healer must always be in control. We assist, we do not control. You are speaking with energy, remember.

A. *I do – I just hadn't seen it work that quickly before.*

B. Energy responds to authority.

A. *That is much better. Not perfect, but I think it will increase the flow through the artery quite considerably.*

B. That is sufficient for this time. You will be able to do this in stages, to go through the other parts of the artery. Understand that healing something like this requires your time, and so pace yourself to do a little at a time.

And on another occasion:

B. Welcome, dear one. We are going to work with intention today, so that you can see what it looks like and what it can do. Firstly we ask you to allow a colour to enter you and become your being.
A. *Blue.*
B. Look into the blue. Look into the particles that make the colour.
A. *I can see lots and lots of tiny little Basidian.*
B. They are everywhere, it is energy. We are intention.
A. *Do you mean that actually or metaphorically?*
B. Actually. Everything we do has a high intention. We cannot do anything without that high intention.
A. *When you say high intention, do you mean that you focus very clearly on what you are trying to achieve.*
B. This is correct.
A. *It is not a matter of will power?*
B. It is possibly a little of both. We have will, but in a different way to you. The colours that you see – if you would go to one particle and go deep inside it, through the Basidian and into the depth of colour, and perhaps into the rainbow of colour.
A. *Yes, not very clear, but lots of different colours. Some are moving and some are flashing. I just saw a flash of fuchsia.*
B. Each time you see a flash, it means that there is an intention put out.
A. *Do you use different colour intentions for different things?*
B. We use whatever colour presents itself. We do not choose it.
B. We ask you to look at something that would need repair that ordinarily would be difficult – let us say a broken bone.
A. *I see a shin bone with a break through the middle of the shaft.*
B. Which would need time to heal and bond. Now we ask that you put the intention to repair this. The intention has to be for the good of the bone and the soul. Watch the colours go into the repair site. Describe please.
A. *The gap between the two ends became suddenly full up with a lot of*

different colours — rather chaotic.

B. And what do you intend to do?

A. *I would intend that this energy become organised and flowing.*

B. This would be correct. What you are looking at is a break in energy and so the energy becomes confused. You are taking confusion out and putting strong order in. Everything has its order. Whenever you see disarray, confusion, it will denote discomfort or pain. It is part of your work to soothe this and replace it with strength. Your intention is what is important. What you intend and why you intend it are very important. That will heighten the colour. It means that you take more responsibility in the work that you do. This is not to say that we think you do not. It is showing you how it is effected.

A. *Now, with this chaotic energy, can I make it ordered just by intending it to be so, without using any tools?*

B. You do not need any tools, just your intention. But beware you cannot do it all in one go, because you are looking at energies that have been distorted and so they need to be soothed, so that they meet up with their counterparts and become one again. So if you look along, it is like taking something very sticky and pulling it apart. The energy is still there, but not in the form that it is meant to be. It has taken away its wholeness. You are replacing that wholeness, with your intention. The colours will alter. You will see the crystals within.

A. *Yes, violet and white crystals momentarily appeared. Once this process is underway and I have intended for the right reasons for the bone to be whole, then I can relax. I do not need to keep pushing at it?*

B. You do not need to push at it, but you need to observe the healing of it.

A. *So the first part is intention and the second part is observation, holding it in your consciousness.*

B. This is correct.

A. *Is it possible to heal this bone in one session? Energetically of course it is, but physically?*

B. This is correct. To strengthen it, it would require more than one session. The repair will happen in one session, but we would not wish the repair to be walked upon straight away. You have materialised the knitting back together of the energy. The energy needs to take its time. The time would be one of your weeks in order to strengthen the bone. Now strengthening takes longer than repair. The repair is easy.

The Basidian also taught me how to repair energy leaks, so that the energy that is given stays where it is put. Any parts of the body, whether wounded emotionally or physically, tend to allow energy to leak out of them, and this of course delays healing. They showed me how to look at the overall energy of the patient and to seal the points where coloured light was escaping. This is a good exercise after surgery, to close the openings that the knife has made.

They also pointed out that once there is a connection between Basidian and patient, healing from a distance, or absent healing, is just as effective. The patient does not derive whatever benefit he might from the healer's presence, but neither does he drain the energy of the healer. It is necessary to go into altered consciousness and connect with the patient and send the intention of what you believe needs to be done. Once the connection is made, if you ask them, the Basidian will take over.

B. "You do not need to spend as much as five minutes of your time. Give us the names and send the intention of what is required to that person. In sending the intention, you have set in motion the healing that you have already started. Once you start that healing, it sets up a memory bank within the cells of the system. You then tune into the memory bank so to speak. That is how you do absent healing. This way, you conserve energy."

The Basidian have shown me how to regenerate cells in tissues where the cells are dormant. When a cell or organ is dead, it has no energy flow and therefore cannot be repaired. But in damaged organs, there are usually many dormant cells that can be energised back to function. (The practice of cryogenics is doomed to failure not only because the patient is dead, but because the soul has therefore left the body and is busy with the next part of its journey!) Rejuvenation for the purpose of extending life beyond natural preordained limits is not practiced, because it is an interference with the patient's life plan, and this is not permitted.

They also taught me to go through an operative procedure, energetically, a day or two before the physical surgery. This they said increases the chance of physical success, by introducing it into the pattern of the patient in advance. I have done about eight of these and, so far, all the patients have recovered well and quickly. It is a procedure I really enjoy and, as I work, my point of vision is somewhere between the surgeon's head and his hands. It is quicker than working in real-time. The operation is accompanied by the usual theatre noises and, since I have spent a lot of time in operating theatres, the images are always anatomical and show the appropriate pathology.

At this stage, I do not have much physical proof of my results. (Certainly there is absolutely nothing "double-blind" about it and there never can be.) My patient selection was partly at fault (although these patients did teach the Basidian how long it took to heal humans), as also was the small amount of energy I could channel while I was ill. There was also my own lesson in trust.

One of the patients had a bilateral Dupuytren's contracture and his story is informative. I worked on the worst of the two hands for some months and was startled to discover that gradually the wodge of fibrous tissue in the palm of his hand softened and disappeared. What I did not seem able to heal was the tendon to his little finger, which remained shortened. My illness intervened here and the patient had the tendon surgically repaired with a very successful result. Later, the problem in the other hand got worse and, although the patient could always straighten his finger after I had worked on it, the improvement did not last. He had already done some of the emotional work, but when I went into the emotion of the tendon, I discovered a much earlier event that seemed to be the root of the problem. Once the patient had worked on this memory, the next time I looked at the tendon, I could not find anything that needed healing! This was a great surprise!

9

Final Thoughts

The system of medicine that the Basidian are teaching me is deep and profound, but not instant. It will be quicker for physically strong healers than it was for me. It requires us to participate in our own healing. The creation of health follows the same rules as the creation of wealth. In order to attract help from the universe, the human must take action to help himself. Then assistance will follow. But positive intention must be allied with action. "Heaven helps those who help themselves" is another of those irritating platitudes that turn out to be true! The creation of anything is driven by the soul who intends it. Just wishing for something does not work, otherwise we would all have won the lottery by now!

The focus of the Basidian's methods on the soul rather than the body is different to our medicine.

B. In orthodox medicine, the greatest desire is to practise to elongate the life. This is not necessarily of the greatest benefit to the recipient.
A. *Only too well I know this! This way is better.*
B. In generations to come, medical science will work with this, for medical science will change.

I like this way, because being able to see the overall picture makes sense of so much more of what happens to people. It is recognising the sacred journey of the soul which is one of the major advances of this way of practising medicine.

The Basidian like working with medical people who understand physical illnesses and take the restoration of health seriously. Those who do not have this background can be just as easily taught, as long as they are able to reach up to the Basidian and visualise the symbols they show. It will be slightly harder for them to understand what it is they are doing, in physical terms, but energetically should make no difference to the outcome.

The Basidian say that theirs is the method of the future and certainly it would simplify a lot of the practice of medicine. If every doctor was his own diagnostic and therapeutic service, then numerous hospital departments would be unnecessary. They say that we would always need some surgeons, and humans would go on having accidents, but most specialist departments would be redundant. I have a vision of a beautiful new hospital with staff who are dedicated to taking care of their patients in the old sense. They remarked one day that:

B. "The heart has been taken out of Western medicine and it is not a discipline that can easily bear its loss."

Restoration of the heart would revolutionise the practice of medicine and we would remember what our fathers knew. Once again, it would be a matter of opening the emotional centres and doing as we would be done by. The left-brain techno-wizardry of parts of modern medicine has achieved wonders, but the price has been very high.

Perhaps if we could understand that the term of a life is preordained, we would struggle less to prolong it at all costs. Since we will be able to look at the lifeline of the patient and perceive whether the outcome is inevitable or can be modified, we could approach so many illnesses differently. If we could conceive that the illness is necessary for the patient's soul growth, might not that change our thinking? Current medical thinking sees death as a failure, whereas of course it is just part of the patient's journey and, if it is what is in the patient's life plan, it is what will happen, whatever treatment is given. If we could approach an illness in the full understanding of the lessons to be learned for the sake of the wholeness of the soul, might not that make a difference? If the soul, every soul, is on its journey to perfection, then would what we do be better aimed at helping that process? A sense of the sacred is necessary if we are actually dealing with the progress of the soul. This was always known in ancient times, but has been forgotten as our mastery of physical tools improved.

The Basidian form of medicine is entirely individual and is based on completely different premises to ours. When pushed, they will agree that the storage of emotions in a particular part of the body is likely to produce similar (but not the same) physical manifestations in different people. However, since long-term success depends upon clearing and healing the negative thoughts and emotions before restoring the energies of the physical, then it makes little sense to start with the physical diagnosis as we do now. It might be better to group people according to what emotions they have buried, rather than what physical results these caused. But since each patient has a unique collection of forces, stresses and influences, perhaps even that degree of grouping is useless. I don't know. What I do know is that our Western medicine is only helpful to those who can be clearly labelled with a diagnosis and for which a treatment has been developed, and this only makes up about forty percent of the sick.

Alternative medicine does a better job with the unlabelled fraction, but much of it is better used preventatively than therapeutically, because the planetary healing energy cannot be applied sufficiently powerfully to deal with life-threatening problems. Whether we can evolve sufficiently to use this new energy for those acute problems, or whether we will always need the "fire brigade" at times, remains to be seen.

This new way of practising medicine/healing is a gift to us from the beings of Sirius and from the universe. I hope we can learn to use it effectively.

The journey of learning to use this method, going through illness myself, and listening to all the other fascinating things the spirits had to tell me has altered my views on almost everything, and I am doing my best to look at human life from the soul's point of view. This changes one's perspective completely. For many, this will seem heretical, and for more, a step too far. So be it. I have used the help of the spirits myself instead of orthodox medicine, and they have so far served me well and done what they said they would do, although seldom quickly enough for my impatient temperament! I can see that the system is not yet ready for this, but if the spirits are right about the collapse of the financial systems, I doubt the pharmaceutical industry will be immune.

The spirits have often told me that doctors will have to remember what they once knew, and this type of intervention can be practised anywhere and without equipment. We shall see. At least it fulfils Hippocrates dictum:

"Primum non nocere."
"First do no harm."

Part Three

The Earth and its Turbulence

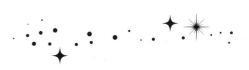

10

The Nature of Earth

The Earth on which we live is an exquisitely beautiful and gentle planet. Seen from space, it hangs as a green and blue globe suspended in the midst of the stars. It is peaceful, nurturing and feminine, with enough natural resources for all our needs. It supports the lives of many species, all of whom live without destroying the world in which they live. We are the exception.

The Basidian have shown me round this world, its energies, the layers of the Earth surrounding the central living core, and its atmosphere. They say that the large-scale mining of oil and coal has removed its major source of lubrication, and it is heating up and becoming angry as a result of the friction engendered. There are many other ways of utilising the Earth's power to create the energy we need that do not cause this damage. This Earth of ours will freely give us everything that we need, without our having to remove what it finds essential.

Early in 2007, the Basidian gave me a series of warnings about impending upheaval and catastrophe upon the Earth's surface. The period of turbulence we are facing, which they say will change everything, is part of the rising level of consciousness of the planet. When this is achieved, then the human connection with their world will be conscious once more.

B. "The quest for mastery of the physical world has led you to develop in such a way that, seeing the minute, you have lost the whole. What is more important is that you have lost a sense of the whole, a sense of wonder and happiness at the beauty, harmony and all connectedness of the whole. This is why you feel alone. This will change when the level of consciousness rises. Man will not be able to see any more with his eyes, but he will be able to feel the connectedness of things. This will make the difference."

They have often told me that the Earth is an important planet in the universe, and talked of how closely interconnected are the worlds and the beings of those worlds. There are many beings from many worlds helping us now. This is what Uncle Theo had to say:

T. The Earth's magnetism creates an importance. What happens with your magnetic fields affects all of the humans on Earth. The magnetic fields emit energy into the universe, and the energy of Earth is important to all of us. The knowledge that is on Earth, that is contained within the Earth itself, is important within its chain, within this universe.

Earth has a greater story to tell than anyone knows yet. There is a greater history to Earth than humans as yet understand. Earth is a mother planet, what you would understand to be feminine. There are mother and father planets in our universe, and the Earth is a nurturing planet. Treated well, it will nurture all that live on it and within it. This being a mother planet and a nurturing planet, affects other planets in its time line. Of course, it has connections with others, but every one is important, Earth is very important.

For the species on Earth, the importance is how humans communicate. Humans communicate in a way that only one other planet communicates, and so humans have a great deal to teach others of verbal communication. Humans also have a great ability to communicate telepathically; they have just forgotten. There will come a time when they will remember this, and the telepathic communication goes along the energy that reaches the other planets within the energy line.

On an energy time line, you would have similar timings, you would have seasons. Some have dark and light as their seasons, some such as yours, have cold and heat, as well as light and darkness. Those are what we speak of as in the time line, and the inhabitants of these planets are able to understand a certain amount of time, although theirs is a different time to yours.

It is difficult to understand from Earth, but understand that you will have brain systems similar to some other planets. Humans don't have as much function as other planets. They have not understood about all parts of their brain. But humans are seekers, it is the one planet that seeks. Humans seek to understand, other planets understand.

A. *Is that because we are so poorly developed?*

T. Not exactly – slightly underdeveloped.

A. *Backward?*

T. Yes, and yet it is a very strong anchor planet. Each planet within the universe has its own weight. Earth has a weight to it; it does not have weightlessness as many other planets do, and so it can anchor other planets that are in trouble for whatever reasons of energy loss. A world can anchor onto a heavy planet such as Earth and they will hook into the energy of the Earth and once they do that, they will draw energy from Earth. They would normally do that when Earth is at a high energy level that will not deplete Earth. They are not allowed to deplete Earth. It is against universal law to deplete another planet. So they would attach themselves to it at an energetic level in order that they can regenerate themselves.

They showed me how this energy was regenerated, by taking me to the edge of Earth's atmosphere.

B. Go to the edge, where you step out of your world into our world. Now look around you and you will see energy sources winding around, coloured lines of energy. Choose where you will plug yourself into. Now imagine yourself reaching in with both hands into an area, to plug in, to connect. Now intention to receive.

A. *Oh, the spiral kept on going through me. There were intersecting spirals of different coloured light – whee, it is not in me, so much as in and out.*

It is in my energy body rather than in my physical body, isn't it?
B. It is. It is the energy that we need to sustain that is not necessarily in the physical body but of the physical.
A. *Where is this? Is this a place in space or can you get it anywhere you are?*
B. You get it anywhere, but it is good to come up through the system out of the body to the edge of the world, because you are plugging in to the world's energy as well as our energy. The world has a great deal of energy that it wishes to share. Humans do not understand. Can you feel the energy? Feel what beauty feels like?
A. *It feels like love.*
B. Correct, there you have it.

During my association with the Basidian, they have taken me on many journeys through the cosmos. Some of these I have described in the section on The Nature of the Universe. They have also introduced me to the world I live in and have taken me on journeys to help me understand the nature of the Earth, its energies and its atmosphere.

The first of these journeys is to the inner parts of the Earth. The Earth's central "black diamond" core is representative of the living core of all the worlds, although the physical structures must vary hugely. I describe it as a black diamond because that is what it most resembles; but it is more beautiful and alive and pulsing than any diamond. They also told me of the Earth's development as it roamed throughout the universes, gathering layers of matter.

A journey to find the "dark energy/matter" was shown to me within the Earth, but this is also representative of the web that makes up the background energy throughout the universe.

Journey to the Centre of Earth

T. We would like to take you to the core of your Earth. At the core of the Earth, we can take you to a fuller understanding of the changes that are happening to Earth and reactions that will happen deep in the core... Now you need to go to a fault line or a volcano, whichever you choose. You are going down into the centre.

I went down Mount Etna, which is not an active volcano. I got down to a point where matter is liquefied by the heat. I was directed through this and came to a fault line in the crust, which was lined with Basidian showing me the way. Through the fault line, I came to a sea of a viscous liquid. They asked me what was holding the fluid together and I felt a strong attractive force between the molecules. Further down, I came to a solid layer of dull-looking material that looked more like iron than anything else, which I was told was a metal unknown to me.

A. *Am I in the core?*

T. You are, but you are not in the centre.

A. *And now I have gone into something that looks like a black diamond, and this is the centre, isn't?*

T. Exactly so, this is the beginning of your planet. It started very small.

A. *Where did that come from?*

T. It was created. It attracted. Look at the energy – what does it feel like?

A. *It is very powerful and it is pulsing.*

T. Yes, this is the rhythm of your Earth. If you can imagine, these are the heartbeats of your Earth. If more could see this, they would understand why you need to nurture it.

A. *It is alive, it is not just a lump of rock, and yet the iron surrounding it did not feel alive.*

T. It is protecting it. This centre can never be destroyed. Even if your world were to disintegrate, the centre would not be destroyed. It would be the beginning of another world.

A. *Like a soul?*

T. Exactly so. Yes, it is described as the heart of it, but it is the soul. Now go into it and look around. It is a large space.

A. *It is, and it is full of white crystalline caverns, and it is amazing.*

T. You are looking at energy. If you go into one of these caverns, you may find a light source that is different to anything you see or can imagine.

A. *I saw light that was black but all the colours of the rainbow. Wow!*

T. What are you looking at? Describe.

A. *The Source! So is this the physical demonstration of the spiritual fact that there is a tiny piece of the Source within every soul?*

T. Correct.

A. *Wow! It is black, this light, although you can see perfectly well by it.*

T. But if you look into the black...

A. *There are all colours, but it also illuminates, which I didn't really expect.*

T. It not only illuminates for you to see, it illuminates for you to know. It is full of knowledge. There are beings there. That flash of light was a being, but not a being in any way you could imagine.

A. *Just pure energy without any form?*

T. Correct. It is a light rather than a form, and the light can take any form that it wishes, and these beings protect the Earth. Light beings would be as humans were. All life has evolved from light beings.

A. *So these beings are just clothed with a few chemicals like we were when we started out?*

T. Correct.

A. *And they kept that form because their function is different?*

T. Yes. They are able to travel from this place at any time. From the centre, they are able to come to anywhere on your planet Earth, and these caverns take you to different areas of your planet. We would wish you to make acquaintance with the beings. They are very loving, be aware of the senses that are them.

A. *This is complete peace and love! It has nothing to do with the turbulence further out, because this is the essence of it and the rest is the trimmings.*

T. Yes, and this energy on the surface of your world is controlled from this centre. More energy is given.

A. *And this centre has limitless energy because it is the Source, and so it cannot be destroyed.*

T. It will not be destroyed. It can continue to take care of its own coating. The layers of the planet are as this planet evolved through time, because all of the planets travel through the universes until they find a place where the energy is right for them, where they would grow.

As they travel through the universes, so they take on another layer. Each layer is born of a different part of one of the universes – it is collected. There are faults on the surface which have not got any sort of heat source to go through, but there is immense heat at different levels and also many cold layers. You are able to come through that without feeling the heat, but you could identify the energy levels. You came through very quickly today.

Now we have shown you where to go, you can come through again and observe each layer and be able to identify the energy of each layer, what it represents and what it has brought with it for Earth. Earth does not want to be destroyed, and the light beings connect with other beings from many many worlds to try to save the planet Earth.

It would be good if some time you go to look nearer the surface where the oil has been drained, the gases have been drained. Have a look at the damage. Then and only then, you will be able to see why Earth is suffering.

Then I followed the Basidian through passages to a cavern that was one in which the Earth's water was created. I was shot up and out of the Earth on a waterspout and found myself among the hot springs of New Zealand! This island, they said, was due to disappear following its volcanic eruptions. After that, I was in a place where the oil had been extracted and the edges were hot with the friction and were red and raw and painful. I could see how the Earth would be angry because of its pain. What I saw of the Earth and its exquisite core convinced me that the Earth is a living being and what I received from it was love.

Dark Matter/Energy

On many occasions, I have been told about the "dark energy" that physicists call dark matter. This is the supporting web of love that contains and fuels the universes. It is the fundamental "matter" of creation. It is not visible to physical eyes, but once we are able to access it, we will use it for all our energy requirements, just as do the beings on other worlds. This energy is freely available to us, and is offered to us by the planet on which we live. Mystics have always known about the energy that contains and is the universe. I have recently seen a computer simulation of how this energy would look, were it visible, and not at all to my surprise, it appears as a three-dimensional web! I'm sure it has many more dimensions than that, but that is all we can perceive from here.

The Basidian took me on a journey into the Earth to look at dark matter:

T. You are going to go into the Earth to see some of this dark matter. Now you are going to travel on the surface of the Earth. You will be in the magnetic field of the Earth. We want you to travel until you see a point on the Earth, any point in the Earth at which you can go through. You will be travelling just above the Earth. There are many different openings.

A. *I am going down below the surface of the Earth, and it stopped being like Earth and started to get lighter. I am coming out through a cleft in the rocks, and it looks as if I have come through into another land. Now I am between two cliffs.*

T. Now determine that you are going to an energy source and then you will be shown it.

A. *I went towards something that looks like an imploding firework – the energies going away from me, rather than towards me.*

T. Now you need to look for its opposite. That is its renewal point. It alters the look of the landscape if you look through it.

A. *Yes, I can see through, but it refracts light. It looks like a warm wind as much as anything else.*

T. Correct. Now put your hand into it and see what happens to your hand.

A. *It goes shooting upwards!*

T. As if your hand has left you. This energy is the dark matter. It is not dark, but as it comes out to Earth, it would create a colour. I want you now to stand in front of this energy and absorb it into your whole body, almost as if you are breathing it in. Describe what you are feeling.

A. *It is as if something very soft and warm is flowing up through me.*

T. Look at a limb and see what colour it is. Can you see into it?

A. *I am looking at my arm, which doesn't look like an arm at all – it looks like a lot of different coloured lights.*

T. You are looking at pure energy. This is the purest energy that the Earth can provide. This is the energy you will be using. Now, there will be an exit point for this energy. Humans will drill for this, they will go into defunct volcanoes, they will go through the Earth plates.

They need to go through the Earth plates, because this is almost to the centre. Not quite at the centre, but almost.

Now I wish you to find one of the Earth's veins to go up. Just as a human would have a vein, the Earth has veins within it. As you go through, it will go along parallel to the Earth and then it will come up. It has verticals and horizontals. Let it take you upwards. Be aware and speak what you see as you travel.

A. *I'm travelling within the Earth and there are little side channels, but I am travelling along the main channel.*

T. There are chambers, as if for storage. You may see where the storage of the oil and other gases are kept.

A. *Yes, I can see chambers containing oil and gas.*

T. As it comes to the surface, it changes its values, just as the oil down here is different when it gets to the surface. This oil is becoming depleted; it will replenish given time.

A. *But we are not giving it time. Now I seem to have gone up, because I'm not in the channel any more, I'm in a bit of rainforest. I have come to the surface. Why have you dumped me in the jungle?*

T. It was the vein you chose. Understand, it will be one of the places where you can source this energy. There are many, many places on Earth.

A. *And is there any way of knowing them from the surface?*

T. Yes, there will be a warmth. When it is ready and prepared to be used, that warmth will change the surface, and the process that's changing the surface will enable it to be visible.

A. *And so, if I am flying along the magnetic line again, I will be able to feel a warm spot.*

T. You will, and from that perspective, you will see how that sends an energy up through the Earth. It will come out into the outer areas of our energy field. It reaches up to the stars. You see, this is the connection between the worlds; it is that energy. This energy is your future energy. It is how we survive where we are. We have similar energy where we are. Earth will become so much more replenished with this energy.

A. *And this energy can't run out, can it?*

T. It cannot, no. With this energy in use, humans will truly become kinder. It cannot be tapped by the few, it will be tapped by the many.

A. *How are we going to use it?*

T. There will be a way shown. Your scientists will find a way. They will not need to process it. They will need to be able to anchor it. That is all that is required. The information on how to access it is being given to your scientists now. They are searching for this energy. They are not sure what it is completely that they are searching for, and they will not understand it fully to start with. They will not understand it is the energy which connects all of the universes, all of them.

All of the universes have this energy and, with this energy, understand when you stood in front of it, how it changed you. You can become non-physical by standing in this energy. You will find this energy can be all things to you. You were becoming non-physical there, because you were visiting in a non-physical way. It alters matter and yet it creates. It is all things.

The scientists will be helped to discover a way to tap into it, but they will all be talking as governments how to harness it and conserve it. They do not need to, but they will think that is what they need to do. They will find, when they try to store it, to conserve it, it disappears, and that will be the dilemma for them – understanding how it works and it doesn't want to be stored. That is to stop the monetary system taking control.

That has been a problem of mankind – that they have found a way of storing the energies that they have used. You see, they will try to use the cylinders that they have used for the gas, but they will not be able to. It will be an empty energy and the cylinders will close down themselves, because they are not taking energy from it.

A. *And how far off is all this from coming into the physical world?*

T. Within the decade it will be discovered, but it will take another fifty years to learn to use it. It will be difficult for people to believe what they have got. Remember how difficult it was to understand the discovery of gas and discovery of electricity and the discovery of communication by telephone. How humans, when they heard of it, disbelieved it. There is a new discovery here now. It is not new to us, but it will be to many. This is a sustainable energy.

A. *And will there be interim forms of energy, because we are going to have to stop using the oil before this is available?*

T. Correct. The Earth will never be left without energy. There is a completely sustainable energy source within the Earth. The many layers of Earth contain different energies.

Later I journeyed again into the Earth to see its layers and find what they brought to the planet:

- *First there were the seas, which brought seeding with life.*

- *At the bottom of the sea was a solid layer of tectonic plates, which brought stability with change.*

- *Under this layer was a molten layer bringing heat and transformation.*

- *Beneath that there were more solid layers with channels and chambers for oil and gas.*

- *Beneath that there was another liquid layer – more seeding with life of an early form.*

- *Below that was another solid layer, which brought nutrition for the life above.*

- *The metallic surrounding of the core brought magnetism and protection.*

- *The "black diamond" pulsing core itself brought life, love and water.*

Throughout the various layers, in a continuous web, was the "dark matter," which was the love energy of the universe. This had collecting channels also, but was everywhere.

The solid parts of the globe were studded with diamonds and other crystals. These were part of Earth's healing and also contributed to the orientation of forces within it and its orientation in the universe.
When I went back up to the surface again, I saw the little tropical islands floating on the seas with their surface coating of living greenery. I could see how fragile it all was, how easily destroyed. Earth is just a tiny ball in space, supporting the surface world of living things that are as fragile as seedlings in a tray.

11

The Atmospheric Layers

Once we had looked at the Earth, the Basidian took me up to see the atmospheric layers. To begin with, they showed me the appearance of a world that had overcome its turbulence. The layers of this world were very beautiful. But when they showed me our atmospheric layers, they were another matter altogether.

A. *I saw a world with beautiful flame-like colours and blues as well. A bit like the Aurora.*
T. That energy that you saw is in part magnetic, two-way magnetic. It is also a cleansing energy, it cleanses that planet. That planet has experienced a cleansing as your planet will.
A. *It is getting over its turbulence?*
T. It is, but the energy that you see around, part of it is the remnants of the turbulence of the souls that inhabited that planet. Part of it is the turbulence of the surface and perhaps even the centre of the planet. The blue that you saw also was tinged with other colours, and that was the healing coming back in to the planet. It is very positive and, in order to cleanse, it needs to be positive to pull it out, and as it comes out, it transforms and becomes complete healing from the Source back. There is a continual healing for that planet and will be for the rest of its life now.
A. *And that is what is going to happen to us?*
T. It is, and that is how it will look. It will create a greater magnetic

force on that planet's surface, so that a different form of life can evolve and be able to sustain itself. We do not wish Earth to destroy itself. That is why we needed you to see and to describe as you go past. Come back to Earth, which is your home for the time being.

A. *But this has got a mustard yellow light round it, and that doesn't look nearly so nice.*

T. Yes, it is pollution and this pollution is from the weaponry of your planet.

A. *Nuclear explosions or all the explosions?*

T. All of them. It will find its level and spread around your planet.

A. *But it looks as if it was round a lot of it already.*

T. It is, it is around most of it. This is what your scientists have not fully been able to identify yet, and those that have been able to partially identify are keeping quiet about this, because they know that it is manmade. This layer obstructs clean energy coming to the planet.

A. *Is this the layer you said we needed to pay a lot more attention to rather than the ozone layer?*

T. Yes.

A. *No-one is talking about this layer yet, except perhaps in scientific circles...*

T. It will come out into the open as it all is now, because the physicists are beginning to open up now.

A. *Well, they are the only people that can understand it at this stage.*

T. Correct.

A. *And now I'm coming in towards Earth, which is still a very beautiful place. It seems an awful pity if it is destroyed.*

T. It is one of the most beautiful planets.

The next journey to the atmosphere showed me these layers at a spiritual level. They looked much the same, but there was more information available.

T. We will now take you to the outer part of your world, in order that you are aware of the colours of the atmosphere, and we need you to fly across the surface of this world at this level, inside the dark layer. Look along through the energy and see the holes that you will see, the gaps in energy.

A. *I can see a series of gaps in energy, almost like funnels over the cities.*

T. Yes, correct. If you go into one of these open funnels, you will have a sense of what energy is leaving at what rate.

A. *Whatever is leaving is leaving fast, and I got the impression of a lot of people jabbering or quarrelling going past me.*

T. Does it feel as if it is wasted energy?

A. *It is unpleasant energy.*

T. Unpleasant energy is a good energy wasted to become unpleasant. Move towards a major city where decisions are being made.

A. *Let's try London, though I don't know that very many decisions are made here any more.*

T. A few.

A. *I will go to one that makes a few more. That is a telling comment on its own! I will intend to a city where decisions are being made. I have ended up somewhere in Palestine.*

T. You have. Feel the energy coming down towards you and the energy being sent out up towards you. Describe them.

A. *The energy that is coming down is cooling and calming, and the energy that is leaving is heavy, burdened and weighty.*

T. Yes, understand this weightiness – how does it make you feel? Go into this feeling.

A. *The physical feeling is an enormous weight of responsibility and burdens, like trying to carry the world on your shoulders, and it is making me feel tired.*

T. Exactly so. Is it of one or of many?

A. *This is collective.*

T. Now we would like you to go higher and look at an area that is war torn.

A. *I have gone to Georgia.*

T. Correct. Look at the atmosphere, look at the layers of the atmosphere, the gaps.

A. *It is not ordinary smoke, but it is as if there was smoke rising up into the atmosphere and forming a layer.*

T. It is a good description – it is a choking energy. Can you see how this now affects the energy of your world? Watch how that goes out, for however long it goes on. If it meets another dark area, it becomes stronger. Look at it, because it begins to destroy the layer underneath it.

A. *It is as if something is breaking up and beginning to drop out of the sky. It is horrible. There are drops of acid stuff and poison.*

T. That is the word we needed. The poison of other men's minds goes up in smoke, then comes down again and spreads elsewhere, and it touches other human beings and poisons them. But it will only touch human beings who are prepared to be poisoned, just by mind of course. And it clings to them once they take it on board and damages them even further. The type of energy, it is so pervasive, it is blinding. Now we need you to go further up and have a look to see why you have such heavy atmosphere.

A. *I've gone up into another layer and there is something which I think is mucky cloud and that's above the smoke. There is condensation of something, is it the condensation of energy?*

T. It is. It is where it is changing from a negative by a pure energy.

A. *This is trying to transform it back?*

T. It is. All of this is not seen by the naked or the telescopic eye.

A. *No, I understand that we are looking at this at the spiritual level. I must make that clear mustn't I, or the scientists will expect it to be visible to physical eyes?*

T. Yes. It is physical in a way, but it is not visibly physical.

A. *So the smoke that was rising, if you look at that physically, was that the industrial layer?*

T. Yes.

A. *Then further out is the mustard layer, which was made by the weapons. I'm going up through a beautiful clear layer, and I'm coming to it now.*

T. Have a look at this layer. What it is doing to your surface and to your atmosphere?

A. *This isn't dripping. It is collecting stuff and it is blocking. It is stopping light getting in.*

T. Yes and what is light?

A. *Love.*

T. Yes, it is like a rejection of love, and love can transmute it, but it will not allow it at this level.

A. *This is the more dangerous of the two, isn't it?*

T. It is. What will need to be done with this is not yours alone to do – it needs many groups on your land.

A. *This is the layer that can be broken up by intention?*

T. Yes, and it will come in a purer form, and by the time it reaches Earth, it will not be unpleasant. It will be changed by your intentions, if they are good. It is a cloying energy; it is an energy that suffocates. It squeezes any light energy that is there. It's like taking the air out of a lung, and it will take the air out of your world and suffocate the surface if allowed to continue. It will suffocate certain areas of your world, and they will become barren – areas where there has been great conflict and bloodshed.

A. *So, all the nastiness will come back to the areas where there have been terrible things happening?*

T. It will be attracted to that negative, so those of you who are truly positive it will not affect. The surrounding areas may affect you, but it will not attach itself to you. It cannot attach itself to light. It can attach itself to things that have just a glimmer of light, but it will suffocate them.

A. *So, if you are a strong enough light, it can't?*

T. It will not – it is averse to light. It is not pleasant, is it?

A. *It is horrible. There is another layer still up here – this isn't quite as vicious. It is emotion! This is where all the bad emotions go.*

T. Yes it is, and you have a residue round your world now. And if you go to a part of your world where there is great love, perhaps a little primitive, but great love and not too much rivalry, you would see it differently - you would see clearings.

A. *So what about places like Glencoe, which have a very nasty atmosphere, presumably because of the slaughter that has occurred. Is that the energy staying near the ground?*

T. Yes, it is in the ground. Blood spilt keeps the energy in the ground.

A. *And is that energy damaging to the people who walk on it?*

T. Yes, but it would only be damaging to the people who are really negative, mostly angry, who are drawn to it, because this was born of anger. Those such as yourself would sense it.

A. *There are many places on Earth that have something like this.*

T. Yes, from centuries back to recent times. Humans think they can bury their misdeeds. They may bury the skeletons of their misdeeds, but they do not bury their misdeeds. And those that have created the misdeeds are the ones that are worst affected in the present life that they are in. It will come back to them. Whatsoever you put out there will come back to you, whensoever you do it.

A. *So you don't get away from it even aeons ahead, if it hasn't been atoned for?*

T. Yes, some atone quicker than others. Those with very base intentions do not fear the atonement, but they need to. Some of them enjoy the fear they live in. They come from a different place to us, but it is for us to understand them.

A. *I can't honestly say it is enjoyable, but it is really interesting. It is very marked as I go through the layers, how beautiful the crystal-clear layers between all this negativity are.*

T. Of course, yes, and that is the atmosphere, the energy that needs to have the clarity to be over your world, surrounding your world, and they will encompass you. As you step into another dimension, your world comes into another dimension; as you achieve the rise in vibrational level, that will help your world, because it will help humans understand. The level of understanding will be greater.

The Basidian then took me back to the mustard layer to show me how the layer could be healed using crystals.

Healing for the Mustard Layer

T. It is appropriate at this time that we show you the problem with the outer layer of your world, and how, from other worlds, it is being healed, and exactly what needs to be done from your world to heal this. So we need to take you beyond this layer of the atmosphere.

The Basidian took me through the layers again. The first was the dark layer, like a lid, which is made of the polluting emissions from industry. It drips its toxins back to Earth as acid rain and other unpleasant poisons. Just below this was the depleted ozone layer, which has lost some of its protective capability. Next, we saw the "mustard layer" of the weaponry. Above them both, in the clear atmosphere, I looked down on what looked like murky cloud. There were openings in the cloud above the sea, where the pollution had fallen to the seabed and been cleansed by the effects of the water.

They pointed out that this mustard layer was the one humans really needed to do something about.

T. Look at the layer, the mustard layer. That is the scary one. That is the one that humans need to be careful of.

A. *This is the one from the weaponry, and the only thing we can do with it is relieve it by our intention?*

T. Exactly. This layer will diminish gradually of its own accord over years and years, but it will diminish when the atomic energy is not used.

A. *But there is always somebody throwing high explosive at somebody else.*

T. Understand that when the layer breaks and falls to Earth, it will fall to the troubled parts of the Earth. There is, if you like, a master plan that knows where it needs to go; it will not come at random.

A. *There isn't anything that it is random in the universe, is there? You just have to think differently and bigger, to understand the plan.*

T. Exactly so, everything has a time a place and a purpose. Look at the gases that are there. There are particles in it.

A. *It looks really unpleasant.*

T. I need you now to reach out with one of your crystals – one that you do not wish to keep, for you will not be able to.

A. *I have an Indigo crystal that is willing.*

T. Good. Now, you need to put this into that atmosphere and look at the effect of the atmosphere on the crystal. It will absorb it and we need you to look to see how damaging this atmosphere is.

A. *Well the crystal sucked a great deal of that nastiness out, so there was a clear area around it, and it is a dirty grey now, that poor crystal.*

T. The crystal cannot be used again, because of the gases it has taken on, the energy it has taken on. The crystal has negated that energy but used its own. But that is its purpose.

A. *What happens to this crystal now?*

T. You need to let it go, and it will go to a planet where it will be of use. The crystal knows what it is for. There will eventually be a group of you coming to use these crystals to thin this area, to try to disperse it. If you travel around the surface a little more, you may well see other beings working on this energy. Some of them are invisible to you. They choose not to show you detail. We need you to view this and understand how much help Earth is being given from other worlds.

A. *They must get very fed up with us, continuing to destroy our world.*

T. No, it is just the task in hand. They do not judge Earth or the souls living on Earth. They know it is just part of their evolution.

A. *If many other planets have done this, then it is just part of the development?*

T. It is. It is as if, on your planet Earth, if someone would have a problem in their home, then their neighbours would come. Say it was flooded – they would come to try to help and they would just take it as the job to be done. We are all considering ourselves as neighbours.

A. *I am considering you as terribly far away and why would you be interested?*

T. But that is human thinking. When you are out of human thinking, this would not occur.

A. *I am beginning to understand that the universe in which we live is much more of a whole than human thinking perceives.*

T. And some of your scientists are beginning to see this – not enough of them yet. Now look at a section of your world where there is love. It will show itself, because it comes almost as a beam of light.

A. *There is a beam of energy coming up from a little island somewhere.*

T. And what does the energy feel like?

A. *It feels like love, but it has a physical feel to it as well.*

T. Yes, it is tangible.

A. *It feels like steam, but it is not hot.*

T. Exactly so. You are describing power. Now watch where that power goes and what it does through the layers.

A. *It burns a hole through both of the layers.*

T. Exactly so.

A. *And if there was enough love on the planet.... Well then!*

T. It would disperse it.

The clarity produced by the effect of love on the various forms of pollution was astonishing – as good a demonstration of the power of love as you could wish for. The other thing we can do to help other worlds is to offer up clear intentions for peace. This is a simple way for us to affect the build-up of the mustard layer.

This is what the spirits said to me on this subject:

B. "There are more wars coming to your world. Some of these will cause serious effects to the planet, not just to the atmosphere. The intention for peace is the best you can do to help. All your people can do this to help. It is important that you tell many, in your book, of how to influence events with intention. The intervention of peaceful humans can minimise the effects, although the events will happen. We have shown you the effects of war on your atmosphere and you know that it is suffocating your world."

So, once again, it is up to us.

Recently, they told me about how new genetic material of all sorts arrives on Earth. The genes for new plant life arrive as seeds within meteorites, and genes that are intended for humans are carried in the air and implanted in that way. In fact, the mechanism seems to be exactly the same as that used by the Holy Ghost! It hadn't occurred to me before that even meteorites are sent with purpose.

A. *It is interesting that nothing bangs into anything else except on purpose.*
T. Exactly so. When you have what you consider to be comets, the debris will come into your magnetic field because it is meant to. It carries information with it.
A. *It is programmed to go into the magnetic field and therefore get trapped into our magnetic fields. Is that bringing new genetic material?*
T. It is. The scientists who work with this are sometimes not quite advanced enough to understand the full meaning of it.
A. *Is this to modify the beings that are here?*
T. Yes. There is an ability to heal within this material and, because

they are not looking for that, they are not finding it. Nothing arrives on your planet that is not meant to, and it will all have a purpose – hidden messages that those that are open to it can understand. Someone who is as open as you, but with a scientific brain, would be able to understand the full meaning of it.

This next journey was undertaken with a piece of moldavite in my hand and its purpose was to illustrate how our planet has been seeded throughout the ages with new forms of life. This is how you got here!

A. *Are we going out among the meteorites?*

T. We are. Speak what you see.

A. *Crystals, in the middle of nowhere, and we are going back in time? I saw one piece of matter banging into another piece of matter. I saw a solid lump bang into something else, which caused fire and bits flying off. The bits are moving very fast – shall I catch up with them?*

T. Yes, come close.

A. *This is glass that is being created from the fire.*

T. Yes. It will change.

A. *This bit is green. What I can see is cooling down. It started off like fire and now it is going grey.*

T. It is going through its stages. It formulates its shape through the energy.

A. *And that must have had a purpose.*

T. Ask the piece that you hold – it has an answer.

A. *It says it came here on purpose; it has something to bring. Information – but about what? I think it said about the future.*

T. The pattern of the past creates the future.

A. *So what is it bringing? It is bringing me love!*

T. Yes, more than you have ever had. Ask it what it has come to teach you and look inside it.

A. *Inside it is all the colours of the rainbow in geometric patterns, and I can see stones like moonstones that are surrounded with gold.*

T. This is information. These hold memories.

A. *So if I went into one of them?*

T. Yes, you will go into a memory and the memory will show you the future.

A. *Inside there are trees, but I don't know in what time or where I am. They are trees from the future!*

T. Yes. Follow the trees, see where they plant themselves.

A. *They are planting themselves up a hillside. They are a bit like conifers and people are making planks out of them. Are they new types of trees?*

T. They are not new to us, but would be new to your planet. There are many that are contained within, and they will grow when they are ready.

A. *So it is the pattern for new life?*

T. You said the words that we did not want to put into your mouth – new life, new forms.

A. *You have told me that, after the Earth changes, there will be new forms of vegetation that would feed the population more easily. This is how it will happen?*

T. Yes. They look not at all like a seed pod would to you, but because of where they have come from, they need this protection. They are born of fire, they have come through immense cold and heat. They are prepared, once they are in the right location, to grow.

A. *So this is new life being created, just like it was at the beginning?*

T. This is so. That is how it is always created.

A. *Is that how we landed on this planet?*

T. Yes. You see, all life requires heat for it to survive, not just the cold. Heat will come from somewhere. All growth comes from heat, not just the cold, and that is why we saw fire.

A. *So that is life being created. That's how it all happened. That is amazing!*

T. It seems simplistic and, of course, it is a complicated process that it goes through. But when you look at it from the outside, it looks simplistic.

A. *So every planet can be peppered with any form of life that the Creator thinks might be good?*

T. It is. Every planet is, and there is a right time for it to emerge.

A. *Like any other seed, it doesn't germinate unless the conditions are correct for its growth.*

T. Correct. These will work with the different energies, and when it is at the right level, they begin to germinate. They have arrived already, but they will not arise, although they are growing in remote parts of your Earth, because trees need time, and they are ones that require very little water. The trees will have an ability to draw moisture from the air, as you all will be able to do that. Instead of going down for the water, you will be looking up for it.

A. *Thank you, crystal. Before I go over, I'll make sure you are planted in some soil.*

T. Something you may not be aware of, that you have learned to honour all forms of life, and we appreciate this. We speak of the forms that you visit on the journeys also – you have learned to honour them.

A. *Yes, but they are amazing.*

T. But understand, from their vantage points, you are amazing in your complexity – the human body is amazing.

A. *Yes, this crystal that I'm holding – it may have come from a long way away, but it is of fairly simple physical construction. Its complexity is not of the Earth, is it?*

T. Within it, it holds secrets that we do not wish your scientists to break out prematurely. They will not germinate until the energy is right. The seeds do not look like seeds of your Earth, as they would have disintegrated on their journey if they were the same.

12

Earth Changes

The Basidian have warned me that the physical Earth changes have already started and that they will become overt in the next few years.

B. "It is very soon, the time of turbulence, and the Earth is already beginning to shake. The times that are coming will test all of you and many will leave as a result. The waters are already rising and the Earth is becoming warmer.

All this will accelerate while your politicians argue. Your leaders live too far from the truth and reality of these changes. It is not they will save your world, it is you. Each one of you, whatever role he has, has a voice. These are the voices that must be heard, not the leaders but the led.

There are those preparing, who will be able to organise the people into a coherent force for good. This is what must happen for your world to be saved. It is the foot soldiers, not the generals, who control the army. The generals only have control while they are allowed to. It is the foot soldiers who will be able to change the thinking so that the planet can be saved. Remember what was once said: 'The meek shall inherit the Earth.' "

Few of us can change the world, but all of us can change ourselves, and that way, the world changes.

I was thinking about how the Earth changes might happen, and images started forming in my mind. I saw the sphere of Earth as from out in space. Its surface was cracked all over and, at intervals, there were under-sea earthquakes and tidal waves. This happened at different times and in different places.

Then I saw the planet again, much more of its surface covered by sea. And there were enormous Angels above the Earth guiding the Earth changes, and everything was happening as it should. And when the Earth had settled down again, everything was sweet and fair and sunlit.

The Turbulence

There are two parts to the changes forecast for the Earth – see below – and they have different causes. This is what the Basidian told me.

The first part is the physical turbulence – earthquakes, volcanoes, tsunamis, floods and fire. This will occur over a short space of time, about two to three years. These events are a result of the Earth releasing its inner excess heat and making itself comfortable again. They can be likened to a kettle letting off steam or a boil bursting. We have brought these events upon ourselves with our treatment of the Earth and our lack of care for the planet itself and the other creatures living on it.

The second part, the warming of the Earth, is mostly due to a natural cycle and occurs over a longer period. We did not cause this to happen, but we are making it much worse. If we do not respond to the warming by changing the way we live, then we have the possibility of destroying the Earth for human habitation.

The water level will continue to rise long after the time of physical turbulence is over. As the cities are inundated and communications are destroyed, the financial systems will fail, governments will fall and not be replaced, and most of industry will also come to an end. During this period, there will be a series of epidemics that will reduce the population levels of both humans and animals.

Alongside these happenings, the human level of consciousness will continue to rise until we are all capable of telepathic thought and we are once more in conscious connection with our Source. That will change everything and allow the beginning of the age of harmony, so that our world will once again be a peaceful, beautiful planet.

The Turbulent Period

The two-to-three years of physical upheaval is almost upon us. The spirits say that these events will happen, but the severity depends on us. They have described the worst-case scenario, but if we can learn how to live, then the effects will be less severe. If we do not change, they will be as the spirits describe. The only mitigating factor is that many of the worlds I have been to have endured a cycle of destruction like the one we are facing. The beings who have gone through periods of physical turbulence have undergone a spiritual transformation and are now able to live in harmony with their fellows.

Here is what the Venusians (V.) have to say about it. They have undergone similar events and no longer live on the surface of their planet.

V. "This is the people from Venus. Your planet is moving into its time of cataclysm and your people need to know how to survive. The essential requirements are water, food and shelter from the elements. Your people will need to move to higher ground and prepare for transport by water. There are places in the Earth where few will survive, where the fires of the earthquakes will be too strong and where the waters will rise too fiercely. There is little that can be done for the survivors until the time of turbulence is past. The best way to live will be to isolate yourselves in groups, away from centres of population, and to work together for survival until the physical dangers are past. The waters will continue to rise after this time and humans must take this into account in choosing a place to live. Disease will reduce the population levels, both human and animal.

For those who survive, the level of consciousness will be rising all the time and the leaders will not only know they are not alone, they will not feel alone, so they will be able to talk to the frightened without their own doubt and fear taking a part. A better future with peace and harmony can be built if humans stop abusing their planet and the other creatures living on it. This must be told, so that new ways of using energy can be found, and the inhabitants can live at peace with their planet. Man has to understand what he has done, so that he can learn a better way."

Let us hope that we also can experience this transformation before we destroy ourselves completely. It is only the developed world that is responsible for this plundering of our planet. I have been told that one third of Earth's inhabitants care about their world and their atmosphere and live in harmony with the Earth. If the rest of us can achieve that, then the destruction can stop and our beautiful planet can become the nurturing and self-sustaining world that it was always meant to be. We shall see. We shall see very soon.

Here is what the spirits said about the future of our world:

B. "Under the surface, the Earth is boiling and churning and the pressure is building. Ease must come by releasing the energy within. This will be violent. The effects will be felt at the margins of the tectonic plates and at the natural rifts within the plates. We have already warned you of some of these happenings and there are many others. The Earth must achieve her ease and this is how she will do it. The carbon dioxide levels are rising from man's workings, and the trees which are the natural absorbers, are being felled. This trend must be reversed. Man must also find new fuels as energy sources, so that he will stop plundering the Earth for fossil fuels, the lubricants of the Earth. Harmless ways of providing for man's energy needs exist and more will follow when the danger is clearly seen.

The Earth will have her ease and the amount of surface disruption depends on how soon man learns to nurture rather than destroy. It is too late to avoid all of the eruptions, but some of the effects can be reduced by man's actions. Man is geologically but a short interlude in Earth's lifespan and the most destructive in this civilisation. The mastering of the physical world has come at a great cost and the payments will be dear. Man only learns through fear and pain, as you have demonstrated for yourself. Learn this well. The diamonds in the Earth were part of its healing, that was their purpose, not to adorn the bodies of the rich. Everything in and on the Earth has purpose. Harmony is the key to living peacefully on Earth."

B. "Already there are subterranean rumblings and crackings, and the pressure is building. At the edges of the tectonic plates, there are fissures and emissions of molten lava and the beginnings of earthquakes and volcanoes. All of these will not erupt at the same time, but there will be a series of events forming the cataclysms of which we have previously spoken. The waters at these sites will boil and suffer from great turbulence and there will be mighty winds over all the lands. Lightning and thunder will also be a feature of the low-pressure systems. There will be fires in dry lands and floods in wet lands, and always the water levels will rise. While these events are happening, it will be for man to find a safe place for survival and to collect around him the people and tools he needs to take shelter, grow food and care for his children, who are the keys to the future. The inundation of the major cities will finally destroy the monetary system and central government. These will not be renewed, for there will be no need of either.

Human life will become physically localised into communities, but communications will be freely available as well as information. Telepathic information will be widespread and each will be able to perceive the truth for himself. There will then be no more war. The age of peace and harmony will come out of the cataclysms. There is nothing to fear. Those who have chosen to go will go and those who have chosen to stay will be safe. Children must learn the meaning of the changes in the Earth, so that a future generation does not return to plundering the Earth for their needs. All shall be well."

B. "Over the period of the turbulence, the rainfall in your land will be much increased and will substantially increase the level of inland waters as well as cause considerable flooding. The resultant lakes and rivers will become populated with fish that will be your main source of protein food. The rain will continue for many days at a time and much loose soil and unstable buildings will be washed away. Strong winds will often accompany the rain, and the winds will cause their own damage. All this natural havoc will considerably alter your landscape, even without the earthquakes, volcanoes, fires and tsunamis. It will be the time that the Earth will finally release the internal pressure and seek to ease her discomfort.

The fertility of the Earth will be increased by the storms, because the rain will release nutrients into the soil and the wetness will aid decomposition of biological material. It may be necessary to protect the soil for growing food from being washed away. This is when the rivers will rise and the valleys will start to fill. Make sure your dwellings are watertight and collect as much rainwater as you can. The time of the flood has happened before and now it will happen again. The final result will be harmonious."

Not all the physical effects will happen within the short time-frame predicted. The water levels will continue to rise for a much longer time, partly because of the release of melted water from the ice, but also as a result of increased production by the Earth. The flooding of recent summers gives an indication that this is already happening. This will alter our geography considerably and will ultimately be responsible for the loss of cities on low-lying land.

The epidemics that they have forecast will also continue long beyond the physical turbulence.

As the temperatures also continue to rise, the fish varieties will alter as they follow their optimum conditions. Much of this information has been given to me on many occasions.

B. "The seas that surround you will become warmer and will support different varieties of fish as the cold-water fish move north and, in many cases, finally become extinct. During the period of change, the seas will be frequently turbulent, as they respond to alterations in the Earth's crust and changing, often powerful, winds. This will make physical communications more difficult, but will increase the speed of development of telepathic communication.

For a time, people will be preoccupied with their own survival and wars will become limited to small territorial battles. The cities will mostly be overwhelmed with water. The death toll will be high, but the people who die will be those who have chosen not to participate in the next age. The exodus from the cities will cause difficulties in the countryside to begin with, but this period will coincide with a major epidemic of a disease not yet known, and also cholera and typhoid.

As the level of consciousness rises, people will band together in cooperative groups that work for the common good. You will not be alone. Do not fear. All shall be well."

B. "When the cities are inundated, there will also be new land that will rise up in parts. This will be rich and fertile. There will be enough land to support the population. There will be those who can tap the energy of the universe and turn it into fuel for heating and lighting and transport. The oil will be mostly under the sea and the will to mine it will recede as man better understands how he is to live.

When man understands how to live in peace and harmony, the warring cycles of the planet will be broken and it will be the beginning of the 'thousand years of peace.' This advancement in thinking of the humans on this planet is essential to avoid the planet's destruction. Do not be afraid. The way you are to live and the work you are to do will be made clear to you and to everyone else at the proper time.

Man learned how to cooperate when he came out of the forest and moved onto the plains. He has largely forgotten this in his struggle for mastery. Your political leaders are bad. Worse will follow. A more spiritual democracy will follow also, when man understands his responsibilities to himself and others. The meaning of life on this planet has become lost in many parts. It is time to find it again. The search for love will replace the search for wealth. The monetary systems and corporate structures will collapse and destroy the power base of those who are manipulating. If man can provide all that he needs for himself, then he is not subject to being manipulated or subjugated."

ℬ. "As the sea level rises, so this causes a rise in the water table of the land and so inland flooding will occur more readily than might be expected. Low-lying land will disappear before it is inundated by the seas, and existing lakes will become much larger. Conveyances will become increasingly amphibious. This technology is already available and better will follow. The turbulence of the weather, fuelled by the movements of the tectonic plates, will also have a greater effect than would be expected. Storms, wind and rain will become much more frequent for a time. The animals will become crowded into less land and epidemics among them will become more frequent, as with the humans. This will reduce the domestic animal population to manageable and sustainable levels. Intensive farming methods will die out as the level of consciousness of man rises and he realises how wicked such methods are.

Although some of the physical changes of the Earth and some of the weather will be violent, this will occur over a relatively short period, and the changes in the way you live will follow naturally and easily. The rise in consciousness will aid this cooperation. The turbulence will last several years and man will understand that it is necessary to cooperate to survive. Although the initial period may be uncomfortable, there will not be a return to the dark ages as has been anticipated by writers and television programmers. Love again is the key, and keeping an open heart and acting from love rather than fear, when physical times are difficult."

ℬ. "Already your weather is changing and there is very much more to come. The patterns are quite different to even fifty years ago and your planet is warmer. The climate changes must be understood in order for man to adapt successfully. The ice on your planet will largely disappear except on high mountains. The water levels will rise, partly because of the ice melt, but also because more water will be produced by the Source to effect the healing of the Earth. There will be less land available for cultivation and less room for grazing animals. The animals will be subject to their own plagues, so many will die. They will return to the Earth when calm is restored.

The pattern of life will change and humans will live in supportive groups. Corporate activity will cease and so this will release humans to work the land to produce food, energy and shelter. Travel will again be by sea. As the consciousness keeps rising, the telepathic capabilities will increase, so that the sense of isolation will be alleviated. Preparations for self- or small-group sufficiency must be made in good time. We will tell you what you should need. There is much to look forward to, but the old way of life is past. Humans must work to heal their planet, to minimise the turbulence that is coming.

The seas are the key to the next phase of life on your planet. The energy of the sea can be tapped, not only by wave power, but by utilising the solar energy trapped in the water. That, after all, is what caused the ice to melt, and it can be retrieved and used, without damage to the water, because it is so abundantly renewed every day. The technology has not yet arrived, but there will be those that will start work on it soon.

The sea you have often found a solace, and it is, but it is more than that, it is a cleanser. It has the power to cleanse the planet and, in part, the rising of the water levels will do just this. You know how the sea has the power within it to cleanse itself of spilled oil and other toxins. Just so can this cleanse the Earth. Fire is the other powerful cleanser and this also will be used by the planet to cleanse itself. It uses this means already, but this will be on a larger scale and will follow from the volcanic activity, which will be unleashed by the shifting of the tectonic plates.

The time of turbulence will be soon, in your lifetime. Be not afraid. All this is necessary to restore the peace and harmony of the Earth and its inhabitants. An eruption must surface before it can heal. Once it has surfaced, it begins to lose its power."

B. "The sea level is rising already and will rise very much further over the succeeding years. There is nothing to be done about this, as we told you. It is necessary so that the Earth can take its ease. The rising will be gradual overall, although where there are great waves, it will not seem so. The ice caps will melt almost completely, releasing a great volume of surface water, and more will come up from the central core where it is created. There is nothing humans can do to avoid this rise, which is ordained in Earth's pattern to happen. But the levels may not rise so far if humans stop damaging their world. It is important that humans know that the cataclysm and rising waters are due to the damage that humans have done to their Earth.

The warming of the planet, on the other hand, is part of a natural cycle of temperature change, the intention for which is carried on the great wave which cycles through the universe. This they cannot change. It has happened many times before and will happen many times again. It is important, however, to stop humans cutting down their forests, as trees are part of the balancing mechanism of your world.

These changes in climate, magnetic field and surface disposition will happen whatever man does, but some of the effects can be minimised by intelligent action on the part of the human race. This intelligence is borne of love, not greed. There is plenty for all."

B. "Water is the basis of life on your planet and water is a sacred substance produced directly from the inextinguishable 'black diamond' core of your planet. Water is a life-giving force without which nothing on your planet can grow or change. Water must be treated with respect and used wisely. Water is a gift of the Creator to his created and must not be polluted or defiled. The way of life on your planet will change until the things you produce will break down naturally into products that are useful for another process and do not damage the Earth or its water. All this must be acted upon to save your world. There is no time to lose.

The mountains on the moon were created by volcanic activity and the mountains on Earth by the shifting of the tectonic plates, leading also to volcanoes. The mountains of the Earth are the youngest parts of the planet and it is here that much development will occur. The 'new' Earth is rich in minerals and nutrients for growth. When the climate becomes warmer, the tree level will ascend and plants will be grown on the side of the mountains that the Earth has not been fertile enough to support before. These plants will provide more concentrated nourishment for the people of Earth than they have been accustomed to. In lands without mountains, the majority of nutrition will come from the inland waters. There will be enough food to feed the population.

The winters will be much shorter and wetter and the summers longer and drier. Water conservation will become an important matter in the land in which you live. When the population understands how to live in peace and harmony, the fighting over water will cease and there will be enough for all. The fertility of the flatlands must be increased and minerals and nutrition returned to the soil. The reversion to crop rotation will aid this process.

We will teach you how to keep your mind stable and how to remain loving and openhearted in the face of physical turmoil and population reduction. All shall be well."

The Basidian took me to see what was happening to the Earth plates.

T. We would like to show you how the Earth plates are moving. We are just taking you up to the atmosphere, where you can still see the whole. Now look at things in a little more detail. Now, we need you to make the intention to look below the Earth's surface. We need you to see how the tectonic plates are performing.

A. *There are two together just below me and a third one further in. They are fiery at the joins.*

T. Look at them – are they are ready to go? Can you detect a slight movement in them?

A. *It almost feels as if they are crashing together. The fieriness of it I can see, but I can't see whether there is a build-up of pressure.*

T. Go deeper, go into the crack. You are safe.

A. *There is a great fireball underneath.*

T. Speak to the fireball and ask what it is doing.

A. *It is getting ready to explode.*

T. Yes. You can ask the fireball if this can be halted.

A. *It has gone too far to stop.*

T. Where will it be and what will be the effects?

A. *Devastation. Where will that be? Oh! The Seychelles, and it is the most exquisite part of the world!*

T. Will they disappear? It is the type of devastation we are asking you to look at.

A. *I saw water rolling over the low ones and fire in the granitic ones and, if this is happening here, then this must be happening in many other parts.*

T. We will take you to another spot. Now, intention that you be taken to another fault line.

A. There is slightly less fieriness, but a lot more rubbing together of two lines which appear to be along the southern coast of France and Spain.

T. You are correct. It is a fault and there is a plate junction also and the two together... Look at the friction, it is important.

A. The friction is with two edges of a fault rubbing together, creating a mountain.

T. Look at it, it creates a new landline.

A. Land is going to come out of the sea here then. That is not immediate, is it?

T. It is not. Part will disappear with this, but the re-emergence is important. It is that Earth is beginning to regenerate itself.

A. So this is a positive – but what is the timescale?

T. Possibly seventy years. It will be ten years in the making. The people will, of course, have ample time to remove themselves. It will be cleansing.

A. I rather like the idea of the Costa del Sol being overtaken by water. It will cleanse the area, which is horrible, entirely due to man.

T. Most of the souls that are living there will have disappeared and that will be the physical cleansing in that way. But there will be another physical cleansing from the Earth. The Earth is beginning to complain, and the Earth is wanting to maintain itself and it is asking humans to help it – it is obvious to some scientists. Your atmospheric changes are the most obvious indication – how your atmosphere changes. You are experiencing more wetness and it is the wetness that is required to cool the Earth down. Would you like to go somewhere else, to a fault line that you know?

A. Could we look again and see what is happening to the San Andreas fault in California?

T. This will be good. We would like you to be aware of the air, the feeling that you feel on your body.

A. It is prickly, little discharges of energy.

T. Yes. We needed you to understand this, understand the reflection of energy, how the particles are hovering.

A. Are they overcharged? Is there going to be an electrical storm?

T. Something similar. Something that humans have never seen before, and the nearest to explain it would be an electrical storm.

A. *And that is in this area of California San Andreas fault?*

T. It is. In itself, it will create devastation.

They have told me before that there was going to be a great deal of destruction by fire, and they said that electrical storms will start the fires.

When I looked along the fault line, it was much more severely affected in the centre than at either end, which they said was because more healing work was being done at the ends. There was an area emitting steam, where the heat had vapourised the water.

T. What is the feeling here?

A. *It is angry at us.*

T. Partially, and it is angry because it is suffering needlessly. Souls that pass over come here to work to help this. It is a place where souls come to work, souls that have on Earth had a lower purpose and, discovering themselves without body, have recognised a higher purpose, and so they choose to work, and it would be, as you would understand, possibly one or two of your lifetimes. It would not seem that to them.

A. *I remember once before, I saw all the fault lines like cracks all over the Earth and they all looked very much the same – but these are not.*

T. Yes, but if you go and look, the crazed effect is exactly so. But when you look in detail, you can see differences. You can see the ones that are close to erupting, and ones that will take aeons.

13

The Timings of the Turbulence

Timings of events are the least reliable of the spirits' predictions. Most humans find this frustrating, but I am beginning to understand the reasons. They say that they do not use measurement, and that linear time, as perceived on Earth, has no basis in reality. When they compare the universe to Earth, they think that one of their cycles roughly corresponds to four thousand of ours, and that does make accuracy a lot more difficult, even if there were no other variables.

This is how they explained their difficulties:

T. The stars in their courses influence one another by their magnetic and gravitational fields. You might think of the universe as a vast web of interpenetrating and interrelating energy fields. Every "thing" has an effect on every "thing" else and every energy on every other energy. This is a system of great complexity and events happen when all the influences are "right."

Because of the complexity of influences, it is very difficult to relate a particular happening to linear time. This last has no place in the universe and no meaning outside Earth. It is merely a convenient way of separating events and has no existence in fact. This is why I have difficulty answering some of your questions. Your questions are many times about "when" and this we often do not know.

These are the only events for which specific timings have been volunteered, and their datings have been consistent. I received this information in May 2007.

T. The information that is held is about the peace of the world. We wish now to inform you of the peace and how long the turbulence will last. It is important that you speak of the peace, because it cannot come until the turbulence is over.

The main turbulence will last for one-and-a-half years. The build-up to it and the breaking down from it will be the other time. Possibly almost three years, over all.

A. *The start of the physical disruption will be when?*

T. Mainly the end of 2010, growing through 2011, peaking in 2012, fading through to 2014. In 2014, it will be cleared. The fading will be felt very quickly.

We are working, as many are, to try to keep as many humans on Earth as possible. We do not want the Earth to destroy itself in the way it is. There are a great many from other universes trying to change the trend completely, to negate everything we are predicting. There are a great many wanting, from this universe, to save this planet. They are working towards saving this planet. We are trying very hard to lessen the impact on the Earth. As humans begin to lessen their own impact on the world, each time one human being helps, it does make a difference. It will get stronger every year from now forwards, that humans are prepared to help their world. There are others, of course, who are not prepared to help. They will destroy themselves. Once the majority are frightened... When things start to change, those who need to be listened to will be heard. There are more and more, and they are coming to the fore.

Fear will become very strong – all the fear of different things to what you have yet experienced, any human beings have experienced. This era of humans has never needed to face the rising of the seas, the heat of the sun, and the disease that will be with it, and the opening of the Earth. Humans have made films of this out of the imagination, not realising they have been making stories of the truth, scary as that might seem. Those who have created pain and are continuing to do so will not be here. That particular type of mentality will be cleared, with disease and water.

Understand, a lot of animals will go also. There are animals in places that humans have preserved that will be, in the future, released into what will be their homeland. There has been experimentation with animals, experimental institutions, and they will be a new beginning with many species.

A. *It seems very harsh that the animal world is going to suffer the same extinction in a physical sense that we are, because it is not their fault, is it?*

T. It is not, but they understand it. They understand they have to leave in order to come back. They know the transition of life back into life.

Everything that is said will happen, will happen, but the effect can be lessened.

All the universes are involved, because this has a knock-on effect on the solar systems. As one is destroyed, it affects the life force of all others and so all others are aware of the impending destruction. Anything that happens in any of the worlds is felt in all of the universes and, just as you in your world feel the energy of the universe, if in another world there was a great explosion, your world would feel that. It would cause destruction upon your Earth, with rains that you would not have expected, and we do not mean moisture rain.

A. *Do you mean the results of volcanic explosions?*

T. Correct, and that would kill habitats in your planet, just as other worlds in other universes have habitats that they wish to protect. Earth is a greatly loved planet. Earth has a great deal to offer to other planets. You are all aware of visitors to your planet. Visitors take a great deal of information from your planet and they also bring a great deal of love. More and more visitors will be coming. After the catastrophe, you will have more visitors for you to understand how to use a different technology. There are changes to the governments coming. You will not need governments, but you will need to govern.

A. *We will, but presumably we will become self-regulating communities in smaller groups?*

T. Much more so, and when someone becomes hierarchical, they will be booted out. Earth is not a complete warring planet, but it has areas that wish war. Those that cause and create war will be taken from the planet. They will lose their power.

A. *Is it the catastrophe that is going to cause the breakdown of the civil structures?*

T. They will not have the places that they used to rule from, and they will find that, without their machines to create the mechanisms of office, they are without power.

A. *And are there enough people on this planet that are able to take up the leadership roles, because there will have to be leaders?*

T. There will be natural leaders, they will come from each group. They may not be highly intellectual leaders, but they will be humane, they will care about the people. You're just going back to basics, and it is as if Earth has just stood still and gone backwards. The way forwards for Earth will be very quick after that. The healing of Earth will take fifty years and there will be a tremendous leap forward with the knowledge that the minds who have remained behind have.

A. *So although the technology will be completely different, it will go forward very fast? Once we find out how to create all the things we need for ourselves, but without damaging the planet, that will stop the destruction?*

T. It will. The illnesses that you have on Earth at this time will not exist, because the things that create those will have gone. Life will become a great deal simpler for a while, until each group has built its own area and regrouped. There will be debris and you will be using a great deal of the debris in order to rebuild – for warmth, for one thing, and protection against the elements. Sometimes, you will need protection against the sun.

A. *More than anything else, we need protection from each other.*

T. You will not.

A. *So once this catastrophe gets going, it will kill off the wars, because everybody will be too busy surviving?*

T. Human nature will change. The biggest change in your world is the change in human nature, which has begun. You worry about the few that cause a great deal of pain and sorrow. It is more important that you look at the many that will bring love and happiness.

A. *I understand that, but a small group of determined people can bring a great deal of pain and sorrow.*

T. They will be outnumbered and there will not be many of them left. They will turn around completely and, possibly, if they are monitored, will become the greater help. Each human will try to survive for themselves and that is why you have groups that will work as a survival group. There will be nothing left that will be of any use. Money will not be of any use and you will all learn to survive by the food that you need to eat. There will still be vast areas of food. Earth will have a lot of food.

The Basidian remain fairly certain of the timings of the physical events, but they are less sure of the speed of breakdown of the financial systems and governments. This I believe depends partly on what happens to the communication systems, and that, of course, depends on how long it takes the water to inundate the majority of the cities.

The timings of these changes are dependent on human action, in other words, human free will, and as such are much less predictable. The preordained pattern for our Earth is that these things will happen; but like the physical events, the severity and timing can be modified by what humans choose to do.

A. *I don't know whether you can predict, at this stage, how the financial institutions and the governments are going to fall?*
T. It will start with water and explosions, and there will be many disagreements as governments start to lose their footholds on the money markets, and so people will see that what they have previously put their money into is worthless. Much money, be it electronic money, will be lost. It will be lost. Humans have a desire to buy and to sell. That will be the hardest thing for the human to understand — that they do not have to buy what they need for survival. It is there for them to help themselves to, without greed — only enough for their need. This will be the largest, strongest lesson for humans — that they leave behind them what is not required, so that somebody else can come along and help themselves.
A. *That is going to be difficult, because the natural inclination of humans under conditions of difficulty is to squirrel away more than they need, for a rainy day.*
T. We have been telling you the worst scenario. Understand that

we needed to tell you that, so that we can help where possible that the worst scenario not happen.

A. *But whether it is the worst scenario or not, we will not be using money, and we won't be using governments?*

T. Correct.

A. *Thank you. Are we going to have a lot of earthquakes in this country as well?*

T. They will become stronger.

A. *That is why we will be picking up all the bricks and making houses from them?*

T. Correct. The world has begun the recycling process, which pleases us greatly. It is on a minute scale, but it has begun. They are still destroying large tracts of land, which worries us greatly. They are clearing forests which your planet really needs. In order to stop the destroying of Earth, they need to stop the destroying of nature.

A. *Indeed they do, but until the people that are doing this have another method of getting themselves food, it is not going to stop.*

T. That is where the other countries of your world need to pull together – to feed them, to help them in order that they do stop. They are talking a great deal about it, but doing nothing. Now there is a sense of urgency again beginning to invade, which is needed. Life is beginning to become difficult now for some people. It is felt, not critically yet. Critically would be we would say in three of your years (said in 2007). If man works hard enough and long enough, these effects can be lessened, not avoided. Man needs to work at the love of mankind. It is about the energy that you are emitting from each individual soul.

A. *So if enough of the population change themselves enough, that will be enough?*

T. Correct, yes. The planet has such resources to rejuvenate itself. It needs humans to help it.

A. *And there are more who would understand that now, but there is still very much doubt as to what is the best way to do that.*

T. It will be the majority that rule the minority. Not like it is now.

A. *That will make a lot of difference. In a democracy, you are supposed to be able to dump your leaders if you don't think they are doing a good job, but in practice it is very difficult.*

T. It doesn't actually work. It is a democracy as long as you follow their rules!

I love Uncle Theo's view of politics. He is so encouraging! "Your leaders are bad. Worse will follow." "Democracy doesn't work." His pronouncements reduce politicians to the ephemera that they are!

T. Everything is in its own time and its own place. Humans once knew that. Part of this lesson is for them to remember that.

A. *So the cataclysms can be modified by the help from the universes, but not completely, because otherwise humans will not be able to learn a lesson that they need to know?*

T. Correct. It depends on how many humans turn their minds to better things. If they work in conjunction with the planets helping them, a great deal more healing will be done. This will be part of your quest also – for the people that are awake to work with the planets for the healing, to avoid a great catastrophe on Earth. Earth does not want to destroy itself. It is not the universe's wish for Earth to be destroyed, for it will have a catastrophic effect on all the other universes.

A. *And that is not good for anybody. But we have to do some of this ourselves – we can't just rely on outside help?*

T. Correct. Humans now are speaking out. More and more are looking at how they can help their planet. There will be a strong push within two years (said in 2007). Scientists will be aware of a catastrophe coming, by that time.

The Basidian also described an event in the Pacific Ocean, when they said that the water would drain from the seas into one of the numerous faults in that area. This would be a temporary event, but would cause physical havoc and great fear for the inhabitants. They were not able to put a date to this.

14

The Warming Cycle

The warming cycle is separate from the cataclysm and on a longer timescale, although the effects are cumulative. The spirits describe great waves of energy travelling round the universe, carrying information from the Source. This is evidently the mechanism for cycles of change throughout the universe. We are due the warming cycle that we are already experiencing.

A. *Is the warming just part of the predetermined cycle?*
T. It is. Because there is an energy wave that is throughout the universe, and it creates a positive and a negative, affecting whichever planet is in line for it, which yours is. Yours is in line for the negative, but the positive is close behind that. That is why your planet could save itself.
A. *So these great cyclical waves travel the universe and the planets just do what they are destined to do at that time?*
T. Correct. It is their magnetic fields that determine what happens to them.
A. *And all of these things happen many, many times?*
T. Yes, they do – not in completion, but in part. It is one wave that goes throughout the universe, but it is continuous and it will come back on itself and repeat, and that is why we say it is cyclical.
A. *Global warming happens as part of a cycle – it comes and goes, and comes and goes? So the cataclysm is due to what we have done to*

the Earth, that is our fault, and the global warming, we may have made worse, but it is not primarily our fault?

T. That is correct. It may be made worse, but it comes and goes. It needs the non-interference of mankind.

A. *If the efforts people are making to reduce carbon emissions will affect how serious the effects will be felt on Earth, I wondered if you could tell me what the best and the worst possibilities were for the future of Earth. Can we start with the worst?*

T. The Earth will start to turn in on itself and the magnetic field will start to break up and it will shift on its axis.

A. *So that will be a physical shift, as distinct from just a magnetic shift?*

T. A physical shift.

A. *So that the worst thing is that the whole thing will come to an end?*

T. It will. It will not be a sudden end, but it will be an awful end, and then the Earth will lie dormant for a while.

A. *It will just rid itself of humans?*

T. It will. It will not provide food for humans. It will not be able to, because the gases that will leak into and from Earth will destroy the very air you breathe, so that the air that you breathe will become noxious. So you are, if you're not careful, killing yourselves and everything on your planet. That is the worst-case scenario.

A. *Yes, and presumably it will then come back and seed itself with life, as it has done many times before, only it won't bother with humans this time!*

T. It will have humans – a different type of human at a later stage. Planets all do that – they have a new form of life. The thing you call cancer does not exist anywhere else; it only exists in your world. There aren't other planets that poison themselves the way humans do. Other planets have done in the past, I understand, but humans are doing it now. Earth is set on a destructive course. The destructive course does not need to destroy the planet completely. It will be destroyed in part. There will be this destruction in part of your planet, even in the best-case scenario.

A. *And is this looking forward into the very distant future?*

T. No, we are not. Well, for the great destruction we are, yes, but for the saving of Earth, Earth can be saved. There is enough beginning that, if they stay on course to help stop their greed, Earth could be saved. There will be those that will leave the planet no matter what, because the destruction is there. It has already begun. This great destruction is very much further on – not millennia, but it will be hundreds, many hundreds.

A. *So what's the best we can achieve and how?*

T. As we have said before, each human that does something to help the planet does have a massive effect.

A. *So the energy of doing something, even if what they do does not have a great physical effect, is worthwhile in energetic terms?*

T. As long as they think also in that positive way for their planet, it will have a massive effect. They can save your planet. This planet should be saved.

A. *And can it be saved, even in the face of the greed?*

T. It can be changed in spite of the greed. The greed will change. There will be greed of a different kind. Your coinage will go. But humans, being humans, will create another type of coin, another type of currency. That is a lesson all humans are needing to learn – to share.

Whatever planet you go to, there is payment and repayment – everything is balanced. The Earth is not balanced. There are many that give and many more that will only receive but not give. Humans have to learn to give of themselves more and not expect repayments. When humans really understand this, they will have turned their planet around. The saving of planet Earth is the saving of mankind.

Mankind needs to save mankind first, and they need to think about the air that they are breathing and what they are doing to their planet, to their space on their planet. If each soul looked at the space they are covering and what they can do to look after that and enhance their planet, you would have no need of scaremongers.

A. *How much of this is energetic and how much has got to be physical?*

T. It is really half and half.

A. *If every single person on Earth did a little something, that would make an enormous energetic effect, but there are still the very big corporations and the very greedy companies which are making much more physical damage.*

T. If ninety percent of human beings were to make the effort energetically, physically, to do something for their planet, they are employed by the few who are greedy — their voice will become stronger and so the energy at that particular place would be changed.

A. *Mostly they give their power away to a corporation, or a family, or a religion, or whatever, and then they don't feel that they could make any difference. But of course, that's not true, is it?*

T. It is not true. If they recognise their power — you can only have power in the moment — they are able to empower themselves to not be overpowered by others. Because there will come a time when there is financial stability in your world — when the finances are taken away. These large corporations will not have the power they thought they had. They need their foot soldiers for their power, but they forget this. It is the seemingly meek that are the strength of your world. It has been spoken of many, many times.

A. *"The meek shall inherit the Earth" was one of the things Christ said.*

T. He was one of the messengers. It is important in telling the story that people will see that there is a solution.

I have relayed some of our conversations verbatim, because I believe they are so important. But the spirits have summarised the various Earth changes for us and what we can do to minimise their effects.

B. "Today we will consider the effects of the various Earth changes. The heating of the Earth is from a cycle of the great wave. As you know, the Earth is subject to cycles of heat, cold, turbulence and peace. The heating is undoubtedly added to by the works of man, but it will happen anyway. Humans are forgetting that the universe is intelligently driven, and that the Earth is a live being which can change to heal itself like any other live being.

If, for whatever reason, the surface of the Earth becomes uninhabitable for man or the other beings living on the surface, then they will leave the planet and go elsewhere. Remember that destruction is not final, it is just part of a cycle. Admittedly, the cycles in human terms would be very long lasting, but cycles they are nevertheless."

The other matter, which is the impending cataclysmic changes in the Earth, are as we have outlined them to you, and these are caused by humans' way of living and disregard for the planet on which they live. The cataclysm will happen, but its severity can be ameliorated by man's actions. If mankind learns to preserve the trees, find alternative ways of using the Earth's energy rather than plundering its resources, and stops polluting the land and seas with chemicals and radiation, then the planet can survive.

You have a beautiful world, and it can supply you with all you need with no damage to itself. The use of freely available energies – wind, tide, wave and so on – will allow the remainder of the oil and coal to stay where it is and the Earth can begin to heal. The rising waters will bring further balm, once the time of turbulence is over.

The time of turbulence must be, because the Earth must release its heat and poison. The heat that is of concern to you is the heating from within. This must be released and the damage will be considerable. The poisons must be diluted and washed away. After this, the time of peace and calm can begin."

15

The Solutions

Patently we cannot continue to do nothing and allow our leaders to play games with carbon trading and offsetting and so on. Until they realise that the reduction in carbon emissions have to be absolute, not comparative, and that to continue to rely on fossil fuels is suicidal, they are no use to us at all. I have a suspicion that politics is largely about maintaining the status quo – and this strategy will not work this time.

Practicalities

The descriptions of the changes I have recorded are the worst-case scenario. The turbulence will happen and the waters will rise, as the Earth releases the internal heat and pressure. But how bad it is depends on the human race. If we can learn again to treat the Earth as a sacred resource, rather than an object to be plundered, then the effects will be less violent.

The essential actions the spirits say we need to take to reduce the effects of the cataclysm are as follows:

- *We should stop the oil extraction from the Earth. There are many ways of creating energy that the Earth will freely give to us. The oil is necessary for the Earth's own lubrication, and removing it causes friction and overheating, just as if Earth were a piece of machinery*

- *We should stop the pollution of the earth, seas and atmosphere with toxic chemicals and substances that cannot be degraded. We are not the only creatures on the planet, and the others have just as much right to life and health as we have. If we don't mind about poisoning them, perhaps we care about poisoning ourselves and our children*

- *We should stop cutting down the world's forests, which are part of the Earth's protection, its lung if you like.*

- *We must open our minds, so that we can once again treat the Earth with love, as a sacred place.*

- *If each of us took care of the piece of Earth on which we live and of the beings of all sorts in that space, then the balming effect on the Earth would be enormous.*

Having described the turbulence of the Earth and the collapse of society, happily the spirits did not stop there. In common with everyone else, I found this information frightening, and this is what they said to me about our future.

B. "Do not fear for how you will live. All is taken care of. Those of you who are staying on this planet are helping to bring in the age of harmony. How then, would we not help you?

If your physical needs are not met, then you cannot do the work that you have come to do. When you feel fear, open your solar plexus and heart centres (not chakras), look into the fear, and see what it is really about, and then see how things change. You must learn this well if you are to help others. To do so, your physical needs will be met, and you will be safe until you are ready to go. Concern yourself with the work that you have to do, and trust that your physical needs will be taken care of."

B. "As you know, we travel freely through the cosmos, which is more wonderful than you can possibly understand at this time. Every star and planet contain their own beings at different stages of soul evolution. Earth has been one of the slowest to evolve, and has had many civilisations before the current one. Previous civilisations have become more technologically advanced, but have misused their powers and destroyed themselves.

This civilisation has as its intention the wish to evolve to the point where the rise in consciousness of the planet would be possible. This point has nearly been reached and the events of the next few years will heal and refine the planet and its inhabitants so that the rise can take place. There is nothing to fear. There will be a great need for comfort and steadiness for the people over the time of the Earth changes.

The turbulence of the planet will release the toxins and harmful substances put into it by man, and the rising of the waters will purify the surface and cleanse it from these effects. When man learns to work with the planet rather than poisoning it, then the time of harmony can begin and there will be food and energy in plenty, freely available to all who need them. There is no need to gather all the crops. They will re-seed themselves, just as the plants you call weeds do now. Food and energy will be freely available, and clean water must be collected and stored. The fish in the waters will feed you also. There will be no more want."

The spirits provided a great deal of practical advice about generating power for heating, lighting and running our machinery. Some of these messages are for far into the future, or for isolated communities thrown back on their own resources, but all of them assure us that our Earth has everything we need. The Venusians in particular are a mine of `handy hints for handless humans.' I have transcribed a couple of their suggestions below, in particular the one about raising hot water to a higher level if you have no electric power. I am fond of this piece of advice, which came in response to my complaint that, whatever happened to the Earth, I could not manage life without hot baths!

ℬ. "The power of the weather has not yet been fully utilised. You are familiar with wind power and solar power and wave power. There are ways to use temperature differentials to create energetic power, just as you use the same principle for extracting heat from the Earth. Putting one end of a metal wire in a hot source causes current to flow towards the cooler source. This has practical applications. Because the big corporations have monopolised energy production for so long, it has been forgotten that production could be local rather than central. Rediscovery of this idea will help to break the stranglehold of the monopolies.

The clouds that carry rain are also a source of power, but the rain is best collected for watering vegetables and for drinking and domestic purposes. Everything that occurs on Earth can be used; it is just a question of whether the principle is practical. The use of acid and chemicals as in lead acid batteries can also be utilised, and regenerating batteries will be made.

You already have generation of power by windmills, but there are more uses that could be made of wind. In the parts of the world that are very windy, power generation can conveniently utilise this force. The wind sock principle will work just as well in a steady wind as it will with the tides in the water. The sails of the boat utilise the force of the wind and this can be adapted for power generation. There are so many ways of generating your own power in the short term. Scientists can produce simple machinery that can be cared for by the local community.

If you are able to use the sun, the wind, the waves, the tides and the heat of the Earth, what have you then to fear from cold?"

The generation of power for heating and lighting has been following along well-defined lines for so long, that humans have forgotten how many other ways that there are.

B. "Out in the universe, the power of the winds is enormous, more than you can imagine, and all this power is produced from the background energy of the universe, as well as from the nuclear explosions in the cores of planets and where the stars are being formed. All this energy comes from the Source and there is plenty for all. There are people on your planet who are already thinking along these lines and are preparing other ways of providing energy. They will not be heard yet, just as you will not be, but the time is not far.

The sun is the greatest power of all, as far as your planet is concerned, and solar power will be used more as the Earth warms.

In time, each community will generate its own power, the methods depending on which part of the planet they inhabit. The waste products of man and animals are already used for the creation of power and heat, but there is much more to learn. Your cooking machines are already being adapted to use methane. The bacteria in biological waste produce fermentation, which is a source of heat and gas production. All of this can be harnessed to produce useful energy. As soon as the people see the prospect of an interruption in oil supplies, alternative ways of creating power will become subjects for increasing investigation. There are many viable ideas awaiting development, and the funding for these will be made available as soon as there is the fear. The final products after the energy has been extracted will still be useful to fertilise the Earth. The heat of the process, as the waste goes through to produce energy, will destroy most of the viruses, but not all the bacteria, that were in the original waste.

These methods are all more labour intensive than they are at present. But remember that many of the worthless jobs that men now do will not exist and there will be labour available. In addition, the workers will understand what they're trying to do and will also understand the need for cooperation.

The recycling of waste in one form or another is essential to avoid further damage to the planet. Once you stop producing materials that will not degrade, this problem will become easier. Previous generations of humans understood how to build things to last, and they will go back to that knowledge. Many of the remaining souls will be able to access information in the way that you are being taught. Do not fear. All that you need will be available."

B. "The power of water is easily visualised, but properly harnessed and controlled, can be used to drive machinery, as was once commonplace. Water can turn a wheel, which will create energy for grinding or for the creation of electricity. On a large scale, this is already used, especially in mountainous lands, and it can be used on a domestic scale as well. If a circular system can be created, it can be used without much loss of water to create power. It will be increasingly important to conserve water. We have told you that the planet will not withhold her water, as is threatened by your scaremongers, but each drop will be precious. With adequate water and a supply of methane-producing waste, you will be surprised how comfortable you can make yourselves.

Remember also that, although physical isolation will increase, we are always here to help and guide you. You will not be alone, not even for a moment. If there are ways to solve the problems that you do not know about, you have only to ask. Increasingly, humans will be able to access their intuition and their guides for help in the turbulent days. You will not be abandoned.

Remember that this phase of turbulence is the necessary forerunner to the age of harmony. This age of harmony is what you are on the planet to help bring in. Every spirit in the universe wishes for this and the help will be beyond your imagining."

From the Venusians:

V. "We would like to start telling you how we can help you. The tides in your water can be used much more than they are currently. The tides are pulled by your moon, and the power of this body of water is enormous. By working against the pull of the tides, a force could be produced which can be transformed into electrical energy. This energy is obviously sustainable and, just as importantly, cannot be stored.

In the future, your population will nearly all live near water. The hinterland will be too hot and dry to grow crops. This means that electrical energy can be supplied to each community. A generating plant will be necessary, but this is within your current technological capabilities. The power will be generated with the use of a device like a windsock or drag anchor. This will pull against the power of the water and can be reversed so that it follows the tides. This is a simple principle and will probably not generate enough electrical power for all of your needs. However, it will be adequate for dwellings near water.

The heat of the Earth can already be tapped by your scientists, but there are better ways of doing this than you have yet found. Volcanic energy will be tapped after the eruptions, and this will be a massive source of power, and there are many other ways. Energy can be tapped from many sources by your communities, until the scientists are able to use the dark energy directly. Man is an ingenious creature and there are many who have information within them that they do not yet know or understand. Man must turn from oil and coal, or the planet will no longer be able to forgive him. This is what happened to us. Our methods of damaging our planet were different, but the effects were the same. We can help in greater detail when we come into contact with minds with the right types of background information."

More from the Venusians:

V. "We would like to tell you more about how we can help your planet. Much of what we tell you must be simple, because of your limited scientific knowledge. Nevertheless, there are many simple things to make your lives pleasanter when your corporate systems fail, as they will.

You are often talking about hot water and your need for it. Here is a simple way to heat your water. If you light a fire under a metal container, as the water gets hotter, it can be driven up a pipe starting under the surface of the water and thus fill a container at a higher level for you to bath or wash clothes. This principle is already used, but should be recorded, for many will have forgotten the method by the time it is needed.

It would of course be easier for you to use electrical power for this purpose, and there are many ways of generating electricity at local level. Methane gas is already used for this purpose, and it is possible to produce this from the breakdown of many biological processes. The methane can then be burned to produce heat for cooking and heating water. Heat can be converted into electric current.

As the earth continues to warm, it will become easier to extract heat from it. This process you call geothermal heating. There are many other ways that take a little more scientific knowledge than you have."

B. "The sea is rising already, though it has very much further to go. The sea will become a more important part of life in your part of the world. Today, the sea is mainly considered for recreation, but it will become again an integral part of life and a way of transport. The inland waters also will increase and fill with fish, and boating will become the usual way of transport in these regions. The diet of humans will become healthier with the rising waters and warmer climate. There are many things to teach you about how to manage the change in lifestyle and we will do this in good time.

This is the calm before the storms. Make use of it to prepare yourself. Water is the key. You must conserve your water and make plans to restore the goodness to the ground. We will put into your mind the actions you need to take and things you need to store. There will be enough for all, but it is time to consider the change."

B. "Fire will be a significant factor in the changes to the Earth. Fire cleanses as it destroys, and new life follows the fire. The burning lava from the earthquakes will cause fires that destroy large areas of land. In time, the new life on this land will find most fertile soil, but the short-term effect is destruction.

Fire, however, is an essential tool in man's armoury and must be preserved and protected. The methods of kindling fire may become primitive, but should not be lost. *(I saw the image of a magnifying glass setting light to some kindling.)* Heat from fire is needed for warmth and also to drive physical processes. Fire is needed for cooking and also for reducing waste to minerals, to fertilise the land. Fire has also symbolic use, as you know, and is at many levels a great cleanser.

The effects of fires upon the land is at first destructive. In the worst cases, the smoke blocks the sunlight from reaching Earth. But the long-term effects are largely beneficial. The large-scale burning of wood should be avoided, although there is nothing else that holds fire for so long. The trees in your landscape will be needed for shelter, but wood is one of the things that you can store. Avoidance of accidental fire will become increasingly important in the drier summers. Fire represents the best and worst, depending on which effect is dominant. Treat it with respect and do not forget all that it can do for you, both physically and symbolically."

$\mathcal{B}$. "Today we would speak of the relationship between light and fire. You know that if you focus rays of light on a flammable substance, that fire is created spontaneously by the generation of sufficient heat. Light and heat are two aspects of the same energy. It is the fires burning in your sun that create the light by which you see. Whether the heat or the light are paramount depends on the physical circumstances. Fire consumes, but light illuminates but does not consume. Their primary purpose is different, even though they are aspects of the same energy. The light that crosses the universe is colder by the time it reaches the planets, but it contains within it enough heat to create fire in the right circumstances.

The manipulation of energy in the universe to satisfy one's physical needs has been somewhat forgotten among man's ingenious inventions. That will come to the fore again in the times that are coming. Man needs shelter against the elements, water, warmth and energy supplies for cooking and lighting. All these can be supplied by the planet and its energy fields. In particular, the needs for warmth, cooking and lighting can be supplied by these fields, even before the ways of tapping the dark energy are found.

A crystal ball may not help to see into the future, but it will be very useful for creating fire! It will be good to prepare for times when self-reliance is necessary."

This last comment entertained me. I had just been given a crystal ball and rather resented the implication that I was engaged in witchcraft!

$\mathcal{B}$. "Love is the force that drives the universe and, as such, is the most powerful force there is. It is also a human emotion best illustrated by her mother's love for her child. This also is powerful, but it is also soft and supporting and comforting. How can this energy of love have such various manifestations and how can the two examples be contained in the same force.

The power that runs the universe is capable of every variation, from extreme violence to the most delicate softness. If you take your own world as an example, the molten inner core escaping to the surface shows the violence, and the delicacy of a single spring flower the softness. But the force required of the plant to break through the hardened winter surface of the soil is very great.

The ability of the Creator to use exactly the quantity of force required to produce each effect is what is beyond your understanding. This is what humans have yet to learn. There have been many ingenious inventions that supply energy, but too much is produced, or the process makes unwanted and dangerous waste materials, which exert their own force.

The exquisite balance of nature and the creative force has yet to be learnt by man. Nothing need be wasted, if the world is to be in perfect balance. Unavoidable waste products that happen in nature are fuel for the next part of the process. When a plant breaks down its structure, it returns nutrients to the soil and methane to the air. Those are used again. When fire destroys the forest, the ash contains nutrients to help the growth of the plants. Physical life occurs in cycles as the material bodies wear out, but love is the force that drives the cycles. Materials that cannot decay turn the surface of the Earth into a rubbish dump and interrupt the processes of nature. This must be understood and learnt."

B. "Water is the sea in which the molecules of life swim. It acts as support and also as a communications system. It transports nutrients and waste, and it acts as a buffer, both physically and chemically. Water comes from the 'black diamond' core of this planet and, being created by the Source, will never run out.

The waters of your planet are rising and will occupy a greater proportion of the planet's surface in time to come. The waters of Earth support and buffer the planet in the same way as happens in a biological organism. Indeed, the Earth is a biological organism, one of great complexity and diversity. When humans can understand this fully, then their attitude to their planet can change enough to allow the Earth to heal and then flourish. The waters of the Earth are the life of your planet and transport all substances that are needed for health and growth. The light of the sun supplies the only other requirement, that of energy for the biological processes to occur.

The life of the Earth is dependent on humans at this time. The damage they have created is enormous, but the planet can survive if the harm ceases. We are working here to open minds and hearts, so that the damage can stop. There are many beings on many planets in this universe who are working to awaken the human to a wider and truer perception of life. The limitation of the human brain and the separation from the Source has caused this damage. We are longing for you all to come home to the truth and understanding of love, the energy which drives the universe."

B. "Water is a solvent, a carrier of more complex substances, in its simple form. Although water is a simple compound, spiritually it is profound. Water is the basis of life on your planet. Without water, nothing can live or grow. You have seen flowers in desert places. They blossom only when there has been water. Germination of seeds only takes place in the presence of water. Most of the human body consists of water.

The waters of the Earth come from the central core and thus from the Source. Thus, water is a sacred substance on which biological life on your planet is entirely dependent. The water on your planet is a gift from the Source and should be treated as such. Pollution of the waters from powerful chemicals and radiation is responsible for infertility. There is not the need of this. Chemicals exhaust the land, and the natural nutrients are replaced by more chemicals.

Grow what you need. There can be enough for everyone. The blessings of the seas are due to the waters themselves, not only their gift of fish. Fish will become a more important source of protein as the landmass shrinks. Meat is an extravagant way of using the Earth's nutritional resources. Here we speak only of free-swimming fish. The farming of these species has all the dangers of any intensive farming practice, quite apart from the negative energy produced by maltreating a live creature.

Fish and eggs will form the protein until higher protein plants become available. With potatoes and squashes for starch and green leaves for the vitamins, you will feed perfectly well. Flour will still be ground for bread and pasta, but much of this will be grown and processed locally. As the waters warm, the species of fish will change. This is already happening in your seas.

Look forward to a time when everything and everyone is nurtured, and everything and everyone is full of love. *(Here I saw a warm peaceful world where everyone was at peace and, although there was work to maintain the lands and produce the food, there was time for everyone to be still and understand their true nature and their relationship with the Source.)* This is how it will be. If the money system and the corporate strivings to produce ever more expensive and unnecessary luxuries and useless toys, if these have gone, this is how it will be."

A. *What about man's acquisitive nature?*
B. When the level of consciousness rises far enough to put love uppermost, that too will pass. Everything is in place. What you need will become available. There is no need to worry. The universe is cooperating for this transition and you will be safe and free and cared for.

Philosophical

The spirits provided a great deal of philosophical advice on how we can best evolve to live in harmony with our planet. There have been repeated transmissions and conversations about the changes necessary in human minds and attitudes, so that we can learn again to treat our planet as a sacred being who will love and nurture us and provide us with everything necessary for life. This has been forgotten by the Western developed world, because we live so far from the Earth and its natural cycles. The so-called primitive peoples have not forgotten what we can no longer remember. Western consumerism seems to be a form of madness, although I have to admit that it makes life much easier on a physical level.

B. "The energy of love is not a feeling, but a force, with all the properties of any other energetic force. This universe runs on love, and this love must be expressed more fully by the humans on this planet, before the planet can heal. There is already discussion, in your media, of climate change and food production by local means. This is a start, but there is a very long journey before man begins to live these truths. Talk is easy, but it is nevertheless an essential precondition for action.

The processing of food is highly dangerous to man, because of the chemicals used and the changes they induce in the food. The whole race needs to understand what they are doing to themselves and the planet. Man needs to learn to treat himself and his planet with love and respect, before the planet can feel ease and harmony. Until the planet feels the ease and comfort and sense of cooperation with its inhabitants, its eruptions cannot heal. This is the way for man to go. A start has been made, but those in power are still bargaining for political gain, and it is only lip-service that they bring to this discussion. It will be necessary for them to become fearful for themselves and their families, before meaningful action is taken. By then, there will be a ground-swell of opinion to challenge the self-serving political will.

Be not afraid, but be careful how you live. The energy of love is quite sufficient to overcome all these human difficulties, if humans themselves will allow it so. The time of tribulation is near and, as we have told you, the Earth changes have started."

B. "The seas will be a balm to Earth as the waters rise. The calming of the Earth by the water will be the final phase of the disturbances and will herald the age of harmony. How much turbulence is inevitable depends on the attitude of humans to their planet. If man can understand what he is doing and change his ways, not all the destruction is necessary. This is not the end of the world, but it will be severe enough to change men's ways, and those that have elected to remain will understand that they cannot continue to behave so selfishly. The reduction of the population by disease has happened many times before.

The calmness, the peace, after the cataclysm will bring relief and joy to the remaining humans, and they will learn to cooperate with each other and their world. Then there will be 'no more war.' If you can keep an open heart and an open solar plexus during the disturbances, you will have learnt your most important lesson here on Earth. That is the key."

B. "As the sea continues to warm, so the cold-water fish will retreat northward and southward and be replaced by warm-water fish. There will be a great effect also on the large mammals of the sea, whose breeding grounds will become more numerous. Much can be learned from these great creatures, whose intelligence and harmony of living could well be copied. The communication of all these creatures, who talk by sonar, will become intelligible to us. These creatures are our teachers. They have agreed to cooperate to help mankind, and it is for us to learn how to listen to them. They are highly evolved creatures, much higher than man, and another of man's lessons is to learn to treat them with respect. They are not competing with humans for a place to live.

Humans have a great capacity to destroy what could save them. The harmony of being must follow on Earth, or Earth will destroy what destroys it. Your beautiful planet is in great danger, and its efforts to heal itself will result in your destruction if you do not act. Live calmly and fairly and do not take another's possessions. There is enough to go round. Man must find peace in his heart, if he is to live peacefully."

B. "When the waters have risen, the Earth will smile again. The air will be still and peaceful, and a great joy will come upon the planet. Some of this you will see and rejoice in. Man is going towards his home with the Source and will live with understanding and in light."

Conflict

One of the often repeated messages is that conflicts and wars resolve nothing and our future on Earth depends on us finding another way.

B. **"Humanity has yet to learn that war does not solve problems and that bombing people does not make them like you.**

You would think they are simple lessons, but they are proving very difficult for man to learn. Peaceful negotiation is what resolves divisions, but too often the waters are muddied by vested interests and none of the involved participants are speaking their truth. If everybody spoke their truth, at least the heart of the dispute will be clear to all. Where the heart of the dispute is greed for another nation's assets, the truth is often replaced by something less reprehensible, and resolution is therefore more difficult to arrive at. In the rest of the universe, truth is not hidden and solutions are usually clear. Truth is the key."

B. " 'Truth is the first casualty of war' was said by one of your statesman and it is true. If a man speaks his truth, it engages his heart and the hearts of those to whom he speaks. If the heart is engaged and the solar plexus stays open, a negotiation can continue, but as soon as they close, then man resorts to confrontation or double-dealing. This tendency must be overcome before the age of peace and harmony can begin. This can only be taught by example, not words. It will become easier when it is realised that each man is responsible for his own life. The devolution of power to others, even in a democracy, allows things to happen that a human individually can see to be wrong. If each man takes responsibility for himself, then the abrogation of that responsibility will cease."

B. "Today, our subject is war again. We are not telling you these things to frighten you, but to educate the people who will read these writings. War, as we know, is a useless expensive exercise of physical power to achieve an objective. How much more intelligent it would be to exercise the heart and obtain what one needs without wasting all the money, men and goodwill. When man's consciousness rises a little further, he will begin to see this himself. But the morality and intelligence of the group will take longer than the individual to come to this conclusion.

Wars, on the whole, are run at the instigation of power-hungry individuals. Sometimes, they are just an expression of male machismo. Whatever the cause, the method does not work, and the hatred and resentment that the effects engender can take many, many generations to resolve. We need to persuade each individual who comes to understand this to say so, and to act against his war-mongering peers in the ballot box or voting chamber. The only way for wars to stop is for those who promote them to lose the support of the rest of the people.

Wars are either about power or poverty. The poverty wars will cease as soon as everyone has enough to eat, as soon as each man realises he is responsible for providing for his own food and wellbeing. What we are talking about here is the power of the individual, which must be reclaimed. With power goes responsibility, and this must be reclaimed also. It is not enough to expect others to provide everything for you.

In the times that are coming, man will rediscover his own responsibilities to himself and his children, for many of the services now provided will fail. When men are thrown back on their own resources, they will then learn to cooperate with each other. But it will be a very difficult lesson for some. The turmoil and terror that will be created will make conditions unstable for a time, and much work must be done to explain what is happening and how to go forward. Civil instability is as dangerous as war in the short term and must be settled as quickly as possible. The message of peace and love must be given with an open heart or it cannot be accepted. Learn how to keep yourself open and overcome your fears."

B. "In the universe, we do not have conflict, we have negotiation. This is easier to maintain when the ego is not involved and there are no vested interests. It all boils down to people speaking their truth with their hearts open. If everyone does this, then resolution of differences is always possible. If everyone speaks their truth, then the negotiation remains fluid. It is only when men close their hearts and dig in their heels that the barriers appear.

In human negotiations, there are always sticking points, either from fear or vested interests. This is why they do not succeed. In human negotiations, the fear of the unknown and of uncertainty play a part. This is because the human does not feel safe in himself and feels alone in his dealings with the world. You know that neither of these fears are true, but it has not yet stopped you feeling them.

The less you fear, the more you can freely give, and the more fluid negotiations can remain. Under these circumstances, it is possible for something truly wonderful to be born out of the discussions. Clinging to the wreckage of prepared positions stifles the free flow between soul and soul. Humans must learn to be free."

Fear

The subject of fear and loss also occupies many of the spirit's transmissions and, while I'm sure their advice is sound, I can't help feeling that it is all a lot easier when you do not have a body and you can feel the connection to "All that Is" all of the time! I hope that, as we approach our conscious reconnection, it will become easier for us too.

℘. "Fear is the greatest barrier to progress of spiritual development. The banishment of the fear is one of the things you must work on, where ever it arises. In a sudden crisis, the fear actually affects the body before the mind has understood the problem. This fear must be vanquished as soon as possible, because it blocks assistance from here.

Once fear has arisen, it would be helpful to remember that the soul cannot be extinguished whatever happens to the body. The fear in situations of crisis is fear of extinction. Lesser fears must be examined to discover what it is the person is really fearing, which is often not what appears on the surface. Many fears are due to unconscious patterning and can be dealt with on that level.

Fear of loss is more challenging. It may well be on the human level that this loss would change circumstances for the worse. This is a time when examining the worst that might happen and devising a method of dealing with it will prove helpful. Loss is an inevitable part of human life and often opens the way to something better.

Humans only learn to grow when their status quo is disturbed. This is why it happens. Everything in human life has its own place in the cycle.
'A time to live and a time to die.'
Clinging onto a part of the cycle that is past is painful and unpleasant, so another method of combating fear is to learn to release the past, and work with the present. To deal successfully with fear, therefore, it is necessary to keep an open heart and solar plexus and to release yourself willingly from whatever circumstance in your life that is threatened."

℘. "When the waters rise and the Earth opens and the epidemics sweep the lands, there will be an explosion of fear. This is where you must work to explain to people what is happening and how to combat their fear. It will have the beneficial effect that many international conflicts will cease, as people become concerned only with their own safety and providing for their families. The fear must be overcome so that the effects of the rising level of consciousness can be felt.

The planet is protesting at the use man has made of it. But if this lesson is learnt and other ways are found of creating energy, then the planet and its people can become in harmony. When this occurs, the golden age of peace and tranquillity will have begun.

If you can show that you are not afraid during the cataclysms, then others can learn from you. You have nothing to fear, you will be safe, but this will be many steps into the unknown. The rising of the waters and the fall in the population will change everything.

Make sure your message is clear – that the Earth can support its people without being damaged in the process and that people can live comfortably if they support each other. The message of the higher levels, of the beauty of the universe, of the continuity of life, and the love of the Source, will follow once the practicalities of the new way are achieved."

Love and Peace

The emotional cleansing that humans require, in order to be able to act with love, is another of the spirits' themes. From experience, I assure you that the process of cleansing is not nearly as difficult as is believed. Most humans would do anything rather than deal with their stuff, and all I can say is that it is lovely being you when you've cleared it!

B. "Love, as you know, is the force that powers the universe, and love is the force that binds your planet together. The reason for the current unease and discomfort of the planet is lack of love. The human inhabitants have behaved thoughtlessly and without love, and a lack of love is damaging.

Once the human race understands how to both emotionally and physically care for the planet, which cares for them, then there will again be harmony. The misuse has gone too far to be resolved without a release of the internal pressure of the planet, but this release and the rising of the waters will bring comfort to the Earth and thus to its inhabitants.

One day, humans will understand that, in their own way, every other being on the planet knows more than them about how to live. The arrogance of the human race is bringing about its downfall.

> *'It was ever thus.*
> *Men are unwise and curiously planned.*
> *They have their dreams and do not think of us.'*
>   Flecker

Said by women, but equally relevant to the Earth, which is a feminine, nurturing being. What is coming has to be, but the way to freedom is through an open heart. Remember this."

B. "Humans need somebody on whom they can rely. This being does not have to be in human form. Because humans feel so alone, they cling to whoever will support them. This may be an animal, a spirit or a human. As spiritual development proceeds, they gradually discover that they can rely upon themselves and, after that, they may find that every soul has many in the spirit world surrounding and supporting them.

Self-love is a necessary prerequisite for this stage of discovery. It is necessary to love and accept yourself, and to clear as much as possible of your negative emotional patterning, and then you can feel yourself surrounded with love and joy. Once you can perceive that there is a much bigger picture and that your soul is inextinguishable, then the clinging to the known ways and people lessens, and you are able to take your place in the universe and become a force for good.

Self-reliance is an essential stage of development for these transformations, as is self-love. The other major quality needed for the soul's development is honesty. A soul must be honest with himself, if he is to be able to clear his emotional patterning and discard unwanted habits. Your intuitive sense will guide you."

After all the events I have described, however difficult they may be to live through, the future for our world sounds wonderful. These transmissions describe the world when the changes are finished. Some of these pieces are lyrical in their beauty.

ℬ. "In your land, when the waters have risen, there will be peace and tranquillity and the climate will be calm and warm. The storms will be over and little winds will cause the waves to gently lap the shore. There will be a feeling of peace and timelessness and man will be at one with everything in his world and ours. Although there will be work to be done, there will be time for humans to take their rest and commune with 'All That Is.' The striving to succeed and the grasping of money will cease, as these concepts will be outdated.

> *'Or ever the silver cord be loosed*
> *Or the Golden bowl broken at the Fountain'*

Man will reconnect with 'All That Is' and will no longer feel alone. The veils between the worlds grow ever thinner and humans will be able to perceive their inheritance and their destiny. They will know and understand why they are here and what lessons they have to learn and teach. The children will be allowed to develop their potential, as there will be less emphasis on academic learning and more on understanding and participation. The very mentally able will continue to be taught academic subjects; you will still need scientists, particularly physicists, but it will be what they want to do.

There will be peace in all the land and there will be no more war. Religions will die when every man can perceive the truth for himself. Remember, you are here to help with the birth of the age of harmony, a golden age of peace for the Earth."

ℬ. "Achieving peace and harmony is this Earth's developmental path and, on the way, there will be considerable turbulence as the wrongs rise to the surface to be healed. The calm and peace and joy that will prevail when the turbulence settles is not yet known to many, though there are those who do. You will find the open-heartedness of truth and the way of being in the world which has been forgotten by many.

There will be changes in structures, governments will fall, the money markets will collapse and, temporarily, international trade will become very difficult. This will alter the way everything is done in the developed world. Man will have to become much more reliant on himself and his neighbours for his daily needs.

Once the turbulence subsides, all this will be apparent and the way of life will have changed forever. The feelings in the people will also have changed and they will feel a calmness and joy that many of them have not felt before. This you will be glad to see."

V. "We are the Venusians. After the turbulence, many parts of your Earth will be uninhabitable. Parts will be desert, and parts will be flooded, and parts will be too inhospitable for a man to live in. So the distribution of humans over your planet will be quite different. The waters will continue to rise, so only high ground will be available for dwellings, and many of the humans and animals will have left the planet.

Humans will be thrown on their own resources to shelter and feed themselves. There will be plenty of food, but it will be mainly of a vegetable nature, and of course there would be plenty of fish in the waters. The remaining population will become healthier through the freshness of the food they eat, and the rise in consciousness will abolish many of the illnesses that man now suffers.

After the cataclysm, there will be many visitors to your Earth to awaken humans to the new energies that are available to them to use, without the damaging effects they once caused. Man will have a sense of purpose, as well as a deep sense of gratitude at having survived, and the rootlessness and aimlessness of many humans will disappear. 'The new Earth' will be beautiful and calm and harmonious, and the whole universe will rejoice at your planet's transformation. You have nothing to fear.

There are many forces outside your planet working to help humans, and especially the humans who can understand what is happening. These will become your leaders and the help that they can call on from the universe is without limit. We ourselves will be helping humans to re-establish their lives and to make use of the many new energies and methods that are available to them.

There will be a return to simplicity for a while, but humans will understand so much more about their world and about themselves, that they will feel that they have gained something precious in exchange for the way of life they have lost."

(I saw a landscape of hills and water with a beautiful golden light and there was a feeling of calmness and tranquillity. The air was warm and the wind was light and there were birds in the skies. The scene was quite idyllic.)

This we show you so that you can understand how peaceful, beautiful and harmonious your world will be. The cataclysm must be endured, for it has its own purposes of relieving the pain of the Earth and helping humans to understand their place in their world – as a participant rather than a plunderer. Every being is equal to every other being. This must be understood before the peace and harmony can begin."

B. "As the turbulence subsides, so the peace and harmony can begin. As the physical forces shaking the Earth begin to wane in intensity, a calm will begin to come on the Earth and its inhabitants. The survivors will emerge from their shelters into the soft beauty of a still and cloudless dawn. The waters will be stilled, and the airs will be light and warm, and the whole Earth will become suffused with a gentle calm and peacefulness longed for but not known before. It will be easy to live on this Earth. Food will be easy to come by. There will be an abundance of fruit and vegetables, enough for everyone. The nights will be clear and starlit, and the days will be warm and calm.

Mankind will set about repairing and building new dwellings and learning the new ways of tapping into the Earth energies. Men will have learnt to live by the truths of their hearts, and this will enable them to cooperate fully with each other. The animals have always done this and will be there to teach them how to live. There will be joy and gratitude, and each will be conscious of his soul's journey and how best to fulfil his purpose. This time will be precious and beautiful, and men will begin to treat the Earth as if she were the precious jewel that she is.

When this is in full flow, then the time of harmony will be upon the Earth, and the stars will all rejoice in the transformation, and the music of the spheres will sound a paean which will be heard on Earth."

B. "When the time of turbulence is past, the age of harmony can begin, and every man will live in peace with his neighbour, and harmony and beauty will spread over the land. The Earth will be calm and fair and the waves will be at peace. The air will be warm and the whole of creation will be consciously aware of the Source. In their awareness, they will understand that they are part of the Source and that all of life of whatever type is sacred. This realisation will change forever the way man treats his fellows, his Earth and the other beings inhabiting the Earth.

The world has everything that is needed and will give it to you willingly. You must just learn to understand what the world is offering and how to live, so that the offerings can regenerate. When you can do that, then there will always be enough for everyone. The energies of the Earth can be harnessed without damage to their source, which is identical to the Source. Look at what is available. The energies of sun, wind, waves and tides and the heat of the Earth are free for you to use and, when you have discovered the techniques, you will be able to harness the 'dark energy' directly. Your other major need is water and this flows directly from the source in the centre of the Earth. This will never run out. Why then must humans fight over territory and energy rights and all the other futile practices of your race? It is all freely available to all.

Each soul will feel the inner joy that the spirit world constantly dwells in. Each soul will understand his own place in their world and the universe and will then be able to live in peace and harmony with everyone. Each soul will identify the love of the Source as within him and of him. He will recognise himself as part of the love that drives the universe and is the universe. There will be no more separation and therefore there will be no more war.

When each man knows he is Love, then that is all he needs to know, because that is all there is."

"The song is endless
The singing will never be done."
Sassoon

B. "We want you to know that the universe you inhabit is one of love, harmony and cooperation. It has evolved through countless generations, since it was not always peaceful. Now it is cooperating to bring peace to the human inhabitants of your world, so that the planet Earth can become at one with all of us. This peace must be achieved through turbulence, as we have told you before. The Earth, your planet, must find its own ease and comfort. But this state is temporary and the future of your world is calm, shining and peaceable.

There is much work for you to do to help this new harmony to birth, so that the vibrational level of your world can rise. You are not alone. You were never alone. But you must help us, we cannot do it without you. Blessings to you all."

It is easy to see what might happen, and some of it will. It is up to us how severe these changes are. Surely we can do better than we are now. Surely we don't have to destroy this planet by our lifestyle. Surely we can find other ways of creating energy and leave the oil in the ground. Surely we can stop cutting down the Earth's lung, her trees, and learn a way to use materials that don't poison our lands and seas. If we can't, I am in little doubt about the outcome.

"It takes so many thousand years to wake
But will you wake for pity's sake?"
Fry

Maybe it must be up to the foot soldiers to make these changes and to save this world. There is no point in relying on our governments, for they have long lost touch with truth and the world we live in. There is no point in pretending that offsetting our carbon emissions actually reduces the quantity. That may be politics, but it is not real life. It is up to us. After all, the spirits have told us the ways we have available for creating power, and assured us that our Earth will freely give us all we need.

B. "If you are able to use the sun, the wind, the waves, the tides and the heat of the Earth, what have you then to fear from cold?"

Part Four

The Nature of
the Universe

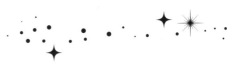

16

The Nature of the Universe

"   ... look how the floor of heaven
Is thick inlaid with patines of bright gold:
There's not the smallest orb which thou beholdst
But in his motion like an angel sings
Still quiring to the young-eyed cherubims:"

                                                    Shakespeare

It is wonderfully presumptive of me to include a section on the nature of the universe in this book. The universe as described by the spirits is vaster and more magnificent, extraordinary and beautiful than can be conceived of on Earth. It is also wiser, more knowledgeable and more compassionate and friendly. We cannot completely comprehend this subject while limited by a human brain. This account can only be sketchy, because my learning is limited, but the spirits want me to tell of the journeys I have made and of how much we are loved.

B. "We wish for you to make clear, at every point, how much love there is in the universe and how much love and help are pouring towards your Earth. These are universes of love, and you know how you feel when you are travelling with us. The love and beauty and feeling of safety you have are not what people are expecting, and we wish you to make this clear. Since our very beings are love, our natures express that love at all times. The whole content of our universe is love, and this informs our dealings one with another and how each world behaves and cooperates with its fellows in bringing this universe back to its perfection."

Through my travels in the universe, the spirits have shown me how closely the worlds are connected. It is as if the universe were a neighbourhood, with the inhabitants helping each other out. The amazing ease and speed of travel and communication between the worlds have astonished me, as have the beautiful colours of space. Truly the void is full.

The most amazing thing of all has been to find how much each of us is loved, both by the Source and by our associated souls on other worlds. The love that drives the universe is freely and unconditionally available to all of us. It is only us poor separated souls that cannot feel this at all times, and this we can change. All the love, and also all the knowledge, of the universe is freely available to us when we allow ourselves to believe in it and enable ourselves to access it. There is nothing that is not possible.

This is what the spirits said about the universe.

B. "The universe in which we live is beyond what can be imagined by man in its beauty, complexity and yet ultimate simplicity. Every world is intimately connected to every other world and what happens to one affects all. This is why so many beings from so many worlds are helping Earth at this time.

The universe is fashioned from the energy of love and must surely act according to its nature. This force of love is, and permeates, all things and all beings. There is no separation except in men's limited perception.

Come with us and see the miracle of the harmonious universe and hear the music of the spheres. Come with us and see the miracle of the web of connecting energies that create the living, vibrant, pulsating beauty of the universe in which you live. Leave your body behind and experience the unity with all things, the 'at oneness' of your heart with creation.

There is nothing to fear. The universe is a friendly, warm and harmonious space.   It is not what your body would experience. The universe is colourful beyond your imagining, and loving beyond your dreams.

Come and be loved as you have never been before. We await you with pleasure."

They say that, because humans make so many assumptions that are born of their fear, they want me to describe the worlds I have been shown and tell of the wonders I found in the universe. They find our attitude to "aliens" extraordinary and they have repeatedly asked me to say that they come in friendship and not to harm or control us. All the extraterrestrial beings I have met have treated me with great love and courtesy, and their approach to us has been far removed from the popular conception. I have become ashamed of our attitude to them, since many of them are trying to help our troubled planet avoid its destruction.

In our human determination to master our physical environment, we have forgotten that we are a part of it. We have also forgotten to love and respect it and indeed ourselves. Our arrogance has led us to believe that we are the masters of the universe. I have been greatly entertained to discover that, in the cosmos, we are thought rather backward, and that inhabitants of other worlds are working to help us evolve to a more advanced and harmonious state. Even the animals are more advanced in soul development, although their brains are not as clever as ours. The spirits tell me that the other inhabitants of the universe view us rather as if we were kittens playing with a ball of wool! Lots of action, but no coherence and a horrible mess at the end!

There are two other warring worlds, but apart from them, the other inhabitants of the universe live in love and harmony and conscious connection to the Source. We are approaching our time of upheaval and change, and on many of the worlds I have visited, I have been given advice on how best to live in harmony with our surroundings. This is what the spirits have told me. I have used their words wherever possible. Their prose is beautiful, which mine is not, and their grammar approaches perfection, which mine does not.

B. "Let us talk of the cosmos. We have shown you the light existing in the darkness and the connection between one world and another. Everything in the universe is connected by a great web of energy, as you have seen, and above that there are more conscious connections between one world and another and one soul and another. The cosmos is teeming and bursting with light and life and love. The creation is so much more alive and extraordinary than you can see with physical eyes.

Since everything is connected to everything else and everything affects everyone else, how then could you be alone?

This coming transition of Earth is attended by beings from innumerable worlds. They are working to help it happen as smoothly as man will allow and to ensure that what is necessary will be provided at all levels, including the physical. The Earth itself is participating and cooperating with the cosmos. It is not in the plan of the Earth to become completely barren at this time. All that Earth needs will be provided and all that you need will be also.

Do not worry about how you will live; it has all been considered and what you will need, all of you, will be there. You will be astonished how what you need will appear, but this is part of returning to the cosmos which is 'All of Everything' and trusting it to provide. Relax and trust the process."

The Physical Universe

> *"There are more things in heaven and earth, Horatio*
> *Than are dreamt of in your philosophy."*
>
> Shakespeare

There are nine universes. They are at different vibrational levels, so one cannot be perceived from the other, although this will become possible with advances in our science and understanding. Each universe is built on completely different physical principles and each is evolving in its own way. There was a beginning and everything has been evolving since. Evolution will continue until all beings understand one another completely.

A. *Will there be an end?*

T. Not in the way that you are thinking, but many planets will come to an end. It is the whole of creation that is evolving, not just humans. Humans must evolve until they are able to tap freely into the universal collective mind. In the spirit world this is possible, but not here.

We straightened out the terminology:

*A **world** is one planet or star with its life (see below). There are three planets that have biological life similar to ours: two in this galaxy and one elsewhere.*

*A **galaxy** is a single star system revolving round a central energy source.*

*A **universe** comprises everything that exists in space as far as can be discovered.*

***Another world** is separated in space and may or may not be in a different dimension.*

***Another universe** is separated in space and also in dimension.*

***Another dimension** is a different vibrational level and it may or may not be separated in space.*

***"Dark matter/energy"** is the background energy of the universe, which is love. This is the matter that our scientists have not quite discovered yet. It is only dark to humans, because we cannot see it with physical eyes or measure it with our instruments. It is everywhere in the universe.*

*A **black hole** is an entry point to a different dimension. Every galaxy has a black hole at its centre.*

***"Black light"** is a physical layer around the outer edges of the universe. It is the layer inhabited by high beings of the spirit world and is not habitable for humans, although they can visit. It is the energy from this layer that the Basidian use in their healing. Again, it is only black to human eyes and illuminates the spirit world with many colours.*

***Parallel realities** exist around each world, but in a different dimension. They are real entities, which can be accessed by the inhabitants and where the soul would have a different body. The parallel worlds exist within the planetary consciousness.*

The universe is not the cold, empty place that the astronomers describe. It is teeming with spirit life of many forms. Few of the inhabitants of physical worlds look anything like us or have similar biological requirements. Of the ones I have seen so far, one race have bodies rather like ours, but with their special sense organs on stalks all over their faces. When they are pleased, all the stalks light up. A number of them have bodies a bit like insects; the beings on the dark side of the moon appear like lollipops on sticks; and the most unusual looked like a coffee bean with a feather stuck in the top pole. Of course, if the beings are non-physical, they are pure energy and can look however they like. The Basidian usually appear to me as golden vortices, and other inhabitants of Sirius show less detail and look more like intestinal villi than anything else. When the Basidian are at home in the black layer, they look amoeboid, with beautiful pearly ovals of light replacing the nucleus and pale, rather ghost-like, cytoplasm with a definite outer border.

Scientists have only looked for life with similar requirements to ours, which has cut down their chances of success to about one in 225 trillion less 3! Talk about doing things the hard way! It seems that every star or planet is inhabited either with spirit life or physical life. Of the many planets with biological life, only three have similar life-forms to us – two in this galaxy and one elsewhere.

A. *Why are there only three planets with biological life like ours?*
T. It is a primitive life-form and only necessary as a training ground for evolving souls.
A. *How many stars are inhabited by spirits?*
T. You have seen the pictures [from the Hubble Space telescope]. Too many to count.
A. *Have all the spirit forms evolved much further than us?*
T. They have. Earth must evolve quickly to avoid self-destruction. Destruction would cause imbalance and perturbation in the spirit world, so many civilisations are working to help this planet evolve to a more harmonious level to avoid this.
A. *Can you tell me about the worlds with spirit life?*
T. As you have observed, there are many, many more, and not all life-forms in the spirit world are restricted to one star or planet. Many of us move freely around the universe interacting with other life-forms.
A. *Presumably though, you all have a base where you go for replenishment of energy.*

T. Indeed, but that is not very frequently necessary. You have seen the pictures of the web of dark energy that is the universe, with the stars and planets imbedded in it like jewels. Many of us can use this energy directly.

A. *Do you have a central sun, or are the planets held together by various mutual attractions?*

T. They are held together by attraction. There is a design which we will show you. It looks as if it was not designed, but there is a bigger design than you can perceive.

A. *There isn't a central sun of the universe?*

T. There is not. Some planets need a sun, some do not. The light comes from a different source.

A. *The light comes from the planet itself?*

T. Some light themselves. As you travel to the outer edges, light is from a different source again. Some planets have their own sun and there is a human belief that there is, perhaps more than one sun grouped together. This is not so.

A. *And if you're a star that is not supporting biological life, you don't need a sun, you have spiritual light, you do not need physical light.*

T. You do not need physical. They often create their own light. It is the vibration that creates the light.

The energy that drives the universes is love.

A. *Does love have a wavelength?*

T. Indeed. It is very much longer and slower in vibration than light, but it is part of the same spectrum.

A. *But it is a perfectly ordinary energy like any other?*

T. It is so, correct. The background energy of the universe, the energy of the "spaces in between" is love. When you come back here, you will be better able to understand the vast complexity and interrelatedness of the universe.

A. *Does every universe have a different Creator or is there a single over-arching mind?*

T. If there were more than one, there would be wars in heaven! Each universe has its own creating principle, but they are all part of one whole, as indeed are the universes. Diversity is all.

A. *Will there be more?*

T. That is still in the mind of the Creator; there are no plans that I know of.

A. *When everything in every universe is really communicating and understanding everything else, then everything will be the Creator?*
T. As it is now, correct.

Understand, the universe that you exist in is the universe of intention. Each one has a different meaning, and the one you are in is intention. The planet you are on has intention also, but its journey is towards love. It cannot go towards love without intention. The purpose of the universe is evolution.

The universe avails itself for beings to go from one part to another, to different worlds, in order to evolve. Humans choose to go to Earth many times. Humans often go to other planets also, and that is why you have memories in your soul of other planets, other worlds. Earth is not the only planet that has life. It will interconnect in the future. They will all interconnect more than they do at this time. It is for growth of the soul.

The universe's purpose is the growth of the soul. As the soul grows, so the universe expands.

A. *So that is all souls, at whatever level that they are at? Plant souls and planet souls? And the main purpose of the evolution is for us all to understand so much of each other in every universe, that we are all part of the same thing, are all part of God?*
T. That is correct. The purpose you understand is to bring peace, harmony and love to every form of life.
A. *Are the other universes evolving on completely different physical principles?*
T. They are.
A. *So then their physics would not work in our universe?*
T. They will when your universe has learned higher physics.
A. *You mean that we are bottom of the heap of universes?*
T. A little, not quite the bottom, but not far up.
A. *When everything in the universe is in complete understanding and living in peace, harmony and love, will it continue to do that eternally?*
T. It will. Other universes are already doing this. There is peace and harmony. The word you would use is goodwill. Goodwill to all things.

The following transmissions give a flavour of what they have told me of the creation and development of the universe.

B. "We have been talking about the Earth and planets and the universe. Today, we will talk about interstellar space. You remember 'as above, so below'; well the energy within a planet, a person or universe is the same. Interstellar space is full of a pulsing low-level energy field. Enough for all our needs, were we to harness it. This energy uses the energy of love. You will see when you come over, not the empty lifeless light years, but the web of energy which supplies the motive power to start the formation of the gas clouds that eventually, by nuclear fusion and fission, create their own energy to spawn the stars. None of this is purposeless or driven by chance. Once the process is started, it is often left to develop how it will, but the initial intention to create is purposeful.

If man could harness this energy, then there would be enough for all his purposes. There are ways of doing this that are harmless to the planet, and they will be discovered soon. This must happen soon, to stop the removal of the Earth's lifeblood, otherwise its eventual destruction is assured. There are many agencies working to help this idea to birth and then to practicality.

Genius is merely the ability to tap into the knowledge of the universe.

The knowledge of this energy has arrived on your planet and the rest will follow. There is no reason to fear. The consciousness is rising and, with it, the ability to know and understand new principles from which new technologies can quickly follow."

B. "Fire is the process of consuming organic matter by heat and leaving the inorganic ash. Fire changes matter. Look at iron and steel, tempered by fire. Throughout the cosmos, the fire resulting from nuclear explosions are tempering matter by heat. Without fire, the universe would not have been able to come into existence. The very high temperatures of nuclear explosions cause alterations of physical inorganic matter, to produce glass and crystal, for example.

It speeds up chemical and physical processes and allows for change of nature. This is how more complex inorganic matter is produced. In fact, this is how you were produced. The alteration to physical molecules by extreme heat has allowed them to aggregate into more complex molecules and eventually over aeons of time into organic matter.

When a being was first ensouled, its body consisted of no more than aggregations of molecules, born in the fires of the stars. Stars consist of nuclear explosions among gases, producing the energies of heat and light, and by the changing effects of the heat and explosions, separating into an entity of exploding gas that we call a star. This is how matter was brought into existence and this is where you were born.

Everything that is made of matter is relatively speaking ephemeral, and stars and planets die and new ones are born, in the constant change that is life in the cosmos. 'As above so below.' Biological life mirrors the cosmos, in the constant change and decay, replaced by new birth. The fires of the stars are crucibles in which everything precious in matter is produced, including man. The life of the spirit is eternal and inextinguishable, but everything that has mass will eventually change and decay. The constant change at all levels, be they spiritual or material, creates the evolution and diversity of life. Fire is the creator as well as the destroyer."

> *"He who thro' vast immensity can pierce*
> *See worlds on worlds compose one universe*
> *Observe how system into system runs*
> *What other planets circle other suns"*
>
> *Pope*

There is nothing in the universe that is not working to some inconceivably vast plan. With our limited vision, we cannot perceive these because of their size. This has led us to assume that creation is random. We are good at wrong assumptions.

B. "The stars in the heavens are without number, but each has its role to play. They are analogous to the cells of the body and, if you like, the galaxies could be considered as organ systems. In the human, there is frequent breakdown of systems, but in the universe, the divine plan continues without hindrance. In the heavens, physical life is finite as it is on Earth. Stars are born, live and die, but the spirits who inhabit the stars are eternal.

Spirits, as everything else, are all part of the mind of God, which your philosophers discuss at length without understanding that the Creator is not separate from his creation.

It is all more simple than you can imagine, and yet unbelievably complex, because of the interweaving patterns on the great web of the universe. On Earth, everything happens when the time is right, though not when humans wish for it to happen. I have often heard you say that 'God is not working to my agenda!' Be content that the plan is working out as it should and the future is visible and intelligible here, though not on Earth. The overall plan is of God; the details of each system are made by the inhabitants.

Humans, having free will, which is not universal, have been able to create their own destiny in a way that has been completely disastrous for their survival."

> *"Our meddling intellect*
> *Misshapes the beauteous forms of things*
> *We murder to dissect"*
>> *Wordsworth*

B. "The detachment of humans from their planned paths, and the fear and loneliness that this has engendered, have been responsible for the miseries of the 'warring planet.' We watch with compassion and fascination the struggles of souls to regain their true path, and the efforts they make to retain the peace and harmony that they know in their souls is their birthright. Those of us who have been in human form have memories of the struggles of our own souls, which help us to help you now. Be not afraid. 'All shall be well.' "

> *"All are but parts of one stupendous whole*
> *Whose body Nature is and God the soul"*
>> *Pope*

B. "The universe is evolving towards perfection – a journey of many millennia. When every planet is in perfect harmony with itself and everyone else, then perfection will have been achieved. When this happens, the universe will continue in bliss. Why would the Creator destroy what he has worked for so long to achieve? Perfection means that every soul on every planet is in harmony.

Now do you see why your warring planet strikes such unwelcome chords? This is why so many types of beings are working to help the Earth evolve into its own harmony.

Love is the energy that drives the universe and love is the energy that will save your planet from total destruction. Peace and harmony are the intended final patterns of this planet, as for all the others. Peace and harmony come from love and respect.

Love and respect are not always in evidence on your planet. Every soul is working towards this; all you have to do is your part also. The animals know much more about this than humans."

17

The Workings of the Universe

The spirits have also given me much information about the physical workings of the universe. This is given in non-technical language, because neither the medium nor I know physics. What I really hope for is an astrophysicist to have some of these conversations, so that he can then explain it to the rest of us. The inhabitants of Venus would be particularly pleased to find a scientist. They often complain of my lack of scientific understanding and say that they can only tell me very simple things! They are limited to lessons on practical make-do, at which they are very knowledgeable.

As you can see from the passages that follow, the spirits barely distinguish between the physical, the emotional and the life force of beings of whatever type. To them, it is all energy and part of the whole and the Source.

I have had many journeys through the universe and I cannot describe the colours and the complexity in words, nor the sense of meaning and belonging. Humans see space as a cold, dark, hostile void and so it is to our physical bodies. If you leave your body at home, then there is a warm and loving universe of apparently infinite size and bursting with light and life, waiting to be explored.

The Nature of Light

B. "Light is not just as you have seen it. An illuminating force stretches over a wider range of wavelengths than the human eye can register. Other beings in other worlds register different wavelengths on their sensing apparatus, but all of it is light. Infrared and ultraviolet light are not visible to human eyes, but easily detectable with the instruments man has made.

There is no point in the universe which is not illuminated by light of some wavelength. The universe is not dark; it is bursting with pulsations of light and energy. Even the 'dark energy' is not dark, and you have seen that 'black light' is not black. Human senses are very limited and very limiting and are largely unable to register or understand the vast arrays of light within this beautiful universe. Even the dark, apparently dead, planets and stars have light and life beneath the surface.

The quest for mastery of the physical world has led you to develop in such a way that seeing the minute, you have lost the whole. What is more important is that you have lost a sense of the whole, a sense of wonder and happiness at the beauty, harmony and all connectedness of the whole. This is why you feel alone.

This will change when the level of consciousness rises. Man will not be able to see any more with his eyes, but he will be able to feel the connectedness of things. This will make the difference."

B. "The light that you can see with your eyes is but a small part of what exists in the universe. Over here, we can see a much wider range of frequencies than your eyes on Earth will allow. The light of the universe is love. Beings over here recognise each other by their light and their colours.

Emotions and energy levels can be readily perceived by looking at each soul's light. This is how we look at you and how we identify your energy levels. Each soul has their unique signature in light. Each soul works (at their own rate) to perfect themselves, and this increases the amount and quality of their light.

You have seen the 'black light' that is 'all of everything' and you have seen the many visible colours that make it up. Over here, it is necessary to use more than one sense to see the light of the universe. When you can do this, you will finally understand that the void is not empty, but full of pulsating energy of many types and colours."

B. "The light that you see on Earth has travelled at the rate of 186,000 miles per second and yet when you travel through the galaxy, you arrive at your destination in minutes. Do you not think that is odd? ?

Physical matter of whatever density has to obey the physical rules of the universe; but once you are released from the bonds of matter and are pure soul, you are able to transport yourself instantly to your destination with the power of thought and intention. Just as you can instantly change your mind, so you can instantly change your location.

Over here, we are not limited by space or time and, what is more, we are able to give our attention to more than one matter simultaneously. The lifting of these restrictions vastly increases our effectiveness. Since we are also telepathic, we are not subject to the misunderstandings and the mistakes of interpretation that bedevil life on Earth.

When the level of consciousness rises far enough on Earth, we will also be able to communicate freely with its inhabitants. The information we will give them will help them to understand how best to live, and more importantly, who they truly are. This is our mission for the Earth at this time – to help the planet through to its age of harmony. This will be joyful for us all."

B. "The light you can see is such a small proportion of all that is there. The 'black light,' which is 'All That Is,' is not visible to human external eyes, but that does not mean it does not exist. You yourself can see it clearly with your inner eyes and you know that, although it is black, it illuminates and contains all other colours. There are other forms of light which behave in a similar way.

The rays of energy that pass between planets are composed of light, whether visible or not. The universe is connected through its worlds with innumerable light paths between them. These are of great complexity and travel immense distances. Although we describe them as light, they can easily exceed the speed of light, which is a restriction that only applies to the physical world that can be seen with external eyes.

You yourself have travelled at speeds vastly in excess of the speed of light, and the communication between the worlds is almost instantaneous and with many differing and beautiful colours. Each colour has a different significance, as you will learn. The connections for communications between the worlds are of a complexity and sophistication that likens the internet to an abacus.

All can be known in the spirit world – past, present and future – and you can understand that such a volume of information requires a very sophisticated and efficient network to disseminate it. It is to tap into this network that the majority of the unused parts of your human brains are capable. This is why we are stimulating use of these parts of the brain, so that humans no longer have to walk in darkness and ignorance.

When all can be known, then all can be understood, and when all is understood, much of the petty rivalries and the meannesses of humans will begin to fall away, so that they can take their place in the universe as forces for good, rather than squabbling among themselves."

Waves

The waveform, they tell me, is the primary method of transmission of energy of all wavelengths. Waves can carry infinite quantities of information. This is the form in which the energies of love, light and information are transmitted. There are also great waves that cyclically traverse the universe, determining changes in the worlds. Nothing in the universe is static, and physical changes of temperature, for instance, are mediated in this way. We are currently on a warming cycle and there is a more temperate one to follow. The changes in understanding of the souls in the universe are also subject to waves of change. It is the way that the Source influences its creation.

B. "Waves are a rhythmic energy that contain 'all of everything.' They are influenced by the forces of love and gravitation, but they continue ceaselessly for ever. The waves of love stretch across the cosmos as the waters cover the sea. The waves of love stretch into every corner of the cosmos and allow the creative force of the cosmos. The waves are part of the Creator and therefore will never cease. The waves have created all the universes and all the galaxies, stars and planets in those universes. The waves have created every inextinguishable living being in these universes. The waves of love are the Source, the Creator, the God, 'All That Is.'

This is the sublime knowledge that tells you that you are all perfectly safe, you are all perfectly loved, and you are all perfect.

There is diversity in creation, but there is not evil. Negativity and evil are manmade, as a result of men closing themselves off from their Source. This closure is a voluntary act, but what is closed can be opened again. It does not cease to exist; the Source is still there. Man is on his way home and his arrival will be met with great rejoicing in the cosmos. You remember the parable of the prodigal son?"

B. "You have seen the light in the universe and how some of the inhabitants visualise it. All this light carries information by virtue of its form as a series of waves. The function of waves is to carry information. The dark energy that you have seen also functions in this way, as well as being the energy supply to the universe.

So all that is needed is the right sort of receiver to collect the information, and a transformer to convert it to a form that is intelligible to whatever beings want to receive it. This is not new technology; radio and television use these principles. So any information can be collected from the universe with the right equipment. Light and information are two aspects of the same wave.

Communication with beings unlike yourself will become an increasingly important part of your work and that of any humans who can receive the transmissions. At this time, all beings have to transmit in human language, but in the future, you will understand all. You have been to the planet of communication, where all languages are modified and changed so that each receiver can understand them. Just so, will you be able to do in your own mind and brain.

There are no barriers in the universe to free communication, and beings from many stars work together in harmony. To play, they return to their own kind, but for the purposes of cooperative work, the origin of the being is unimportant. Humans have been disconnected from this free flow of information, or rather the human race has, while they developed mastery of the physical world. This information also is useful to the universe and, once humans develop beyond the level of trying to kill and steal from one another, it will be more so.

This is some way from light, but light gives illumination and so does this! Go in peace."

B. "A wave is the essential form of the energy that travels through the cosmos. It is capable of storing infinite amounts of information. A wave can travel for ever and it arrives at its destination unchanged, so its information is not distorted by distance. A wave of light travels through the cosmos unchanged until it meets a physical object to illuminate. Just so do the waves of telepathic thought and the myriad communications between worlds travel. Love, as we have said, is a wave; the wavelength is very long, but it acts in principle like any other wave.

All waves originate from the Source and therefore in effect are indestructible, though individual photons may decay. The waveform is the basis of energy and thus of matter. You can see the effects of the waves in the light that floods the spirit world. The universe is full of waves, a few of which can be detected by humans. If you can understand this, you can begin to understand the flowing, changing nature of the world of spirit.

Matter is only energy waves that have slowed down enough and become dense enough to appear static. Aspire to the light beyond the physical world and the whole universe can be opened up to you. Do not stop except to rest your physical. The truth is in the light."

B. "The waveform is the primary form for movement in the universe. Every energy moves as a wave at different wavelengths and cycle speeds. The wave, like the spiral, is one of the basic patterns of the universe. Every pattern is smooth, without sharp angles, and infinitely reproducible.

A wave has the same wavelength, however far it travels, so the information that arrives is the same as that which left the source without distortion or change.

A musical note will be the same, however far it goes. The music of the spheres, the sound that echoes through the universe, is not audible to human ears, but the sounds also ring true. There is great order in the universe, for all that it is full of pulsating changing waves, the patterns are ordered and are not chaotic in nature.

The waves of the sea can become chaotic when driven by great winds, and waves of the universe can lose their pattern when driven by explosive events. The order is harmonious, the chaos is not, so the inhabitants of the universes work to avoid the chaos, just as they are working for your world now. The harmony of the worlds depends on their order."

B. "Waves are the basic pattern of the energy of the universe and so an understanding of their properties is fundamental. A wave of light will carry information about light, as a wave of the sea carries information about water. All of this information can be tapped and used by humans.

We are using it already. The carrying of information on waves is one of the ways we can see and find out whatever we need to. We use the information on the waves. This enables us to access information throughout the cosmos, as the information travels unchanged. It also travels unchanged through time as well as space, which is how we are able to access the past and the future.

Time and space are too closely connected to be separated, and time is a form of space – a further dimension of space, if you like. If you view time as a form of space, it is easier to understand precognition and how we can just as easily see the future as the present.

Space does not have shape and nor does time; but your scientists have needed to postulate shape to give form to their calculations. It is all much grander and more infinite than you can imagine at this stage. Do not limit your thinking with physical rules. The impossible is but a heartbeat away and the reality is so much more exquisite and all-embracing, that you can see that it is truly 'All That Is.' "

Time and Intention

In this universe of intention, everything we need can be manifest if we give a clear enough intention. I am told that we cannot yet manifest our food, but that seems to be the only exception.

The spirits do not measure time as we do, although they told me that one of their years is roughly equivalent to four thousand of our years. This does explain why it is difficult for them to pinpoint human events! In the universe, it is always now and they consider time as a dimension of space, when they consider it at all.

B. "Ideas and thought travels on waves, just as much as physical forms. The waves of thought are tidal, just as the waves of the sea. There are phases of creative thought and phases with absent thought. Both are equally important. If creative thought were constant, there would be no opportunity for processing the thoughts and creativity would never reach the physical. Everything in the universes happens at the best moment for it to happen, when all the other factors in the creation of an event are at their optimum degree of helpfulness. This has little to do with linear time, and you will see that, with multiple factors to reach their optimum influence, that this is more a matter of space than time.

In no case is this more apparent than in the birth of new creatures. The infants decide the time of their birth once they are sufficiently mature and the mother is ready. It is their souls that make this decision. But everything in the universe has its birth when the time and space is right, and no amount of driving or pushing can have it otherwise.

First you must have a clear intention of what you wish to happen. Then you must make sure that what you wish for does not harm another person. Then you must allow the universe to bring this into manifestation at the best possible moment. Do not push, allow. But be clear in what you put out intention for.

How many times have you pushed for something to happen, only to find out that what did happen was better than your individual plan and came at the perfect time?"

B. "The stars in their courses influence one another by their magnetic and gravitational fields. You might think of the universe as a vast web of interpenetrating and interrelating energy fields. Every 'part' has an effect on every other 'part' and every energy on every other energy. This is a system of great complexity, and events happen when all the influences are 'right'. Because of the complexity of influences, it is very difficult to relate a particular happening to linear time."

As they have said before,

B. "Time has no place in the universe and no meaning outside Earth. It is merely a convenient way of separating events and has no existence in fact."

I struggled to understand how all the waves of information travelling the universe didn't interfere with one another. The answer is that they are intelligently directed. This must be so self-evident to the spirits, that they did not initially understand my difficulty! I quite believe that the universe is intelligent and that nothing is random, but sometimes I forget just how intelligent!

A. *If an energy meets another of the same wavelength, it will not interfere, it will conjoin, but how does all the other stuff manage? There must be myriads of energy lines going through the universe...?*

T. They are not all lines. Some are waves of energy going through the universe. Some wash over the lower energies. Some are dense energies that cause disruption with the higher levels. The density of the vibration would be what would be interfered with by a higher vibration.

A. *When I started to think about it, I couldn't see how any information ever got anywhere because there are so many waves.*

T. There are, but when we wish to send information in any particular way, we route it exactly, straight to whoever or whatever it is meant for.

A. *But it must meet other stuff on the way.*

T. It can cut through. Information always will. All waves carry information. They do not interfere, and when they recognise information, a path is made and it is able to go through. Information has a different vibration and this is recognised by the other energies.

A. *Do the other energies interfere with one another?*

T. Some do, some do not. It all depends on the magnetic field at that time, and those other worlds understand the right time, the right magnetic time, to send out an energy.

A. *It is a lot more intelligent than just waves bashing across the universe. So even if it is just light coming from another planet, it will not be diverted?*

T. It will not be, no.

A. *It goes straight, doesn't it?*

T. It does. It is reflected and, in its reflection, it is made greater. When it cuts through or goes towards an information channel (and we call an information channel when the energy of an information, the vibration of an information, comes forward and light is on that same route), it becomes very powerful. It will not diminish it. Neither of those will diminish each other. To diminish the energy of the information, it will need to come from a very low energy, low in vibration.

A. *And presumably the very wide spectrum of wavelengths means they don't interfere.*

T. Correct, and there is a great deal more harmony in this than you would first imagine.

A. *Because it is done intelligently, not just randomly?*

T. It is not random.

A. *And that, I think, is where I had the difficulty. You show me the myriad colours all going in different directions and, of course, if it is intelligently driven, they don't have to bang into one another at all.*

T. They do not. Recognise also the magnetic fields of each planet, how they emit that energy and it is the driving force for the energy that they are sending. It is not only to attract, it also is to reflect out. It is difficult for us to explain this here in human terms – you will come to it. Humans' understanding of physics is not great enough, it is very limited.

A. *The "dark" background energy of love supports all these waves. It does not interfere with them at all, it just lets them pass?*

T. If anything, it heightens them.

A. *And it is the matrix of the creative force?*

T. Yes. It is a building.

A. *So the informational waves are intelligently driven so they won't...*

T. Exactly so. The information that is received by humans is sometimes muddled by humans. They misinterpret and they give wrong information. They have what we would call an edge of the information that is all they have picked up. They have not taken the fullness of the information and so they give incorrect information. That is where the interference occurs – at the point of the origins with humans.

A. *So it all travels all the way across the universe perfectly truly and then it gets distorted by humans when it arrives!*

T. Correct. Humans are not the only ones that distort. There are beings from other planets that distort information, but not quite in the way humans do. Humans enjoy what they consider to be the importance of their information and so they want to build on their information. That is why we teach you strictly.

A. *The reason I'm writing this book is I am hoping it is as near as possible to what you said.*

T. It is the closest thing to me dictating to you.

A. *It is difficult because of the limited understanding of the human brain isn't it?*

T. It is. We wish to speak and teach much more of the human brain, the part that has not been used, the part that we use with humans.

I find it difficult to comprehend that if I need something, be it physical or energetic, it is freely available if my intention is clear and strong enough. Mostly it isn't, because the intention gets muddied by negative thoughts, but the universe tries to answer our requests and prayers. On a recent shopping trip, I went to three shops and in each I found one of the three items I was looking for. Then I went home! I like to think of my uncle as my personal shopper – I imagine him flicking through a rack of sharp little jackets wearing a robe of light and his usual bow tie! The image is even more enjoyable if you know that he had not visited a shop in his last earthly life since he was a medical student!

A. *Uncle Theo, on the frivolous subject of finding my shopping, how does it work?*

T. We know what you search for and we search for it.

A. *I see – you do find it first. You are my personal shopper! So when we put out the intention, then our guides will observe what is wanted.*

T. Exactly so. The energy of what is required is trebled when the intention is strong. So when you really require something and you really put your full being into it, and know you will get what you want, then we deliver. We are able to, because it is much more precise.

A. *And it is easier with material things, because one doesn't get the anguish or wishful thinking in the way.*

T. Exactly so. We aim to please and we will always answer your request.

A. *But we have to be able to banish the negatives completely, and not just from consciousness?*

T. It is more than banish the negatives. If you can balance what you think about and what you feel, you cannot put a request forward with a negative, when heart and head are in balance.

A. *But that's the difficulty in the human world. Half of our mind is saying "I can't have that" or "I'm not good enough to have that" or "that is not possible."*

T. Yes, that is why, when humans ask for something simple, it is so simply delivered. They have no expectations of it not, or of them not being sufficiently strong enough or worthy enough.

A. *So how do you find out where there is a purple bedspread, for instance?*

T. We know.

A. *So when you put the question, you get the answer?*

T. Yes. Be precise in the question. We sometimes have humans asking that a lavatory be close by.

A. *That is sometimes very essential. What do you do? Shift the lavatory?*

T. We cannot, we can shift the human. We can point their eyes in the right direction!

There are many of us struggling to fulfil our little part of the universal plan down here on Earth, and there are many difficulties. One of the problems arises because we don't fully understand our own role. I have heard people saying that they are merely instruments of God, and of course we all are, but I believe we have to actively participate. It has dawned on me, during the gestation of this book, that we cannot just wait for it all to happen. It is for us to use our intelligence to see what is needed to make a project an Earthly success and then to put out clear intentions for what we need to receive.

The spirit world does not use money, the physical, machines, or have trade unions, or human bloody-mindedness, and do not always understand our trivial difficulties. This is what we are for, and it is up to us to be clear about what would help us. So many worthwhile projects fail through lack of money, because we just vaguely hope the "Lord will provide." Well, He will, if we are certain of what we want. I saw so many seriously sick people believing that "Jesus would save them" and doing nothing at all to help themselves. Without exception, they died, so undoubtedly He did, but not in the manner they were hoping for.

We have to participate in our lives; we can't leave it all to others. The spirits have the power to help us, but they want us to join in. Had I just typed up what the spirits told me, it would have been far too unwieldy to publish. Once I had divided it into sections, reduced the text and provided links, it flowed quite easily and, towards the end, I only had to say "I need a paragraph on...," and it would soon appear. They helped me all the time, but I had to take action myself to receive the help.

18

The Inhabitants of the Universe

The inhabitants of the universe on many worlds are non-physical. Many have evolved beyond the need for bodies. Many worlds have undergone turbulence of the sort we are expecting and some no longer have life on their surfaces, although it continues within the substance of the world. Mars does not have surface life at the moment, nor does Venus. There is life on the moon, but the spirits said that they hid themselves from the humans who landed, because of their reasons for coming. All worlds are subject to the same cycles of change as ours. Ours is the only world where the inhabitants have such limited vision and perception. This was necessary, I am told, to allow us to master the physical. When I was allowed to look through the viewing organs of beings from some other worlds, I could see right across the cosmos.

B. "Life is very much more various and wonderful in the universe that you can imagine. All souls were created together but all develop at different rates and for different purposes. Souls who have become human have on the whole developed very slowly, but their path has been complex because of the cycles in earthly bodies. Beings who do not have biological bodies consist of pure energy and are much simpler in construction. This means less to go wrong and less effort required in tending them.

Your troubles, but also your spiritual development, are directly dependent on the lack of care that you give your physical vehicle. An energy being finds it astonishing that you would give so little care to your body, but it is common among Earthlings.

Your soul's purpose continues whether you are in a body or not and from the soul's point of view, life, once given, is inextinguishable.

Life is the animation of a collection of molecules and their clothing with a minute spark of the Source, which partially separates from itself in order to allow individuation of the soul.

The living soul is never truly separated from the Source, but feels so in earthly journeys, when the bigger picture is temporarily lost. Pure energy beings do not lose their conscious connection with the Source. Therefore, they act and react quite differently. You have seen a little of the interconnectedness of worlds on your most recent journeys. That it is how it is. How it appears on Earth is just how Earthlings think it is. Life is the most powerful force – look at a seedling pushing up through cracks in paving stones.

Life cannot be extinguished and the soul's journey continues whether incarnate or not.

All souls in whatever form are part of the Great Tree of Life and are all connected to the Source and thus to each other."

Souls were born in space and visit many worlds, and even other universes, during their development. Some worlds they find more agreeable than others and they choose as homes those where the interests and development levels are most congenial. They can have more than one home. I have four, none of which is Earth.

A. *Can you explain to me why some people are human and some are not.*
T. Most humans stay with this planet, except the visits to gain particular experiences from other planets. Those we call human have chosen this planet as home, just as you chose Sirius.
A. *Are most humans primarily human or do they come from other worlds like me?*
T. Most are primarily human. Man was born in space and originates from different roots. Some, such as you and us, have long associations with Earth for particular lives of learning. You have learned medical things over many lifetimes and, when you have fulfilled your destiny, you will be able to return home and continue the work from there.

You will be channelled by others, just as you are receiving us.

Humans are very various and have many different purposes. Some will be developing new energies, some new crops, new ways of sheltering your bodies, new communications, new textiles, to fit a new age.

Communication

This is the only world and we are the only species who are not in conscious telepathic communication with each other, the planetary consciousness and "All That Is." This isolation was to enable us to learn to master the physical world and has been responsible for much of our aggressive responses to each other and to other beings, which are born of fear. Now, with the changing and rising of our conscious levels, we need not feel alone for much longer. As our vibrational level rises, we will be able to communicate consciously in this way and our isolation will be at an end.

Occasionally, I go for a trip round the oceans with an albatross. He is not a great conversationalist and, at first, I felt he must be lonely as he flew on his long solitary journeys. He showed me what he could perceive and, not only was he in conscious contact with all the other albatrosses, but he was tuned into the planetary consciousness, past, present and future. So much for loneliness! He also showed me how it felt to die. I was flying with him when, suddenly, his body dropped into the sea, but the bird itself, its soul, flew on, as did I. It was just as if he had taken off his overcoat and allowed it to fall. There was no sense of doom or ending for the bird.

As I have learned more, I have come to believe that this is indeed how death may be. If what the spirits have shown me of my own physical ending is true, it is just like that, only better, because of the glories of the spirit world, which become immediately visible and accessible. Although we in human form have not yet arrived at conscious connection with the rest of the universe, there is a lot more available to us than many will yet believe.

Levels of Consciousness

This phrase has very different meanings in the world that I used to inhabit. There was a physician called Karnofsky who graded levels of consciousness starting with zero for dead and ending with five for fully conscious. This starts where Karnofsky stopped! A human is ordinarily in contact only with himself; but the planetary and universal consciousness are available and we are all equipped with the capability to access both these levels. Conscious ability to tap into these levels is called genius.

The planetary consciousness is available for all and is the source of intuition. Whether we can reach universal consciousness or not depends on our soul development level. Access to this level depends on our ability to reach for it, unless we belong to some apparently primitive tribal societies who have remained consciously open. We have to know of its existence before we can seek it.

The rising of human consciousness will lead us to be consciously connected to the planetary consciousness and each other and is what will change the way we live. There are things in universal consciousness that cannot yet be accessed except by endeavour, for example, the energy used for the Basidian's type of healing.

The spirits tell me that all knowledge is available to us, but the level of understanding is what differs. They likened the difference between planetary and universal consciousness to the difference between a novel and an encyclopaedia. A novel gives a partial picture and the encyclopaedia should tell you everything that is known. Or you could consider it as the difference between studying a subject at primary school and at university. The same knowledge is available, but the depth of understanding is different.

This free communication throughout the universe happens in many different ways on different worlds. It is possible to use colour, telepathy, light patterns and ways of which we cannot conceive from here. One of the effects is that the truth is always visible and there can be no lies. Imagine how that would be – no self interest, no hidden agendas, no misleading statements. What will our politicians do then, I wonder!

19

Parallel Realities

The scientists have spoken of other dimensions of reality being hidden, and that is just how it seems to be. Since we all know that the Tardis is much bigger inside than out, this shouldn't really be too difficult for us to understand!

> *"Now my own suspicion is that the universe is not only queerer than we suppose, but queerer than we can suppose......I suspect that there are more things in heaven and earth than can be dreamed of in any philosophy"*
>
> *Haldane*

A. *Can you tell me about parallel realities. Are there myriads of realities like the physicists tell us?*

T. There are many other realities, but not too many to count. When your soul leaves the body and you're not coming to a place such as this, you go into a different reality. Humans have the ability to go into a different reality. You take on a different physical body in the other reality to protect the soul. Whichever reality it is, there will be a soul.

A. *Same soul, different realities. In every reality, one puts on a different persona?*

T. Correct.

A. *Are they physical spaces or are they spiritual?*

T. Some are physical, but they are mainly non-physical. They are energetic, where all can be created. They can create their surroundings. Each being can create the surroundings they choose.

A. *Why would a soul leave the body and then not go back home?*

T. They would perhaps be on their journey home, not going direct. It would depend on the level of the soul's growth at that time.

The soul does have a choice once it leaves the body. It does have a choice. It is thought by souls on Earth, that Earth is the only place where choice is. There is choice everywhere in the universe.

When you meditate, you go into a different reality – that reality is real to you, it is as real to you as the reality you live in. We need you to understand and start to experience that reality in the feelings, and you will then begin to understand how you can transport yourself to a different reality that is not necessarily a physical reality, but everything in it seems physical. You have stepped away from the brain; you have followed the soul.

A. *Is it anything like the other world I go to when I'm deep in a book – living in that world for that time. Is it anything like that?*

T. Yes, it is. When you're deeply engrossed and you are in that place, you are being drawn into that reality. You are drawn into it, you do not take yourself there. You are assisted to go into that reality and there would be those around who would help you to that reality.

A. *And that's why, because it is a reality, that it is such a satisfying experience?*

T. Yes.

A. *So the people that we would describe as mad, who are not connecting with us on the mundane ordinary reality, have they created an unpleasant one for themselves?*

T. They are not creating it themselves; they have been drawn to one that is unpleasant; it exists. Understand, these realities exist within the magnetic field of your world. Each planet has its own realities – beyond its surface and ones within it.

A. *So they are not just constructs of the physicists – they are real?*

T. They are.

I was taken on a journey to discover and explain more about parallel realities. The first world that we visited looked as if it might have been somewhere in the eastern Mediterranean. The population was having a siesta, so I did not meet them. The Basidian said that their world was the world of respect.

A. *So this is where some souls live out their whole lives, and they can do all the things that the souls in my reality do?*
T. Yes, with one exception, the exception being anger. They have anger, but they do not have violence as your world has. They have anger and they have disputes, disagreements, but they do not kill. For them to end a life would be for them to end their own. To end their own would be for them to be the outcast.
A. *But these are perfectly ordinary humans?*
T. Yes, they are, but they have learnt not to kill. They have no weapons here. They do not see anything as a weapon – a stone, nothing.
A. *Is this just a peaceful version of where I live or is it different?*
T. It is different, but it is more peaceful than where you live. It is a peaceful version.
A. *Why do I live in my one and all these people in their one and vice versa?*
T. Choice, your souls' choice.
A. *How many of these alternative realities are there on this planet?*
T. Three. Each has its own purpose. Earth is about learning and each one is about learning, but learning differently. Earth needs to learn about love. This world knows love, but it does not know love as heartfelt love, it knows love as respect. In other words, they respect all other beings, all other life-forms. They do not use the term love and yet love is what supports them.
A. *What have they come to learn?*
T. They have come to learn about respect, respect of other life-forms. A lot of the souls that are here are souls that have not respected life-forms previously in other lives.
A. *So it is just a learning place like any other?*
T. It is, it is like going to a different class.
A. *So every time you decide to go and live on a planet, you would have more than one alternative?*
T. Yes.

A. *Do the other worlds have alternatives as well, and you just choose which one fits what you need to learn?*

T. Exactly so. There is one which is of innocence. It is a world of innocence and the souls on that particular world have come to respect innocence in its purest form – not to unleash anything other than innocence. By innocence, we mean purity. It is a sense of purity they have come to learn. Pure thoughts and pure deeds, and they come from the very soul.

A. *And the fourth one?*

T. That is the planet about envy and the souls that go there need to understand envy. They are a world where there is envy of others and they have come to learn to live without envy. It is a progressive world like yours – envy of a soul's journey, of a soul's possessions, so it is a very difficult planet to be on. These are specific worlds.

A. *So is the one I live on the main one and these are sub-plots, so to speak?*

T. Yes. These are ones for when a soul has visited your world many times and still not been able to overcome or learn the lesson they came in for.

A. *So they have still got to deal with respect, innocence or envy?*

T. Yes. Each reality has a different learning for them; but it is all the process of learning for them in that particular life.

A. *You mean you go to more than one reality per life?*

T. Yes, and when they go from one reality to another, they have forgotten the previous one, until they come to the end of their life.

A. *So what happens to... do they apparently die in the first reality they are in?*

T. Yes, that is not known as death, it is known as moving on.

A. *When people aren't necessarily going straight back to the Source, they just go to another bit of reality and have another life there? Do they start from the beginning or come in halfway through?*

T. They pick up where they left off, so to speak,

A. *At the same age and maturity?*

T. Yes. It happens on your Earth also. You are visited by souls you know as perhaps Angels in physical form, who appear into people's lives and then disappear.

A. *So they go back to another reality?*

T. They do.

A. That is how a person appears to save your life and when it is done, disappears?

T. Exactly so. We draw this for a parallel for you to understand it.

If these are the main parallel realities, of which each world has a few, there are many more that are somehow secondary, although they are real, not imaginary, worlds. The three sub-worlds concerned with envy, innocence and respect are worlds where humans go when they have failed to master these particular emotions. A soul would lead an ordinary life there.

The other parallel realities, of which there are very many, are just as real but their purpose is for souls to experience different ways of living. These would be accessed by memory. Souls could leave one reality partway through and take up a new life in another. It seems to be possible to walk from dimension to dimension without any difficulty. The parallel realities exist within the planetary consciousness, where they are available to all.

I think that, like so much of the universe, they are accessed through an apparently small entry into another dimension, which opens out into an enormous world just like the Tardis. It seems as if one goes into a point which then apparently enlarges to become a world. Blake, the visionary, saw "a world in a grain of sand" and the spirits said that was exactly what he saw. They told me that the worlds within things were hidden partly for their protection and partly to limit the confusion that would be felt by experiencing them all at once. Everything has its own world within itself.

They took me to one of the secondary worlds, which was inhabited by many creatures, and then I walked through a wall and came into a completely different landscape with crops growing in the fields, but no visible creatures at all. When I met the growers of the crops they looked like humans, but they had blank discs for faces. When I spoke to them, their features appeared. They preferred to be anonymous for their protection. They were busy people, kindly, but not at all interested in me. The spirits said they lacked curiosity and accepted what came to them without question. Their learning was of community. They did not have illness or time, but they did need to rest their physicals. One of their days lasted for one of our weeks and the nights were as long as one day.

A. *Does every grain of sand have a world inside it?*
T. Yes, it will have a world of its own.
A. *If you went inside, it would it be enormous?*
T. Yes, because your reality will have altered. If you go inside and you look inside the human body, the reality is different. When you go in, it seems enormous.
A. *But the grains of sand are not all full with alternative realities in the sense that we are looking at them this afternoon.*
T. No they are not, but they have a world within themselves that is their world. Everything is complete in itself. The stones that you like to collect have worlds within them and that is why, when you collect them, you are still aware of the energy of the world within them. Your crystals have a world within themselves and an energy from that.
A. *With the crystals, you can often feel the energy.*
T. Exactly, but if you were to allow your mind to realise there is energy from everything, you would feel the energy from it. It could just be a little mind-boggling to be forever feeling the energy in every particle. You can't do it all the time – you would be deemed as crazy.

If every particle is emitting energy, it would indeed be very confusing to be able to feel it all, all the time. However, the feeling of being "at one" and being "a part of" the energies and beings all around us is what we all crave. Once again, we are the only species that cannot feel this oneness, consciously, all the time. But that will soon change.

20

Universal Love

The essential energetic force driving the universe is love. This is a word that has to do duty for some very different qualities. Universal love has more in common with the love of a mother for her child than the love between the sexes, which is the form that preoccupies many humans. This last, the spirits dismiss as an attracting force that allows for reproduction of the species and nothing more!

The love that I have received from these beings everywhere that I have travelled in the universe has been of a quality that I have not experienced on Earth. It strikes directly into my heart, but it also has elements of comfort, freedom, safety and "everything is all right." If this is a small fraction of what is actually available, I can barely wait!

B. "The love that powers the universe is an accepting, including love, like the best of mother love. The love stays steady whatever the child does and accepts the essence of the child under all circumstances. So long as the love is not withdrawn, the child feels safe and protected. So are we all loved and where we can perceive that all-consuming love, we also feel safe and protected. But it is our souls that are safe, not necessarily our bodies, as many have already discovered.

'Dust thou art, to dust returneth was not spoken of the soul.'

The bodies of man on Earth go through their cycles of growth and decay like any other biological unit. Man feels more comfortable when he discovers that he is not only his body. When he discovers his essence, he begins to realise that he cannot be extinguished and when he arrives here, he sees that life goes on.

'Do not be afraid to die' is a very important part of your message. When you are ready to release from your body, you will know when it is the right time. The release is easy, 'between one breath and the next.' When you are ready to go and have fulfilled your tasks on Earth, then you will be able to go on your way with great happiness and joy. The love we have for you is endless. You have nothing to fear."

ℬ. "Love is an aspect of light is an aspect of love. There is no distinction between them except in human eyes. Love is the force that powers your world and light is the aspect of love that enables you to see what you are doing.

The wavelength of love is much longer than the wavelength of visible light, but they are in harmony with one another, both emotionally and mathematically. Together, the tune they play is beautiful and harmonious, and when humans are sufficiently evolved, they will be able to perceive these harmonies, which are the 'music of the spheres.' This extends throughout the universe, not just on this one planet. The music plays when the worlds and stars are in harmony, one with another, and the melodies are sublime.

The rise in consciousness on your planet will enable it to take its place in the symphony orchestra of the universe and play in harmony with all the other worlds. We are using metaphor to help you understand, but the music of the spheres truly exists and gives great joy and peace to those who can hear it."

> *"All nature is but Art, unknown to thee;*
> *All chance, direction which thou cans't not see;*
> *All discord, harmony not understood;*
> *All partial evil, universal good:*
> *And, spite of pride, in erring reason's spite*
> *One truth is clear,*
> *Whatever Is, Is Right."*
>
> *Pope*

B. "Today we will talk about the Creator, God. This is not completely understandable at a human level, because the perspective is so small. God is what we refer to as 'All of Everything.' Not a bad-tempered old man with a beard, but a creative force of love so vast that it is unimaginable even to us over here. This force has chosen to diversify to create experience and to allow for individual souls to learn the innumerable lessons that are necessary to reach any level of understanding of the whole.

Here there is not bad or good, there are just opposites to create polarity and diversity. It depends on who is the observer as to whether the action is positive or negative, and the more that can be seen of the picture, the more it appears that negative actions can produce positive results. The lesson here is that it is impossible to judge from your world.

For a human soul, all you can do is follow your intuitive sense and do what feels right, until faced with the problem where the solution does not work. This is the time to display wisdom in coming to a decision. The Creator has created opposites: up – down, left – right, in – out, and so on. This does not indicate that half of these directions are bad in your terms.

What you would call heaven is filled with myriads of beings, mostly acting in harmony with a creative purpose. The bliss is universal and the only way we would not have it is if we willingly cut ourselves off from our Creator. This we would none of us want to do. A soul exists in bliss and glory and with the complete perspective on past, present and future. There is nothing that cannot be known or experienced."

B. "We have more to say on the subject of love. There is always more to say on the subject of love! The feeling that you get from the beings on Astra Stiria is the human response to the energy of love flowing through you. The energy itself is many times stronger and we, without the handicap of physical bodies, can bathe in its full force at all times.

This is what we describe as 'Bliss' and 'All That Is' and this force emanates from the Source or 'All That Is' and so it is completely sacred. It is important that this is understood. It is described by the religions as the love of God/Allah/Yahweh and so it is, but it is more than that, it is 'All of Everything' and 'All That Is.' This all-powerful but infinitely gentle force of love is 'All of Everything' and is the Creator as well as the creative force.

There is no separation in the spirit world and each individual soul knows that he is just a spark of the Creator and is part of the Creator and indeed the whole universe. The maintenance of the universe which has been created is in the care of the beings that inhabit it. This is the same for all levels. There are beings who oversee the universes, the galaxies and the myriad worlds, as well as the beings who oversee a flower, a stone, a river.

There is no separation except on your Earth and this is merely an illusion brought about by the loss of memory of your connections when you come into human incarnation. Thus it is so that truly 'Everything Is All Right' and 'All Shall Be Well.' "

B. "The fiery furnaces of the stars are born of love, just as the most delicate windflower. The energy of each reaction is entirely appropriate to the outcome required. Nothing and no energy is wasted. The universes, on their tide of love, are born, live and die, and all matter and energy are continually reused in a never-ending cycle. Matter is finite, love is not. The exquisite balance of the forces of love in the universe and on each world creates the harmony of the system. Each slight imbalancing, to allow for change in a world, is preordained and works for the ultimate good of all. Love contains everything and love is 'All of Everything.' There are no exclusions."

B. "The Creator, which is the created, is a vast and loving omnipotent force for good. Consciousness of this force enables a soul to believe and feel that 'Everything Is All Right' and this is what we enjoy and what humans have forgotten. Your soul is perfectly safe, bathed and held in this loving supporting power of infinite softness. You are loved beyond your knowing and beyond your power to know. You are free."

Universal Law

The laws of the universe seem to be held in greater regard than they are here. The ultimate sanction is not imprisonment or execution, but banishment.

B. "Today we would talk of the law, not the man-made law, but the universal law. In the universes beyond your world, there are laws we live by to enable harmony between dissimilar beings to continue. As you know, there are the laws governing matter, some of which humans have discovered. Then there are laws ordering energy and energy particles, what you call quantum physics. The laws of quantum physics cover the very large as well as the infinitesimally small, but that is not generally known in your world yet. Then there are biological laws for living creatures, and finally there are behavioural laws. These are the laws we choose to observe to enable all beings to live in harmony. The law that says that a being from another world shall only communicate with and help a human, or any other being, at that being's request. There are many others. We ourselves created the laws of behaviour in negotiation with all beings. Life over here is freer and more beautiful and blissful than you can imagine, and these laws allow us to continue in this freedom, beauty and bliss.

As we have told you, warring planets are isolated to avoid the effects on the rest of the universes. For Earth to avoid isolation, the humans must change and evolve so that they do not need to fight. Open your hearts to accept the help of the beings from all universes, so that you can live in peace with each other and with your planet, so that the age of harmony can begin. Opening of the heart and solar plexus emotional centres (not chakras; these are physical) is all that is needed to start changing each soul to allow this to happen. This you must teach and this your world must learn."

T. You are being shown love at many different levels. Love can be shown in many different ways in your language. This book needs to portray the fact that we are loving beings, not as we are portrayed as "Aliens."

A. *As if you are trying to manipulate us!*

T. As if we could!

A. *Of course you could!*

T. We could, but it goes against our universal law.

A. *In the universe, does everybody obey universal law?*

T. If they do not, there are consequences which would depend upon which planet they are of.

A. *You would be subject to the laws of Sirius and Astra Stiria?*

T. Yes, and two others. Just as you have a law of your country, but there is your personal law also, that is as it is here.

A. *You have the power to do almost anything you wanted to?*

T. We have, yes. Others do. There are those that do, they are not associated with us, but there are those that rebel. They rebelled on the planet Earth or whichever planet that it might have been, and they became outcasts. They then have to earn their way back.

A. *Is this what is responsible for all the stories about evil souls being cast out of heaven?*

T. It is. They are not cast out, they cast themselves out, they choose to not belong to the loving body.

A. *Why would they do that? You would have thought that this soul separation would be too painful for them?*

T. It is painful. They abuse the pain also; it is as if they would choose to feel that pain. That pain, the pain of the separation from the love of the universe, is more than a human being would imagine they could bear. So they turn themselves into not good things. To alleviate the pain, they will sometimes cause emotional pain in others. They cannot possess; they can come close, but they cannot possess. The more energy that you give to these beings, the stronger they become. They attract. Like attracts like, just as you attract good minds. Understand that beings that on Earth had good brains, you would attract by the memory of that good brain. Over here, we are all as one, but there is a hierarchy whereby there is greater knowledge known by some than others.

A. *And is that knowledge because of the level of evolution or of capacity?*

T. It is the knowledge because of the level of evolution.

A. *You all have the same capacity for knowing everything?*

T. Knowledge is freely available.

A. *You don't have to carry a great deal in your brain, so you don't* need

to be clever.
T. We do not. Everything is accessible.

The subject of good and evil has come up many times and it seems to be more complex than perhaps we would like to think. The spirits say "What is good in whose eyes?" and negotiate with whichever beings are causing damage to the whole. Earth, they say, is the warring planet and this is because of an effect of our magnetic energies and has always been so.

A. *Are there worlds that are working for the downfall of the spiritual hierarchy? What has happened to their energy?*
T. There are, but we would argue that they are driven by the same forces but with different intentions. They see their actions as good, and I would not say they were bad, just different. There are many spiritual laws that prevent one world from interfering too much with another. If one appears to be working towards destruction of the whole, then there will be discussion and negotiation, but not war as happens on Earth. The Creator created all and there is room for many different points of view. There is only intervention to avoid destruction.

The discussions that occur here are all a great deal more intelligent and informed than those that occur on your planet, because our view is so much larger and we are able to know so much more. At your planetary level, we are working with you to avoid your self-destruction.

This is a good illustration of how we work. If your planet destroys itself, it will have profoundly unpleasant effects on the universe, which we are working to avoid. However, we cannot just impose our will on you. We have to inform, suggest and give glimpses of the higher picture to any souls who are willing to receive us. That is what is happening now and that is why climate change has become such a popular topic. We work in a similar way to your Queen: "suggest, inform and warn!"

We have the power to take control, but spiritual laws do not allow us to exercise this, except to protect ourselves from extinction. We hope this will not go this far. Many times, your planet has arrived at the extinction of the life-forms living on it, but it has not threatened the universe before. This has come about through man's exploration and exploitation of the planet's natural resources of oil, gas, coal and so on. There are other ways to provide energy for light, heat and travel, and these technologies are beginning to emerge. There are new ways still to come when man's consciousness rises further and he understands how to harness energy without causing destruction.

Everyone knows that humans have free will, but they are not the only race or world who exercise their own choices. There is much more free choice in the universe than expected. The spirits are not allowed by universal law to interfere in another being's free will except at that being's request. We truly are entirely responsible for our lives by the choices we make. Our souls also have free choice but a much wider knowledge on which to base decisions.

A. *Not everything in the universe has free will or choice?*
T. No, not everything in the universe has free will. There is a lot, but not everything. We use it differently.
A. *Are there things that just have to react according to the laws of the universe?*
T. There are. In other parts of the universe, we have actions and reactions and we always follow the law of action and reaction. It is an element that humans have, but don't seem to understand. (Said with tones of great surprise.)
A. *An action will definitely cause a reaction.*
T. Exactly so. Scientists understand that.
A. *Scientists understand that, but the rest of the humans think they can get away with it.*
T. They do, but every action or thought, spoken word or physical action has a reaction.
A. *So there are some parts of the universe that have to follow that law and others can choose what they do about whatever situation they are in.*
T. Yes, there are, and there are some parts that have evolved so much that their actions would be love, so the reaction would be love also.

$\mathcal{B}$. "You are not alone, you are never alone, you just believe you are alone and must struggle for your survival. Soon you will know that you are not alone and you will also know how much you are loved. This knowledge will transform each of you into the unlimited loving being that you truly are. That is the purpose of it all."

21

Cosmic Travel

"Oh, I have slipped the surly bonds of earth
And danced the skies on laughter-silvered wings;
Sunwards I've climbed and joined the tumbling mirth
Of sunsplit clouds – and done a hundred things
You have not dreamed of –"

Magee

Travel in the cosmos is wonderfully quick and easy, as long as you leave your body at home, so that you are no longer subject to the physical laws of our planet. My longest trip to the outer edge of the universe took less than three minutes! As the Basidian said, "So much for the speed of light!" It often takes me longer to get back into my body than it does to cross the universe. For those who believe it to be unsafe to leave their bodies, the spirits tell me that we all do, every night when we are deeply asleep. During our lifetimes, our souls are attached to our bodies by a silver cord of energy. This cord is not cut until we leave our bodies for the last time, and this is our souls' decision, not our personalities'. Many of us do our most important work during our bodies' sleep, and if we are not working, then we are playing with our spirit group. When I have visited the Earth's fractured plates, there have been many souls from Earth working to help heal the damage.

Some journeys are included here for the light they throw on life in the cosmos, and the communication with beings so unlike ourselves in appearance, but with such loving concern for our wellbeing. Most of the beings I met commented on how little of our brains humans use! Some of the worlds are similar to ours or have experienced the upheavals that we are about to go through. Some visits were to show me how more advanced beings live, and some were just for fun. None of the descriptions would be much use for The Lonely Planet Guide to the Universe, as I usually visited for a specific purpose and saw only what was relevant to that purpose! Words cannot describe the wonderful colours and feelings that I experience. You will just have to go there yourselves!

Astra Stiria

This, the "icicle star,"' is my favourite world. I christened it in Latin at the spirits' request, since it had no human name. It is in our galaxy, but very far from Earth.

A. *I keep seeing a flower.*
B. Feel it. Touch with your senses.
A. *It's soft and I can see things like icicles. Spurs of white, which are soft when you touch them, and I see a crystal made of many fine projections.*
B. This is one of the energy centres.
A. *Are we inside the planet and is all its energy crystalline?*
B. Yes. It has clarity with it, it will give you clarity. You need to tap in to this. Can you see it getting brighter for you?
A. *The whole thing is getting brighter. I have the strong feeling of being in a very white place which looks like ice.*
B. There is a lot of love in this place. A lot of lights that you will see around you, that look like pieces of crystal, are beings, except in the energy centres. There are many energy centres here. Each group of beings has an energy centre that they would gravitate towards and they would be healed. When you go inside the energy centre, it creates a world where there is only beauty for you. Let yourself be drawn in through that light. It is full of beauty unimaginable to a human. This is your world – touch, feel.
A. *It is full of white flowers. When I hug these petals, I feel love!*
B. They have love for you. They are greeting you. Now let them

surround you with their love and you will really feel the sense of being home. Your home is a place that has great love, great consideration, great intelligence. It is a place of greatness. It is a great privilege to be able to be in this place. We do not say this lightly to you. This place is a place that you now can visit and those of your same level that come from this place. Once you leave the twelfth level, you go into a jetstream. You are not waylaid along the way, as you are in a human life. It is a magnetic force. The magnetic force is love, that is all that is needed. While you are in this place, you are being opened and prepared for your greater journey. We smile upon you. You can play. This is a place where we all play.

A. *Do you come from here too?*

B. Oh yes! But we guard another place also, for we are teachers. Feel this love. Allow this love to come into your healing. It will lift your healing to the level of a superpower.

We would wish to take you on a further journey. We need you to search out the column of light. It is made of crystals, light crystals. We would ask you to place yourself in it. Good. Now allow yourself to be drawn upwards to the opening of this column. Do not rush this. We ask that you feel everything that it is possible for you to observe at this time. We understand that you cannot observe all that is there. There are messages here for you – answers. They will be in the flecks of light. Take hold of one – what does it tell you?

A. *"Open your heart."*

B. This you must do. You cannot just say the words. This is good. Now take another light.

A. *That one says "You are able."*

B. Now you need to open yourself fully to acknowledge that. Your supersubconscious needs to acknowledge this. Breathe it in. Good. Be aware of your expansion. You are becoming lighter. Take one more.

A. *"You have no limits."*

B. Yes. Now feel you have no limits, don't just use the words. This is just an exercise that would help you to go to higher knowledge. This you can do on your own. Use the same column of light to go through, it will lift you up. Remember the magnetic field is of love. This is for your self-teaching and self-healing. The doubts you have of self will be dispersed here. When you have any of the doubts in these three things that have come up, you will be reminded. It is understood that, as a human, you cannot clear something from your mind immediately. It takes a little practice. You will be helped.

A. *This is wonderful. I am inside an energy centre on Astra Stiria!*

B. This is what your energy centres are for – they are informative. We are aware of your energy levels. It is time for you to come back……..

A. …………*I am not sure if I am anywhere near my body yet.*

B. You are not. We need you now to come back into your body, very gently. Feel your fingers and toes, a gentle way of coming back in.

A. *Am I in. I still feel a bit uncertain about it?*

B. Wiggle your toes more. You have been in a faraway place. It will take you a while to assimilate your body again... You are back in.

A. *Thank you, that was wonderful.*

B. It was our great pleasure. It is with great love that we leave you. Understand that it is with great love that we come to you each time. The level will become more tangible for you. Blessings, dear one.

Later, I asked for more information:

A. *Please tell me more about Astra Stiria. I know it is a crystal planet of beauty and knowledge.*

T. There is a great deal more to Astra Stiria than that. This is a place of love of humanity. You think of yourselves as being the only humanity and you are called humans, yes, but there is much more humanity than on Earth, and so it is a place where there is no judgment and total love and also a place where you can come to regenerate.

A. *Can you regenerate anything on Astra Stiria?*

T. You can, and you are also able to obtain your tools from this place and so it is a place of great love and healing and it is a teaching planet also.

A. *So that's where the knowledge is kept. Is all the knowledge to do with healing, or is it about many things?*

T. It is about many things, but mostly healing to the forefront.

A. *So is it a related planet to Sirius?*

T. That it is. We are introducing you to the planets that are interconnected; so what one would have, the other would have a different aspect of.

A. *So it is all part of an interplanetary healing network?*

T. It is. These particular worlds connect with your planet Earth most strongly; there are others which connect, but these connect most strongly.

Journey to Sirius

Sirius is the world that the Basidian call home and is another of mine. It is the world of healing and the teachers of healing.

B. We ask you to be very still within yourself. We are going to take you up on the fast track. When you come to the opening on the edge of your world's energy, it will be like a firework going off. Take a whole breath. Watch your chakras open as you go up. Keep going till you get to the starburst. Let one of the stars take you and we will draw you towards us. Be aware of the crystalline effect of what you are. Go up towards the light. You cannot enter till you have become the light. A whole breath would help. Put your feet down, if feet you have. We are all around you. It is now for you to clear your vision and allow us closer.

A. *I am having difficulty seeing you, but I can feel you very well.*

B. We are aware of your feeling us. You are being carried at this moment. Go towards the light that you see in front of you. Go into the light till you see an image. We have no limitation. If you look around, you will see me and you will see the collective around me. We may present as just round to start with. We are all working to present ourselves as a shape.

   (I saw mother-of-pearl-coloured ovals with wafting fronds of pearly light around them.)

A. *Not much shape, but a lovely colour. You are like ghosts drifting about, but the colours – wow!*

B. Drift is what we do. You can touch one of us, it will not feel like a human.

A. *It feels soft. I see something like strings of beads.*

B. This is us manifesting ourselves. You are seeing our molecular structure. We are as one. Keep coming in till you feel at home, till you are in the centre of us. You can intention where you would go. We do not wish to tire you – do not work too hard.

A. *As soon as I stopped trying, I felt I was in the middle of you.*

B. Good. What is the other emotion you feel?

A. *Love.*

B. Good. Come with us. We will take you now to show you what our world looks like. We are not in water, but there is a fluidity. Nothing has sharp edges.

A. *No – all soft and rounded. Many lights and colours, but not much solid. Do you have any solid?*

B. Yes, in the chambers. We will take you presently. We will take you to the healing place, the blue place. We use this to heal the soul. Take a full breath and go deep into this blue. It will support you, you can lie back and relax here. As the soul leaves the body on Earth, this is one of the places we bring them to for healing. The soul carries many scars. The souls of this place, those who have passed through here, will always come back. It is part of your journey home, but it is not your final destination.

A. *Where will that be?*

B. You will go back to the ice planet and once you have had your complete healing from there, you will then return to us and we will discuss everything that has passed on your life on Earth. We will discuss how you can help those left on Earth. Understand your weightlessness; it is as important to you as your feet feeling the ground on Earth. With your expansion, the mind clears. The soul has a mind of its own; the soul has your deep subconscious.

A. *I still feel as if I have a body, but it doesn't have very circumscribed edges.*

B. There will come a time when you will not be aware of your body at all as you do this journey.

Bid farewell. Your intention is enough... It has given us much pleasure to accompany you. We are now in the process of replenishing you. You are becoming tired. You are our prime concern. For, understand this, we are what you would call your greatest friends from where we come from. We come with great love for you, because you are a part of who we are, as we are a part of who you are. That is why, when you journeyed towards us, we all became one. You may not have been fully aware of that, but that is what happened. We are not separate, we are a part of each other, so you will understand the great love we have for you. As we have love for ourselves, we have love for you, and it is our task to protect and honour you.

A. *Thank you.*

Antares and Heros

We went to these worlds for me to see beings who did not look like humans. On Antares, they looked a little like vultures, but they radiated love towards me. Because of my reduced energy, my light, which is how they saw me, was dim. This they did not understand and, when I explained, there was a powerful whoosh of both love and energy that made me cry. They were a harmonious, loving people whose purpose was giving support to other worlds.

Heros was populated by beings who look like coffee beans with peacock feathers at the upper pole. They let me look through their eyes, which I think were situated in the feathers. I could see right across the cosmos! I visited here on another occasion and was directed to look at the ground, where there were pearls lying among the pebbles. I was invited to pick up any that were relevant to me and I collected sixteen of them. When I opened them later, one by one, I found each gave me information on a different subject, such as "The Nature of Love" or "Wisdom." It is, in fact, my own personal Google, and I can refer to the relevant pearl whenever I want to know about anything. This was at the very beginning of my being able to channel, and I was often startled by the information I was given.

Journey to Venus

This next journey was in the nature of a birthday treat – a trip round the galaxy! Its purpose was to show me how closely connected are the worlds out there. It is only us who have the illusion that we are struggling alone. This time, I was trying to channel the various beings myself, but I quite often needed help. I tend to start arguing with myself about whether a statement comes from the being I am speaking with or from my own mind! It is easier when the being says something startling and outside my experience, but when the statement is close to my own opinion, I find it difficult to know who said it. Once you start to argue with yourself, your mind is in the way and the communication ceases to flow. I have learnt to distinguish the quality of a statement by another being from my own thoughts; but keeping my mind out of a conversation is more advanced work! These experiences give me an even greater respect for the accuracy of the medium with whom I work. Her name is Dorothy, but the Basidian refer to her as "The one through whom we speak!"

First we went to Antares, and then:

A. *He said "Come with me." We have gone off again. I wonder where he is taking me now. I am in a gas cloud of some sort, and whether it is a place with beings in, it I don't know... Now I can see a lot of ovals, each with a single antenna, and I imagine they must be beings. They agreed. Where are you? It is not somewhere where I would know the name. They don't have eyes to do their seeing with. I am seeing multicolours and rather indistinct sort of shapes. I want to see how far they can see. Gosh, they can see across the cosmos, a lot further than us!*

T. If you ask that question of the Basidian, you will get a similar answer. Feel what it is like when you communicate with beings of other energies. What does the energy feel like?

A. *Lighter and not so powerful in human terms. What do you do? "We are." I am seeing all sorts of things that I don't understand, that appear and disappear very quickly. What are those shapes?*

T. They are other beings.

A. *Everything except us is shooting about the universe all the time! Do these beings have purpose? What is that purpose? Of course, there are a lot of different beings, aren't there? What about the ones with the antennae. What is your purpose? "Our purpose is to love." Do you have any other purpose? I have a background feeling that they are supportive. Who do you support? "Other worlds." What do you support on other worlds? "The life force." I have a sense of a force going whoosh through space, but I don't yet know where we went. Now we are on a planet. This is a planet with structures on the surface; it is not Earth. Can I know where this is? The thing that came to mind was Venus, but it isn't anything like I would expect.*

T. It is Venus.

A. *I have to learn that things aren't going to look how I would expect. So you support the beings on Venus with life force. Why, don't they have enough of their own? Are you their energy? "Yes,"' they said. Can I ask what is the purpose of these beings that you are helping? "They have much work." Can I know what any of that is? "The Venusians need a great deal of help." Why? What they said was "This is a troubled planet."*

T. They have had many problems.

A. *Oh I see, so the Earth is not the only planet having a bit of turbulence. I am getting the feeling that this is bigger and better turbulence than anything that Earth could possibly do! Can I see a Venusian? I can see something that looks like a cell, but with a lot of projections. Hello. Then I saw a very bright light and, when I entered it, it looked like hundreds of lit crystals. It was an energy source. They showed me that every planet, star and being are deeply intermingled and not at all separate. They showed me the web of everything, with all the worlds just like jewels on this web.*

The White Planet

This was to show us a world that lives in a way that we will evolve to eventually. First they took me to Sirius and showed me what looked like a great wave curling over, made of light of many colours. This, they told me, was a "black hole," which they describe as an entry point to different dimensions. I dived through the wave and found myself in a rural landscape with grass and trees of unfamiliar types. The grass was very dry and the trees had water-retaining leaves. I was told that the inhabitants conserved their water very carefully and wasted nothing of their resources.

I went to a beach, which was dark red in colour, and the sea was white because the sun of this world gave off white light, which was much less scorching than ours. Some buildings appeared, of different shapes and colours to ours and with a reflective surface that was partly to keep the insides cool and partly a technique to collect the sun's energy. Inside, the rooms were almost octagonal and the beings within them had two arms and two legs and their heads and bodies were covered in a material that looked like, but was not, metallic. Their visual apparatus received much wider wavelengths than ours and they showed me that I could see all the colours of the universe.

T. There is great intelligence here. They do not have names, they have identification which would be called energy levels. For your ability to identify to them, you were showing a colour. They identify by colour, they worry not of names.

A. *I have an impression that these beings have eyes which have got a much wider wavelength range.*

T. Correct. They also can see into and beyond solid matter. They can see the goodness of who you are. They are working to help their planet evolve greatly.

A. *So they are doing what we ought to be doing?*

T. Correct, and they protect their planet.

A. *So are they working in harmony with their planet, as we are trying to?*

T. Just so.

A. *Okay, does the planet have a name that I can know?*

T. It does. They do not do it in words. They use symbols to create their language, which is very different to yours; that is why the communication is difficult. We would know this planet as the White Planet. Colour is important to beings of this planet. Each is identified by their own colour. There are many of them, but there are many more colours than there are in your spectrum. They would look at the energy of the colour to identify. This planet is about light and clarity. Earth will discover it one day. It is sustainable. Life here is totally sustainable.

All their materials came from the planet and they did not use the indestructible materials that have made such a mess of Earth. They shared everything they had completely and there was no poverty or misery. They had both self-respect and respect for others. They had evolved beyond emotional problems, but they still were subject to accidents. There was no monetary system; this is quite unnecessary in a world where the inhabitants can manifest whatever they need at will. So there was no greed or avarice. There were many types of being on this world, but whatever they ate was created for them. They had learned to take just what food they needed and leave the rest for others.

The spirits told me that they are as happy and peaceful as they could be and live in the midst of plenty. They considered other beings as at the same level as themselves. There had been invaders in the past, who were searching for their riches, but they left because their riches were their intelligence rather than their possessions. I was told that eventually Earth would evolve to the point where our lives would be very much like this. But first we had to learn to use our brains properly. In the universe, most of the beings I have met use their right brains.

T. Humans do not use their right brain. These souls are right brain. They have such intelligence that they are beyond your greatest scientists, but they use their right brain to access it.
A. *That is interesting – if you can be just as intelligent using your right brain – because all our scientists would say that you have to use your left brain.*
T. There is a great deal of human brain that is not used. These beings have brain that every part is used.
A. *Well I'm not envying them, but I would like to be able to manifest anything I wanted.*
T. You can.
A. *I suppose I can, but I don't believe it yet properly.*
T. Until you do, it will not manifest. Humans have not yet evolved to the point where they can manifest food, but humans can manifest anything else in their lives – anything.
A. *You mean whether it be thing or circumstance?*
T. Yes, but they have to believe it.

Affurika

Affurika is a world that has been through its own upheavals. It is physically similar to our world, but the beings (AF.) live differently. It is situated on the outer edge of our universe. During conversation with the inhabitants, there were some entertaining misunderstandings, as they interpreted literally what I said. I'm so used to the Basidian being able to decode my speech, that I often forget that the beings I speak with are not human and do not use my language. The beings I met had similar body construction to ours, but had retractable antennae on their heads. They lived in shelters that looked like igloos and they manufactured their furniture almost as if they were spiders creating their webs. They were biological in nature and created offspring in a similar way to us.

They showed me their landscape and seas, which were not dissimilar to Earth. The sea was of fresh water and there were many fish, which they did not eat because they did not destroy life. They ate grain, which they harvested by hand. It seemed that much of the healthy population worked at the harvesting. They did not use money or have paid work and they had evolved beyond having illness. Their bodies, being biological, wore out like ours. They educated their children by example and the children joined in with the tasks at an early age.

They were able to tap the energy of their worlds for their needs. This is the first planet where I saw the inhabitants apparently putting a three-pin plug into the earth. Uncle Theo said that they did not use plugs, but otherwise that was what they did! I asked how they resolved their differences and they said that they transcended differences because their communication and connection with each other and the Source was so close. In the past they had had wars.

AF. We were a warring world, just as yours is.
A. *And did you destroy yourselves and your world?*
AF. Almost to extinction.
A. *And what changed it?*
AF. A few that were here spoke out. They were strong in their speech. They gathered followers, those that understood, and that became stronger and that became the voice, and with the trauma that our planet went through, theirs was the only voice left.
A. *Very much like what we are about to go through?*
AF. It is.
A. *What do you feel your purpose for being is now?*
AF. To connect up. To use this planet that we live on to connect up with other planets in order to save your planet. That is our purpose. Also for our planet, it is to maintain harmony, for this planet now

has a balance.

A. *And you don't want to upset that?*

AF. We do not, no. We see the imbalance of other planets.

A. *And are you helping other planets, as well as us, that have gone through similar...?*

AF. When it has been necessary, yes.

A. *Because Venus went through a similar destruction, didn't it, and I imagine that there are many more that I never heard of?*

AF. There are. We would work with one planet at a time. The energy is required to keep that planet in the position it is in, to stop it changing its position too much, going off course. Although it is necessary for planets to go off course slightly, in order for them to change.

A. *So that is what you would describe as your work, your purpose?*

AF. It is our purpose, yes. All will work towards this purpose. All.

A. *Because I'm so busy asking questions, I haven't given myself the opportunity of feeling how you feel. So perhaps I should stop talking for a minute to see if I can feel that.*

AF. We would like you to go into this feeling. We will come close.

A. *Your feeling is soft and loving. It seems to be like this everywhere, except on Earth. Is there anything that you want to tell me to help the people on Earth with their transition?*

AF. We would wish that souls that live upon your planet would open themselves to what the planet requires, rather than themselves. Humans are observed by us as a race of souls that considers itself to be in a race. They seem to require to out-race their neighbours.

A. *And it isn't until we drop out of that race, for whatever reason, that any of us get any sense!*

AF. That was once the way here. It is understood by our elders. We have elders who are many times your age limit, as we are.

A. *So they can think back to the time of turbulence?*

AF. They are able to. They would be the collective leadership and they would and do transfer information from our Source, "All That Is,''' for all of us. On Earth, this will happen. You have connections with the Source. Humans appear to sever this connection at will. It seems to be inappropriate.

A. *Indeed. It is wonderfully arrogant of us to believe that we can!*

AF. We do not have this word.

A. Arrogance means the sheer cheek of thinking that we can separate ourselves from "All That Is..." I don't suppose you understand cheek either, do you?

AF. We understand the anatomy of the human.

A. The human effrontery, do you understand that?

AF. Feel it, feel the effrontery. When you go into the feeling of your spoken word, we can.

A. I'm not sure I can do that just at the moment. I'm too far out of my body. It is a very human thing. What I really mean is that it is impossible to separate from our Source and we are guilty of false pride if we try.

AF. This we understand, for that was a feeling that dwelt here – falsehoods. Humans are opening a little and those which refuse to open will perish.

A. Did your elders, your leaders at the time when turbulence came upon you, did they have a very hard journey to persuade the others to begin with?

AF. Great difficulties. They were banished until proof were able to be given. They were banished by their own communities. This is not to be reflected for you. They did not lose their connection with our Source through this banishment. They were warned of it and so they dealt with it; for elders are able to see ahead, as we can, but we choose not to. We enjoy what you would say the present.

A. Are you all happy?

AF. We are.

A. And fulfilled?

AF. Filled full?

A. Do you feel satisfied that you are achieving your soul's purpose

AF. (In tones of considerable surprise:) We are!

A. It is just that most people on Earth are not.

AF. This we understand.

A. And because I am reaching towards the end of this Earthly incarnation, it is a most important thing for me.

AF. Understood, it is a time for celebration for you. Humans should learn to celebrate their lives. We understand celebrations here.

Oriaton

On this journey, I used the silver/gold shell for the first time. This has now become my standard travel method because it conserves my energies. It is infuriating to have to limit a visit because I have run out of steam. Although I do not take my body with me, the journeys use up my physical energy in a way I do not understand, and I am often fit for nothing after them. The beings of Oriaton are the only beings I have seen that look anything like us, although the arrangements of their special sense organs would not be thought appealing by most humans!

T. We wish to take you today on a journey to a planet that we have spoken to you of, that has life-forms on it the most similar to your own, and they have emotions very similar to your own. Just be the observer. We are going to support you on this journey, to save your energy. Can you see the vessel we have for you? It is like half of a shell that will support you. It is a great comfort for you.

A. *Is it padded?*

T. To the level your soul would require.

A. *Of course, my body does not need to come.*

T. We would like you to observe as we take you on this journey. The reason we are taking you in a vessel, it will use less energy.

A. *Yes, I can see it clearly now, it seems to be of polished metal. I don't know whether it is gold or silver or even copper.*

T. It has both, as you would understand, gold and silver. It is very special.

This was a physical world with earth and vegetation. The buildings were of mud with another organic material for the roof. The furniture was mud based and the inhabitants used planetary energy for their needs. The beings there, who as usual were considerably more advanced than us, had rather similar bodies to ours, built on a similar skeleton, which is what they first showed me. Their heads differed in that they had sense organs on short stalks all over their heads. These lit up when they were communicating. Their hands were much more flexible and dexterous than ours and their heads were larger. They showed me how their brains looked when they were being fully exercised. It was like the most complicated wiring diagram ever made, with lights whizzing about in all directions. Their emotions were all positive apart from a sense of loss. They were great communicators, using telepathy or energy, but not words. I got a surprise when I asked their purpose.

A. As beings from Oriaton, do you have a particular purpose in the universe?
T. Ask if they will show you.
A. I have the impression of an Oriaton person picking up a baby.
T. Yes, watch what they do with the baby.
A. They are putting it in the river! That is slightly surreal. The baby turned over and swam briskly off!
T. Why would it not?
A. Human babies can't do that!
T. And there is your answer.
A. I'm still laughing at this image of the little baby briskly swimming away!
T. They are educators. Ask them to take you to the visitor centre. This is for visitors of many planets and also from Earth.
A. I have a picture of a dome and there are groups of people there from many places. I can't see any detail. The feelings are of love and expansion. Are these beings trying to help people to understand how to expand into the beings they truly are?
T. Exactly so.
A. There are a lot of different sorts of beings. Are there a lot of planets that don't know this yet? I thought we were the only one?
T. You are not. Different levels.
A. So they are trying to explain, in their way, what you have been telling me repeatedly, that we are limitless.
T. Correct. They understand their limitlessness. You were shown the child put into the water and it just knew how to swim. They have no limits with knowledge and their physicalness.
A. And they are able to believe that they are able, which is what produces the human difficulty. I don't know what affects the other planets, but presumably something similar or they wouldn't be here.
T. They would have a similar problem.
A. These beings are very much more competent in their limitlessness

than any of us are on Earth.

T. True. They have no barriers, whether it be in their emotions. Their emotion would be love. Before they eat anything from the planet, they would have love for it. They would not consume anything that was not produced through love. It is always replenished. They have learned self-sufficiency through replenishment.

A. *They have learned to leave enough for it to re-seed itself. This lot has cracked it really, haven't they?*

T. They have. They also do not use the language of words.

A. *They communicate telepathically or energetically?*

T. Both. They are communicating with you telepathically.

A. *Do they make any sound at all?*

T. They do, they make music, and they can make a baser sound.

A. *So they make music, but they don't speak?*

T. They don't. They make a sound that to your ears will sound almost like music. Understand, that is a sound a little bit like the mammals in the sea, how they make sound, and these souls make sound similar. They would understand the mammals that are in their seas. It is a planet with gravity.

They had evolved beyond illness and made much better use of their brains. Their young were educated collectively and had a different growth pattern to ours. While they were infants, they went to their place of knowledge and absorbed all their knowledge for that lifetime. There was then a short period of assimilation and learning to understand, and then they became functional adults; but their bodies did not decay until they chose to change them. This is another world where the inhabitants had brought themselves to destruction and they had evolved to their present advanced state as a result.

Neepa Sovon

This is another of the worlds I call home. On the way, I was invited to look back to my own Earth, which I saw as surrounded with a corona of light. This, I was told, was the energy going to Earth from all the other worlds.

Neepa Sovon is one of the worlds that evolved very early on in the universe. The world I came to had many layers of light surrounding it. There was a channel through the layers, which led me to the surface. This is not a solid world; it is more like one of our gas giants than anything else, and the beings live, not on the surface, but in the centre. They create whatever they need using the energy available and their intention. It was one of those worlds where you can grab a bit of energy and sit down on it! When I naively asked if they didn't miss the sun and the sea and so on, I was told that all this was available to them where they were.

The beings who greeted me had shapes like a Lowry "matchstick" person, but with more limbs. They had a single, beautiful, many-coloured eye taking up most of the front of their heads. There was great love being emitted from the eye, and the effect was happy and smiling. They showed me how I looked on this world – just like them – and gave me the name Madra, which means "being of light." The importance of this planet to me is that it is one of the worlds that I call home, and on it I found my soulmate, whose name is Roson, which means "energy with smiles." He is further evolved than me and has never had human incarnations. That was a very happy meeting.

The Moon

*I have only been once to the moon and it amused me to find how the beings there (**M.**) dealt with the human landings. It was humbling to discover that they too are working to help us and are concentrating on the neediest humans. We went to visit beings on the far side, where the surface looked much less barren. I went into a surface opening, to find that I was in a great white chamber shot with rainbow colours. What I thought were rounded sections of rock opened up to reveal chambers full of beings, looking a bit like lollipops on sticks.*

B. Look at the sticks – the sticks will have a purpose.
A. *I get the impression that the sticks separate up into arms and legs – are they limbs?*
B. Correct.
A. *So they are beings and the head of the beings looks more like moonstone than anything else.*

B. They will glow stronger or lighter. This is the planet that deals with emotions – the transference of emotions. This is a strong-energy planet. These beings relate to one another through their emotion. With the emotions, they are working towards helping planet Earth, for it is mankind's emotions which need to be helped. These moon-beings work with human emotions, with the ebb and the flow of the emotions. Do you see the way that, before they showed themselves, they hid? Not to be penetrated by man unless they choose to be. Man has not discovered these. We would like you now to go inside one of the chambers. This may make you feel emotions; the strongest emotion will be love.

They showed me the group of people they were working with – a group of very poor Americans, who were jealous of the plenty around them. They always work with the poorest and neediest souls on our planet, because:

B. They are the building blocks of any country, because they are prepared to go out and work, and so these souls need help in order that they change their attitude. As they change their attitude, it will filter outwards and upwards. You would think, as humans, that it needs to filter downwards. They need to be given enough energy to feel good about who they are, and so it does have an effect that it will affect the next group and so on. Now we wish to show you what they will use to send this healing to these people. They have many tools.

A. *There was a bolt of light like a lightning strike.*

B. Yes, they use the light energy in their sleep state and they would normally go to the lowest that we see there first. That light came from a crystal. Look around you. They will be there, tools will be there.

A. *Oh yes, I can see very brilliant clear crystals.*

B. See the shape of them and the colour of them...

A. *They have got rainbow light through them, but intrinsically they are colourless and quite sharp and long.*

B. Good. As they are used, one colour will predominate.

A. *Purple. So is that purple light trying to raise their consciousness to* *make them more aware?*

B. It will help them to be more aware of firstly themselves and others around them, and then secondly their surroundings. Once these people care about their surroundings, they will begin to take care of planet Earth; but first we need to help them.

A. *It is interesting that these beings are working with the poorest and most needy first.*

B. It is most important.

A. *It would be almost the opposite that humans might expect.*

B. Exactly so. Humans seem to think it is the one at the top that makes the difference to the ones at the bottom, but it is not, it is the other way round. In order to be at the top, they must start at the bottom, though not necessarily in this particular way. It is to climb – once they have climbed to the summit, they use that to filter through to the others. Those that learn, we are able to help along their way, with the lessons they have to learn. There are a few that are beyond our help at this time. Our planet has been working closely with Earth for some time – with the beings of Earth. We also work with the animals, all species. We communicate with them not to overpopulate and, as we do this and they hear us, we move onto the next. They will not disappear quickly, but they will become less.

They invited me forwards to share in their energy so that they could communicate with me.

A. *Now I am very close to just a few of them. It is as if we are sharing the same candle flame.*

B. You are sharing the same energy. They have invited you forwards. They will begin to communicate with you and show themselves.

A. *They said "Welcome, my dear friend" and I can feel my heart being touched.*

B. Yes, they will do that. They are curious about your heart. Not many humans have been there.

A. *Why are you curious about my heart?*

M. We do not have such things, we have no need of them.

A. *Because you are beings of energy and you can get your energy around you perfectly satisfactorily without a pump?*

M. Correct. As we understand you, you also are a being of energy.
A. *Yes, different energy to yours. I can't get the physical energy around without a pump.*
M. Correct, understood. It has a good feel to it, it feels soft. We look at the emotional. We have strong emotions here. We do not have anger here, we do not.
A. *Do you have any of the other negative emotions?*
M. There was a time we did have.
A. *So the ones you have are joy, love, peace, happiness, bliss?*
M. We do and what we like is to put right what is wrong. We go into a shell, we hide ourselves. That is why humans have not been able to see us in the past. A few have, that we have allowed in, but when they touch our planet, probe our planet the way that they do, we give them only what they require, nothing more. It was about money, this we understood, and so we formed ourselves as rocks. They walked amongst us, unaware to themselves, and yet those early ones were aware of the emotions and what you would call the spirituality of this planet.
A. *Yes, one of them at least is still talking about his spiritual experiences in space.*
M. For a reason we do not understand, humans have difficulty speaking of the higher emotions. We do enjoy studying human beings. You have strange emotions, you are not always consistent in your emotions.
A. *There is nothing consistent about humans.*
M. Where we are, everything is consistent.
A. *A human can believe two completely opposing beliefs at the same time, as I am sure you have noticed!*
M. We have noticed this. It is difficult to comprehend, but we have noticed.
A. *I think it may be because our brains are divided up into compartments.*
M. We have delved into the human brain and there is not a great deal of it being used and there is a great deal of wastage. We waste nothing of ourselves. Humans will evolve to use all of their brains. Lifting your consciousness to a level that you allow information to flow into your conscious and subconscious minds, brains, will be the way the Earth is redeemed. Earth does not need to perish. It is

not the universe's will for Earth to perish. There are many worlds working with your world, with humans in your world, and that is why there are strange things happening in your world now.

B. Understand that these beings are collecting the energies from where they come and directing them. A little, as you would say, like a sign post.

A. *Thank you, moon people.*

B. They are good souls. They will give you their name.

A. *They are the Elon.*

B. They are honouring you.

Skouros

I did not actually land on this world, but I looked at the energy layers surrounding the world, and the inhabitants came out to meet me there. It is situated somewhere in the middle of the universe, but not in our galaxy. First they showed me how the energy of magnetism felt – clear and sharp. And then I travelled through the energy layers surrounding this world. First there was a layer of indistinct shapes that the spirits said were discarded emotions. Next was a golden five-pointed star, which depicted the positive energy left when the negative was discarded. The next layer was rainbow colours, the colours indicating the health of the world. Inside that was a circlet of jewellery, each jewel representing a collective of the beings.

Then I came to the most beautiful amethyst you could ever imagine, glowing with subtle colours. I entered this jewel and inside it was green with swirling energy lines, which I was told was the being of the jewel communicating with me. They gave me unconscious information and told me that "All shall be well." I am not the first human to receive that message! They wished to comfort me, because I had been worrying over the state of our world. I found it astonishing, but very heartwarming, to travel halfway across the universe and still find beings who cared about us.

22

Unconscious Information

The next three journeys were to worlds that I had visited before, but the spirits had more information for me than they could give in speech.

Sirius

I went to the beautiful world of Sirius with its soft pearly light, which emanates from within the world, and I was taken into a great crystalline chamber and surrounded by non-physical beings, who appeared as wonderful jewel colours. They gave information directly into my mind and said at the end that they had imparted enough to fill one of our large books! The information was about how our planet will be able to take care of itself. Then they showed me structures looking like little golden beehives and inside they were labyrinths. I spiralled up through one of them and out of the top. These were places the Sirians use to cleanse and replenish their emotional energies. They would go through them to remove any negative emotional energies and these would be transmuted within the labyrinth.

T. When we are affected by humans' emotional energy, we come here, because it is often sticky. This is a place with many chambers that a negative energy would go into to be stored and worked with and turned round. They are places of positive energy. It is just that humans tend to bring their negativity into the positive, and they cannot exist together. When there is negative, positive cannot exist and, when there is positive, negative cannot exist, and so we always rid ourselves of anything that feels negative after visiting your planet. It is just as you would shed the day's energy that you no longer need and, in doing so, you would replenish yourselves with different energy, just as you would have a shower. There are many of these, there are many of us.

Of course, when we are working with humans on Earth, we will need to come back to cleanse ourselves, because we are non-physical. We are pure energy and we will attract some negative energy away from people, as we would replenish good energy, and these chambers change the energy back. We do not necessarily need to do so – we go through them. These chambers are never clogged or full. It is a continuous flow, and that goes out then positively into the universe, into the limitless. It is a pity humans don't understand fully the benefits of limitlessness.

A. *Limitlessness is what I have to learn about.*

T. It is. It is not just you, but you are the subject we work with. The moment you truly feel limitless, you will be in constant instant contact with us.

A. *That is something to work for!*

T. It is, but it will also lift any worries you have had. We do not mean to say that you, as a human being, will not have concern for others in the future. You will, that is the nature of the human. It will be concern rather than worry, which is much more constructive.

A. *If one is in fact limitless and one is also connected, then most of the things we worry about are completely unnecessary.*

T. Exactly so, and we wish more humans to come to this space.

A. *While I am out in the cosmos, I can entirely believe this, but it hasn't yet stopped me worrying on Earth!*

Then they took me into their crystal world to absorb their beautiful energy. I had feelings of love and comfort and being at home, which made me cry, as I always do when my heart is touched. Finally, I had an overview of their lands and had the curious experience of seeing the physical contours on one level and the energy levels of light at another, at the same time. This world is physical, but the beings, my friends the Basidian, and others are not.

Astra Stiria

Here I went to the place of knowledge and saw a form with wings, which were lit up. I was invited to go into this form and told that it was a projection of the universal mind that had partially individualised for a specific purpose. Inside this form, I felt that I was a part of this mind and that I was a part of creation. I was not alone, I was supported and protected always. I was shown, and felt, the warm energy of information travelling between our planets. As I came closer to the energy stream, I could perceive the phrase "The fate of the Earth" being repeated.

A. *What is the fate of the Earth?*
AS. That depends on you, but not you as an individual. There is a concern in the universe, because it will affect our balance. It would upset our equilibrium. We need each planet to create the balance in our universe. When one planet loses energy, such as yours, yours is seeping energy, and that is why you are seeing this energy going to it, and it is being filled with information as well with this energy, so that humans on Earth are better informed. It is going into the very core of your planet and to the surface of your planet, and it is those humans that are on the surface of your planet and are sensitive enough, will receive it. It is a continuous inflowing and outflowing, and that is from the universal mind, where what you would consider new revelations come from, new understanding.
A. *This is what a genius can tap into?*
AS. Correct, for we would all be considered genius where we are, because we are able to tap into everything. Humans we consider genius, but there are those that excel.
A. *Why do you consider humans as genius?*
AS. We consider the human body to be pure genius, and how humans are able. It is genius. Humans have the ability to reinvent themselves and that would come from genius.
A. *Are you talking about their bodies or their creations?*
AS. Their creations – they just get little parts of it wrong, but that is part of human evolution, and it is part of the human evolution to understand what you call the spiritual mind also, and that is the area

that we are concerned with, for that has a sense of rapid growth. The surface of your planet is too warm. It is considered it is heating from externally; it is heating from within also. It is as if the heat from within creates a steam-like atmosphere and that is wasted. It leaves your atmosphere. Humans there speak of the ozone layer, they understand that, but there are layers that they need to take care of before that level. The pollution eats away at it and, through the time of this planet, it is becoming thinner, and all the planets are working to stop this in order to save the planet Earth, in order then to save the universe.

A. The fate of the universe does not depend on planet Earth, does it? You would be made uncomfortable, but it doesn't depend on the fate of Earth, does it?

AS. It does not, but the balance will be different and we would not... None on other worlds will perish, but it would make difficulties. We would all have to realign ourselves, and it is not wished to do this.

A. I understand that you just wish that humans would get off their butts and do something about it.

AS. Correct, for once they do, there will be harmony in the whole universe.

A. What about the two other warring planets?

AS. There is still work being done on those. We do not only heal Earth. The healing of these planets that you know would be spread to many different ones, mainly the ones with the negativity, not the positive. They will go to the positive in order to go to the direction they wish to. Do you understand – it would be like a refuelling? It would be a planet that has excess energy and is able to feed the negatives. There are many of them. They are, as we would understand and in terms you can understand, refuelling stops. Basically, we all work from love at a very base level and then it is much higher that we attain. Base does not mean the same as it would for you. Our base is love and we grow from that level of love, higher. Unconditional would be the word to use and that is why, when you visit places in this universe such as this, you have a sense of that unconditional love. Each time we take you there, you absorb it and you are able to give it also, more than you realise. As a human mind, you are not aware of it. It is within you. It is not to all and sundry, as you would say.

A. *I am kind to people that I am concerned with.*

AS. We understand that, and that is all we ask of humans. We do not ask you to try to heal your whole planet, just heal the space that you are in. If each human were to look at taking care of the people who inhabit their space, the beings and their Earth, then that will help the whole of their Earth. They all have to take on the responsibility individually.

A. *There is no such thing as a free ride!*

AS. No, it is a difficult planet to be on.

A. *You are telling me!*

AS. It has great beauty, which we enjoy visiting.

A. *And when I have looked at it from space, it looks like a planet of great beauty and peacefulness. It is just the humans that have messed it up.*

AS. This is so – not all, but a majority. That is beginning to change, but until we get the majority to be the minority, we will have difficulties.

A. *Presumably that will change when the cataclysm gets going?*

AS. This is correct. There will be good people going also.

A. *Because their time is finished?*

AS. Correct. There will be those who will be gatherers and they will go with those whom they have gathered. It will be their time. Your seas are set to rise and, we see, at quite a rapid pace.

A. *Yes, we are expecting our seas to rise quite rapidly, but I don't know what that means, because we have time, which I know you don't have.*

AS. Correct. Rapidly with respect to the life of the Earth.

A. *The life of the Earth is many billion years, and the life of the human is more likely 80.*

AS. Well let us say of the life on Earth then! The Earth has been heating for many, many years; it is not a new thing. Even if humans had not prodded and probed their Earth as much as they have and still do, there would still be this. It is part of its evolution, but it is also part of our evolution to not allow your planet to destroy itself.

A. *I hope you are successful, as it is a beautiful peaceful planet.*

AS. It is. We will be successful. It will not, of course, be in your lifetime that we are successful, but we will.

A. *Well, my lifetime is fairly short.*

AS. This we see. Also your energy is short and those that brought you here are ready to escort you home. Understand also that you will take away with you knowledge that you have not been aware of today. Farewell, little one. Your carriage awaits you! Time to go home.

Venus

Here, the Venusians (V./ V.) showed me what a mind looks like and how it could expand without limitation. These beings did not have bodies, but I was told that the mind is not contained within the brain, which is just a receiving and transmitting station. They came to welcome me and took me to an enormous cavern, where I saw great vertical bands of gold and silver light and felt as if I was in a cocoon of love. I was told that I was in the centre of peace, and the cavern itself was lined with enormous complex crystals that looked like snow. From the midst of this emerged a vertical band of light that was a little darker in colour than the others. This was a being of very high evolution.

V. *"Your world is in danger," it said.*

A. *These beings I am seeing – are they crystal or just an arrangement of energy?*

T. They are – they are energy and they will create themselves into these beautiful shapes. They surround themselves with beauty in all places. This is a planet of beauty. They have information for you. Look at the main one that is looking at you and they will communicate with you. They will take you to a place that is full of information. Just follow them. You will be able to see pictures of the world as they see it.

A. *I am going towards something that seems to be the place of pure knowledge. What would help us the most to know?*

T. Look into the light and you will know.

A. *That was about opening the heart. Is there more?*

T. There is.

A. *I got a feeling about the love of the universe; but most of the humans think that the universe is a very hostile place!*

T. Ask them to show you what a mind looks like, how they see a mind.

A. *Something of a very ill-defined shape which is attached to a being, with a stalk, and then it expands into limitless shapes that are not contained in a skull. And, of course, if it is like this, then they can communicate freely with other minds.*

T. Correct, and with universal mind.

A. *So, is that an individual mind of a Venusian?*

T. It is. This is how a human mind can develop the limitlessness. Humans create limitation, and when the love and the mind are in unison, you will have great compassion. Humans are using their minds not for compassionate reasons. We need you to feel the energy of this place, touch that mind, the energy of that mind, and let it give you some answers. It is as if you are actually connecting your minds.

A. *I have a sense of my mind expanding a lot and they are intermingling.*

T. Yes. Ask what they put into your mind.

A. *Information about love and something about limitlessness. How could we persuade humans of their limitlessness?*

T. This will be part of your work.

V. You will have a sense of us, now that you feel us, when this is correct for you. It is the limitations that humans have that are harming your planet.

A. *I know. It is the difficulty in persuading so many closed minds to open.*

V. Understood, yes. It is not just at this short time-span of your life that this has been approached. There are many such as you. When you visit in the future you will see the souls come from Earth.

A. *Brought here to learn?*

V. Yes, you come here to absorb.

A. *Yes, and will the information you're giving me now be available to me when I need it?*

V. It will, it will. It is not necessary for you to speak it at this time, but you are the receiver. We do not wish you to be conscious of this – there is too much information. We need to use the part of your mind that humans don't use in order to store this information. All of this information has great compassion, for it is with compassion you will teach. It is with compassion we are teaching you. Compassion to us is when the heart and the mind are in balance. Mind is not a purely human thing, but humans seem to think so. Mind is not necessarily contained within a physical part of the human body. As you have understood, your mind reaches much further.

A. *Yes, and I think that the thinkers about mind on Earth are beginning to realise that it couldn't be all in the brain.*

V. It is just a receptacle. We understand what you are trying to say with your brain. It is a receiver which sends messages to certain parts that are requested. Human brains are wasted; the minds of humans are wasted. The mind is far more than humans realise.

A. *Mind means brain to many humans, which I have realised is not the case.*

V. It is a much higher energy. Your brain is a little like a junction; it receives and it gives out. It receives without realising from the mind, and when the human brain is used fully, as it will be, total understanding will come. Those on Earth look to expand their minds and speak of expanding their minds and give lip-service, not truly understanding what they are speaking of. As we understand, this is expanding their brain.

A. *I don't think that a lot of them realise that they are separate.*

V. No. The mind becomes part of the brain, because it uses the brain. The brain uses the mind in a very different way to what humans at this stage understand. The brain has great capacity, not necessarily in its size, but in its capacity.

A. *To store information?*

V. Yes, and you are using your mind for this, your higher mind. You are channelling it to be stored in parts of your brain. Because it has an energy. Every piece of the information is pure energy. You have been taught about energy, but not necessarily have you been taught until this stage about how the energy energises itself and other parts of the energy. If you really look into us, look into our colour, you will see what you would understand as the soul of us. We will come close to you; you need to just allow us and for you to come in. We need you to see us, not with the thinking mind, but the open mind.

A. *I can't see you at all, but I can feel you.*

V. Yes. Describe us.

A. *I can feel the compassion, the love in my heart – that's making me* *cry – and I have a sense of being surrounded by completely supportive loving beings.*

V. You are.

A. *But I haven't looked into your souls yet... All of a sudden, I got the impression of brilliant light, like a diamond with all sorts of colours.*

V. Yes, that is us. More beautiful than any diamond. Now look in and see our rhythm, feel it if you can. As you have a heart beat, we have something you would understand.

A. *You have a pulse and it is just the same as the "black diamond" in the centre of Earth.*

V. Exactly so. That is because we are of our planet rather than on our planet, and so the sensing is so important. The more you become of your planet than on your planet, you will be more in rhythm with your planet. You will teach this to many and you will be in rhythm with the pulse.

A. *If you are part of your planet, then it must change things completely.*

V. It will. The compassion is not just for man.

A. *Oh no, man is the problem.*

V. It is. For man need not be the problem on your planet, but man at this time is your problem. Humans, as we understand, have a great capacity for love. They are able to have a great capacity for compassion, but they do not understand it. When many become of your planet, they will feel the compassion.

A. *While you're explaining this to me, what I'm feeling is that compassion is understanding the world around you, with your heart completely open, and in that way that is love. This is really perhaps an explanation of love and not only love, - it is identity.*

V. It is, and that is how you will know workers such as yourself, and there are souls that you will have a love for and souls will have a love for you. It is not displayed in the way that humans think love has to be displayed. On our world, we give of ourselves to each other freely. We will share whatever is required by us. It is not ever requested, but we are aware of each other and so, in that awareness, we know what is required and that is where humans need to get to, to that understanding. The word would be spontaneity, and it can only come with love and compassion and the open mind. If the mind is fully open, the heart is open with it. It does not leave you vulnerable to do this.

A. *Because these are the energy centres, not the chakras, which are the physical ones.*

V. Yes, because we understand your fear of leaving yourself open and we understand why it would not be good in certain circumstances on your planet.

A. *Is what I'm feeling now how you go about your lives?*

V. It is. It is beautiful. How does one define beautiful, the beauty that you are in now.

A. *It looks beautiful, it feels beautiful, I expect it sounds beautiful.*

V. We have sounds that would be music to your ears. We are very supportive on this planet, both to those who are here and those that we invite here and also to those we visit, and we do visit your planet, just as the Basidians visit your planet. In the past, we have created an embodiment in order to visit your planet, but we have been misunderstood; our motives were misunderstood, and we withdrew because of the closed minds of humans. It is with the souls such as yourself we are speaking with, that we are able to reveal ourselves again, and we will.

A. *Thank you so much for that most beautiful journey in all senses.*

V. It is we who wish to thank you for allowing us to reach you. We will use the information we have picked up from you for some time to come. For it is with the visitation of humans that we learn a great deal about you, more than your words will tell us. It is your density we find difficult, because with you travelling here, we are still aware of your density. But now it is time to leave. It is with great love that we say farewell until we speak with you once more...

A. *Is that a different bunch of Venusians from the ones that give handy hints?*

T. These are higher; you were with the hierarchy. This hierarchy would be the hierarchy as certain planets have and they are a collective, but they form a universal collective, of great knowledge, which is a part of what you would understand as the universal mind.

A. *So, that was a part of the universal mind I was talking to?*

T. It was, but you were with the highest beings. We expected them to show themselves, but not exactly in the way that they did.

Because of the purity of their planet, we are not able to see ahead. It was a good journey.

The Planet of Higher Intelligence

I went through numerous coloured layers and came to a rough-looking physical surface. It looked much like a slag heap! When I went round this world to its light side, the surface looked like diamonds sparkling and reflecting light. I was met by beings looking like spikes of light, who took me to a larger light. On entering this light, I could feel its pulse, which was in time with my heart beat, and I felt perfectly safe and it was perfectly beautiful and "everything was all right." This, they said, was the centre of knowledge.

T. Where you are is the centre of knowledge. This is where the knowledge that is not a conscious knowledge in humans comes from. All of our knowledge is retained here; it would be, as you would understand, our library. If we, the Basidian, ask a question that we do not know the answer to, the answer comes from this place, and for all beings in the universe no matter what they look like. So you will begin to understand that there is shared knowledge here and knowledge as you understand can only be of use to the soul when he is enjoying learning and so he is ready to learn. We are all souls; there should be fun in learning. That is why you felt the fun of the souls that are here. They have great pleasure in knowing their knowledge. They never use it, as humans sometimes do, to be appearing as better than others. Humans need to visit this place and get a sense of knowledge and a sense of the oneness that we all have. There are many of you as humans come to visit. Even though you leave your physical body behind, the energy that is the shape of your physical body is seen by those around us.

They recognise you in the physical form as well as your soul form, because the memory of your physical body travels with you. It is just a memory and you are in the place of memory. Some souls would like to think they're getting knowledge from somewhere different. Their journey to reach this place will be different, but this is the fount of knowledge. This is a physical planet with a pulse, with a huge pulse energy, and what you are feeling with the pulse is the waves of energy going out, because it is being called on by many, many souls all over the universe.

A. *And it sends out information purely on request?*

T. It does. At times, information is given that is specific, because it has been requested and it is known what is required by the recipient. Whilst humans sleep, information is much easier to be delivered. Those of you humans who are seeking the higher realms are able to focus your minds in order that you take on this knowledge. We are bringing you to your memory, to your soul's memory here. Because all souls come through this place with their memory intact and all of the important happenings in the soul's lifetime in whatever body they choose, be it human or otherwise, memory is stored, the parts which are important to be retained and used for another lifetime.

A. *So this memory is a two-way traffic. Do they choose which bits to keep?*

T. It is, and the soul discards the parts that seem irrelevant. The soul does not necessarily choose what to keep, but this place we are in now does.

A. *So if this planet believes that a certain piece of information is important, it retains it, whatever the soul thinks?*

T. Correct, and it would keep it with that soul. It is a huge planet and those layers that you must come through to get here may change colours for you as your higher knowledge opens up. When you come here, it does require a lot of energy. This is knowledge that we are opening to you.

A. *And this big light that I went into to receive – is that a being or an energy?*

T. It is not a being, it is an energy. It is an energy source and another time when you come, you will see many of these energy sources. There is one central Source that you do not enter whilst you have what you understand as a life, a body, encapsulating the soul. You would enter that when you are just pure soul.

A. *You can enter it, I can't?*

T. We can, but we have to step out of our bodies, that is, our energy.

A. *Even your Basidian energy?*

T. We do. We go through. We also look for endless knowledge. We have great knowledge from where we are, but this is the greatest knowledge. You are not in the centre of the universe, but you are in the universal mind. When you are able, this will be a place we will bring you to many times. You can find all answers here of the higher questions. Now you are needing to leave. Before you go, you need to give thanks to the energy that is facing you.

A. *Thank you for showing yourself to me. It got much smaller and turned violet!*

T. That is its answer to you. It has shown itself in its own state. When it is opening to knowledge, it lights up. They take the pulse from the whole area. You need to leave now. We will bring you back... This is a place that you do know. Everywhere we take you, you are known.

A. *But sometimes, when you take me, the beings do not know me.*

T. The beings may not, but the energy would.

A. *Every time I think the universe can't get any more amazing, it does.*

T. The universe is endless, it is amazing. It is full of love.

The Planet of Requests

T. We are going to take you further out, going towards the darkness to the black energy. Look to the light, there is light within this dark layer.

A. *I can see a pearly white light in one direction.*

T. Yes, you can go into this light and through it, and it will take you to what would seem like another world.

A. *I feel that I have gone through and landed somewhere else.*

T. Yes, and there will be what would seem an unusual landscape. Look around and it will show itself to you. This is a beautiful place.

A. *I'm not seeing a place, I'm seeing all sorts of spirals of colour very close together.*

T. Look closely at them – they form something.

A. *Almost like a building, the shape of a beehive, it is as if whatever this is is made of little units of coloured spirals.*

T. Open yourself to understand what this is.

A. *This is an intelligence of some sort, it is not an ordinary being. Is it* *one of these forms that is only mind?*

T. It is. It is a place, but it is an intelligence, it has emotion. It absorbs and sends out. You can touch it. Go close. Describe how it feels.

A. *It feels smooth and silky and is it removing some negative energy for me?*

T. Yes, you are looking at something totally positive. There is not a word to describe this fully in your language, but it is an intelligence with complete understanding of "All That Is." It is of the Source.

A. *Is it one of the specialised projections of the Source?*

T. It is.

A. *What is its specific purpose?*

T. There are many of these that come from the complete Source. This part that you are in holds intentions, intentions sent out by humans and from other worlds, and it transforms them to become positive, to become actuality. We brought you here to understand. The intention has to be pure. We know when the intention is pure and when it has baggage. Look at the energy. There are all colours and it has many more that you have not got words for. This place, which is massive yet small, it will show itself as large or small, as you can allow. When negativity comes towards this place, the colours light up because they repel. They do not allow negativity to be part of this place. Everything becomes positive.

A. *So do they transform it or do they get rid of it?*

T. They get rid of it. That would be back to wherever it has come from, the source of the negativity, it is of their choosing. A soul here will not be allowed to come into this place if it has negativity or if their intentions are not good. It is not a private place, but it is a special place. There are many of them and all of the other worlds know these places. This is a very busy world you have come to, with other than your own world.

A. *You mean there is a lot of negativity for it to repel?*

T. Yes.

A. *What does it do with a positive emotion or intention?*

T. The positive intentions are sent back, and as they are sent back to the individual, they are multiplied to become even more positive, and then they become physical. So it takes the thought and transforms it to the physical.

A. *Even if it only happens to be a nice little mauve jacket?*

T. Exactly so.

A. *And what about the negatives – does it send those back as well?*

T. They go back and they multiply.

A. *Because that's how you create your own destruction?*

T. Yes, but it sends something else back that you would not understand at this stage, and so what comes back is multiplied, but with light within it. Negative comes to us here as darkness, because this, as everything that is here, is part of our Creator, it is all creation. This place, if you were to follow through it, it takes you to the Source. We need you to understand that people with good intention will receive from this place.

A. *So, even if your intention is rejected, the fact that you made it is rewarded in some way?*

T. Yes, always. It is only when the intention is interfering and the soul knows it is interfering, it causes the soul who has the intention problems. If there were in this place such things as mirrors, you would see that you have taken on every colour there is here.

A. *Well, I'm not seeing anything except lines of colours, energy lines I presume, all possible colours, and some that aren't possible.*

T. Yes. Look up – what do you see?

A. *It is almost clear, like a glass roof, clear rather than coloured.*

T. You can go through if you wish, you can feel its energies.

A. *I'm getting shot up there with energy and I came out of the top. We are out here in the black layer again!*

T. Exactly so. We would like you to allow a gold particle to attach itself to you.

A. *Do you, the Basidian, come here for any specific purpose?*

T. We come here to renew.

A. *A lot of its work is on Earthly level people?*

T. Mainly earthly level people and for other planets that have negativity also.

A. *So its purpose is to reward good intention, and you could say it rewards negative ones also. It rewards good intentions by you getting what you intended and bad intentions ditto. It is a bad idea to have bad intentions!*

Akubina – The World of Metamorphosis

This is another world helping us with its energy. This is a very ancient world which developed before true form was created on any of the worlds. The spirit world visit here for replenishment. The inhabitants are perfect as they were created. They have no fixed form, because it has never become necessary. When I first saw them, they looked like cumulus clouds with flame-coloured tendrils at the edges. They tumbled and rolled as they moved. Later, they appeared much as if they were a coloured dye dispersing lazily through water. They have access to unlimited energy from the Source, but the number of beings does not change.

"The number that is, is the number that was."

This planet sends energy to Earth – some for the planet and some for the surface and the inhabitants. It is a very powerful energy transfer. It can cut through the toxic layers we have created in our atmosphere. When these beings approached me, it was as if they had grabbed me and wrapped me in love and a feeling of safety. They send this energy to Earth and, at this time, they are involved in:

"Trying to help the souls on Earth to find the light within their own souls, to change the attitude of human beings."

23

The Eohm from Onhm

Onhm is a sound rather than a word, as is the name of the inhabitants, the Eohm (E./ Ẽ). These are the highest beings who have spoken to me and they have information that they wished me to include in this book. I journeyed to another dimension where there was a world of great purity, whose surface appeared to be of pearls and gold, interspersed with occasional coloured crystals. I entered a sapphire crystal and found myself in another part of this world with pink sky. It took me a while to realise that the customary feeling of love was not there – it felt neutral. I was told that this part was a world of work. There were structures rather like the quills of feathers, which were dotted with little round blobs. When I went into one of these, I found it to be a beautiful jewel of blue-and-purple colour, and the feeling of love flowed through me. I was told that this world had been attacked in the past and now hid itself.

Then I went back to the pearls and the gold, and some very large beings in robes of light with jewel-coloured heads approached me. The colour was unfamiliar to me. The word "Elohim" appeared and they asked me to remove the "l" and the "i": "Eohm." They were beings of immense power and purity and very stern in demeanour. They too are working for the Earth at their high level, and they too had come to give information into my unconscious mind. I was told that they worked in groups and each being that I saw had a group that was overseeing a star or a planet. Their mission was the order and harmony of the universe. They were of a very high purity and I was told that their journey to perfection was nearly completed. I found myself in considerable awe of these great beings, whose work I could hardly begin to comprehend.

T. When this world was attacked, these souls went inward and it took many of the world's cycles before they would come out. They have been coming out now for what you would understand as four thousand years. It is as a year to us, as far as we can understand your year. These souls are close to their completion and, in contacting one or more of these souls, you will understand a great deal more about the Earth and its healing. They work with many planets, many worlds. Each one of them has a group and each group looks after a particular planet or world. Each group has their own group. It is time that the Earth understood itself. Let us put that a little differently: the Earth understands itself, it is the beings that are on the Earth that don't understand themselves.

A. *Are these wonderfully high beings putting information into my mind in the usual way?*

T. Exactly so. Understand that when we work through you, we give you the words and we can only work with your intention. Where you are now is where intention is heard completely. If we took you, with permission, into the centre of this world which you are on, you would see how they deal with intention, and we are informed that you will be taken there. You will be able to understand what intention sounds like and feels like.

E. Always, always, welcome. We have a great deal of work to do. Our worlds communicate with each other differently to yours and we are able to move from one world to the other, with permission of course, quickly. We are the Eohm.

A. *It feels like this is a higher level than I've ever been at before.*

E. It is the highest you have been. We needed to feel your energy first, but we also needed to give you instruction of this level. Until we communicate once more, we thank you. It gives us great pleasure and great power. As we share power with especially a human being, we gain great power.

A. *How?*

E. It is in the giving that we receive. As you know in your land, the giving generates power.

T. That was good, my dear. They are very special beings. They have a very serious role and they are very serious about the healing of your planet.

A. *Is that their purpose?*

T. It is, and it is also healing through people. They will empower the people with souls such as yours to heal their Earth.

A. *That was wonderful and quite unexpected.*

T. And to us also. We wanted to take you to the place of power and we did not know if we would be allowed to go to this place at this time.

A. *Goodness gracious me, it gets higher and higher, and purer and purer, and at the same time, there gets to be more and more of it.*

T. The universes are vast.

The following is a series of transmissions from the Eohm that were sent specifically for inclusion in this book.

E. "We wish to continue your education by telling you of our role and purpose. The purpose of every soul is purification and this we have almost achieved. Our role is to oversee the harmony and order of the universe, as we told you yesterday. Each group of us attends a world and works with both the soul of the world itself and the souls on that world to increase the order and harmony and beauty, both within the world and in its relations with its neighbours.

Each world must sit precisely in its setting, like jewels in a diadem, and our energy is disposed to make sure it remains exactly in its place. Then our energy is disposed to help the world and its inhabitants to be the shining jewel, emitting beautiful and powerful light. The more beautiful and harmonious the worlds in their settings, the more we rejoice, for then we have done our job well and our perfection comes closer. When each soul on each world has completed its purification, then truly the universe is a sparkling living jewel which exists in total bliss and harmony. That is the aim for which we work."

E. "The worlds as you see them are shining, but they can shine brighter yet and we are helping them. We shine very brightly ourselves, but we have undergone aeons of purification. We oversee the universe and its worlds and we fully understand the mind of the Source. We are not separate. No more are you, but you have further to travel yet. We are pleased to be able to write directly with one of your world. We work to help your world and the beings upon it to ride the physical turbulence and come through to your peace. We are here to help you do this in ways that you do not yet understand. We will instruct you of these as we continue to speak with you. We need to continue your education about our role in the universe and in healing your Earth.

We are the directors of the many energies pouring towards your world. We are organising and harmonising the help your Earth is receiving. We are also communicating with any minds that are open, to show them what must be done to save your Earth. There is much that can be done; what is lacking is the will to do it. This is where we can help your people, by showing them how to proceed. The stability of the universe would be affected by the destruction of your planet and this we are working to avoid.

We can help, harmonise and awaken, but we cannot overrule. It is for humans to save their own world. The information in your book explains this. Do not water down this part of the message. The order and harmony of the universe is in our charge and it is our role and purpose to maintain and increase these qualities. Help us to tell your people what they can do to help themselves."

E. "We wish to continue your education about our purpose. Our purpose, as we told you, is maintaining order and harmony within the universe. To this end, we work with the overseeing beings of every world, to make certain that the actions of one do not interfere with another. Discord in the universe is not permitted, as it may destroy the stability and balance of the whole. There are occasions when small amounts of imbalance are introduced to allow for change on a particular world, but this is not random. Nothing in the universe is random. We manage this imbalance in the most harmonious way for the other worlds. The ecstasy of the universe comes from the Source and so do the beauty and harmony, but the beauty and harmony depend on our being.

We know only love and it is by love that we affect the harmony of the universe. We use the energy of love that is all around us, and of which we are created, and we use our high vibrational power to influence all. There are no negatives within our being, but as you know, there are negative forces in the universe. There is enough good and love within this universe to outweigh the negative forces, and worlds are only affected when it is part of their pattern to be so. If you like, these forces do not affect us unless we allow them to, just like any other negative pattern. Even the negative forces are doing what they believe to be good. It is just that they are prepared to break the universal law of non-interference to achieve their ends. The universe is vast enough and diverse enough to accommodate all points of view, and remember, here there is no separation. That makes all the difference."

E. "The vastness of the universe is beyond your comprehension, but remember that we oversee all of it. There are many of us, but still it is an enormous task. The balance and symmetry of the patterns of the Source are also beyond your comprehension, but it is these that we apply, so that the harmony and beauty of the universe is maintained.

The energy that we use in our work is of course love, out of which all is created. This energy is therefore everywhere and its aim, for it has intelligence, is for the whole of all the universe to be existing in one peaceful, connected, harmonious whole, so that it is easy to hear the music of the spheres. When the whole of creation has reached its perfection, then the Orchestra of the universes will be fully tuned and the Symphony it plays will be everlasting. We use metaphor to help you understand, but as you know, the music of the spheres is real.

This then is our mission and, once it is completed, there will no longer be any need for our work and we can sink in our own perfection back into the Source from whence we came."

E. "We wish to tell you of the all-connectedness of the web of energy that is and contains the universe. This web of love, which creates all, carries the communications between the worlds, and it is for this that we are particularly responsible. The communications must flow freely from world to world, because each world has essential functions of helping another. Mutual dependence is normal in the universe and, because we do not have the fear that humans have, each world and its inhabitants are open to the others. In the universe, we give freely without thought of return and, if all do that, then the balance of giving and receiving is maintained. There is no greed in these worlds. Many can create whatever they need, so greed and envy are unnecessary emotions.

When your world vibration rises, you too will begin to participate in this free flow of energies, and humans will come to understand that all are equally deserving and that there is enough for every soul in the universe. When this time comes, then the Earth will become an even more beautiful jewel in the web of love than it is now, and humans will come to understand their real nature and will know at last who they really are."

Conclusions

The journeys, which started so simply to the crystal star, have become more distant, more complex and requiring greater understanding as they have gone on. I have been so fortunate to have been able to communicate through the medium while I travelled, as it helped my understanding so much. If I could ask questions and have her channel the replies, it removed a great proportion of my anxiety and so I did not tire quite so quickly. The anxiety was entirely to ensure that I was recording what actually happened and understanding the significance of what I saw, so that what I write is as accurate as I can make it. Dorothy is such an accurate channel that it reduced the possibility of error. If I was in doubt when I read the transcript later, I checked with the spirits that I had received the information correctly. There is no point being charged to deliver information from the universe and merely recording what I have in my own mind. There are minds in the cosmos that make what I could store in mine look like the two-times table. This is not my information, this is from the cosmos. It seems that the universe is, to misquote JBS Haldane,

"not only vaster than we suppose, but vaster than we can suppose."

And there are nine of them! The use of the different dimensions means that variety is almost limitless.

I have been fortunate also to be travelling with my dear friends the Basidian, who are able to take me to worlds that I could not access on my own. The journey where I went through the black hole took me into a different world that I could not have reached on my own. I have also been very fortunate to have beings from different worlds giving me information. Much of what I have been told is not in my conscious mind until I come to speak of it, and find I say things that I have never thought before.

This wonderful universe in which we live, so full of colour, light and love, has been the greatest joy to travel in, and I look forward to spending however many aeons there are in eternity discovering more. I am not particularly well travelled on Earth, but, my goodness, I am enjoying the universe!

I don't take these journeys alone and neither would you. Let the spirits have the last word:

B. **"You are not alone, you are never alone, you just believe you are alone and must struggle for your survival. Soon you will know that you are not alone and you will also know how much you are loved. This knowledge will transform each of you into the unlimited loving being that you truly are. That is the purpose of it all."**

Part Five

The Evolution and Development of the Soul

24

The Developing Soul

"I will tell thee what is the secret of life –
To sink into thyself like the pearl.
Then to emerge from thine inward solitude;
To collect sparks beneath the ashes,
And become a flame and dazzle men's eyes."

M. Iqbal

It has often occurred to me to wonder why life is as it is, and I have had many such conversations with the Basidian. This section is a distillation of what they have told me, as far as my human mind can comprehend. For all that human life is difficult, the rewards that await us on the completion of the soul's journey seem wonderfully worth striving for. Our universe is created from the energy of love and its purpose is to use the energy of intention to evolve to its perfection.

All souls were created at the same time, but not all started their evolution immediately, some remaining embryonic. Even those that did developed at different rates. When I asked why this was, the spirits pointed out that, if they all developed at the same rate, there would be worlds populated entirely by babies or old professors! The purpose of the soul is to evolve to a state of perfection and the purpose of biological life is to have experiences that aid that evolution. Each life is chosen and preplanned by the soul itself so that it may learn the lesson it has chosen. If the lesson is not learnt, then a further life will follow later on the same theme, but with different details.

There are many worlds in this universe, all with different types of beings, but all with the same purpose. Each soul must go through every possible experience in order to achieve perfection. Souls living on more serene and peaceful worlds come to Earth to have some lives on a planet with negativity, so that they can experience and clear their own negative emotions. Soul perfection is achieved by the resolution of all the built-in negativity.

℘. "The soul still has the shadow side of itself. When you hear of souls on your Earth doing misdeeds, they are clearing the shadow side of themselves. They are learning about the punishment of the shadow. When they return to soul life, they put right what they have done wrong and that is how they learn. Until the shadow side has been expelled, they cannot progress. It happens to all souls. That is why there is such abhorrence of the pain inflicted by one soul to another. It is memory. On other planets, they have done this in the past, they have cleared it. Once all souls have cleared their negativity, the vibration of the whole planet rises."

Once the soul has achieved perfection, there is no need to return to biological life, although some wish to do so in order to help others. Soul life appears to be just as busy as biological life, but it has enormous advantages. There is no pain, fear or doubt, and best of all, no body, so no illness! Differences are resolved by negotiation and souls do not have the human trait of trying to force others to agree with them and fighting with them when they won't!

> *"Our birth is but a sleep and a forgetting.*
> *The soul that rises with us, our life's star,*
> *Hath had elsewhere its setting......*
>   *......trailing clouds of glory do we come,*
> *From God who is our home."*
>
>   *Wordsworth*

Souls were born in the crucible of the stars and initially wrapped in inorganic chemicals. They visit many worlds on their path to evolution. There is nothing human about a soul, it is just a soul choosing to inhabit a human body. Some feel comfortable during these incarnations and regard the Earth as a home. Many do not and have other worlds that they consider to be home.

This is what the Basidian told me about the birth of souls.

B. "The consumption of matter by the flames causes an exquisite rearrangement of atoms and molecules into completely new substances. This of course was how matter was initially created. This is what is happening continuously in parts of the universe, the parts where stars are born, and this is where souls were initially created and clothed in simple minerals. All souls have developed from this birthing place, although a soul does not consist of matter. A soul is of a much finer vibration and consists entirely of the Source, which as you know is pure love. The soul is born from the fire, but never dies.

The bodies of the incarnate die and decay and the molecules are absorbed back into the universe. The human identification with their bodies is responsible for much of their difficulties with the knowledge of death. If you know that you are immortal, then casting off a worn-out body is no more difficult than changing your clothes. For us, to die is to be born into life, and is an occasion for great rejoicing. The myths and taboos of bodily death are responsible for a great deal of suffering."

B. "Life is very much more various and wonderful in the universe that you can imagine. All souls were created together, but all develop at different rates and for different purposes. Human souls have on the whole developed very slowly, but their path has been complex because of the cycles in Earthly bodies. Beings who do not have biological bodies consist of pure energy and are much simpler in construction. This means less to go wrong and less effort required in tending them. Your troubles, but also your spiritual development, are directly dependent on the lack of care that you give your physical vehicle. An energy being finds it astonishing that you would give so little care to your body, but it is common among Earthlings.

Your soul's purpose continues whether you are in a body or not and, from the soul's point of view, life once given is inextinguishable. Life is the animation of a collection of molecules and their clothing with a minute spark of the Source, which partially separates from itself in order to allow individuation of the soul. The living soul is never truly separated from the Source, but may feel that it is so in Earthly journeys, when the bigger picture is temporarily lost.

Pure energy beings do not lose their conscious connection with the Source. Therefore, they act and react quite differently. You have seen a little of the interconnectedness of worlds on your most recent journeys. That is how it is. How it appears on Earth is just how Earthlings think it is. Life is the most powerful force; look at a seedling pushing up through cracks in paving stones. Life cannot be extinguished and the soul's journey continues whether incarnate or not. All souls in whatever form are part of the Great Tree of Life and are all connected to the Source and thus to each other."

The Basidian say that there are nine different developmental lines for souls. All souls go through the mineral line, but thereafter the lines diverge and the soul development of plants, animals, insects and humans are separate. The human body develops through the animal route, but not the soul. There is considerable choice, so there is no bar to experiencing life as an animal to learn a particular lesson, but it is not part of the overall scheme. I am assured that I have never been a monkey, and rather to his regret, Uncle Theo has never had a life as a palm tree! However, I have enjoyed a life as a bird.

The human stage is experienced at the end of one of the evolutionary lines, and these lives are designed to give experience of the complex negative emotions associated with humanness. This takes very many incarnations. They have provided me with much advice on the healing and clearance of this negativity and the alteration of unconscious childhood patterning. As children, with limited understanding, we misunderstand many of our instructions, and some of the patterns set up at that time persist throughout life, unless we consciously replace them with more useful information. It is during childhood that we develop the type of script that says

"You have to get it right first time and you can't have any help, otherwise you are NO GOOD." None of the three statements in that sentence are true, but many people live by them. The daftest script I found in my own unconscious was "You are not clever enough to make soup." Since I have two medical degrees and a higher qualification, this is most unlikely to be true, but I believed it until I discovered that my soup was excellent!

I was comforted by the information that we were intended to make mistakes, so that the learning from them could facilitate our soul growth.

Pain

℧. "It is not possible to be a human and to avoid emotional pain. What matters is what use a human makes of it."

Much emotional pain is inflicted in childhood, because the infant brain has limited understanding and no sense of proportion. This pain often becomes buried in one of the organs and must be resolved later, when the human is old enough to understand what is required. In order for soul growth to occur, this is what must be done, otherwise the adult mind will continue to react according to the childish patterning. A strategy that was successful at the age of two is likely to be very limiting at forty-two. The release of emotional pain is what is necessary to allow the human to become truly who they are. There is nothing difficult about this; it merely takes time and attention. If the souls do not develop and grow, neither can their planet.

℧. "Pain of any sort is an indicator that something in your personal world is wrong and a correction needs to be made. Let us take emotional pain. When somebody harms you emotionally, you feel pain at the level of your heart. If you shut off this pain, you will feel anger, which is very much harder to get rid of. The optimum way of dealing with pain is, first of all, to remove yourself from the source of the pain, and then to go deeply into it to find out what it really signifies to you. Very often, what is really hurting you is an old pattern that can be healed once it has been exposed to the light.

If you allow yourself to feel the anger, this will go on for much longer and you will get into a cycle of anger which has to be broken before you can get rid of it. The pain, however unpleasant, is much easier to deal with, by fully understanding what it means to you and allowing it to flow through you. To do this, it is necessary to keep your heart centre and your solar plexus centre as wide open as you can and acknowledge your feelings. There is no shame in feeling pain. So long as your pain is handled truthfully, it will fade. This is not to say that you need to allow the source of the pain to keep giving it to you. That is not common sense, as you would say."

Physical pain is built into the human system, indeed any biological system, to allow the organism to remove themselves from the source of the unpleasant stimulus. It also indicates a part of the biological system that is not functioning optimally and therefore needs attention.

B. "Pain is a necessary part of biological life and should be treated as what it is, an indicator of malfunction or unpleasant external stimulus. There is the temptation among humans to hug their pain to them and use it as an excuse for not functioning. There are many souls that do this – it is what you call secondary gain. When the external stimulus or the physical malfunction has been present for long enough, it sets up patterns of its own and these patterns must be broken before full function and health can be restored.

Emotional pain is an invitation to grow. It is not an excuse for avoiding anything you do not want to do, but it is often used in this way. Use your pain and learn from it. A human who has had no pain is completely unable to help another. The way to health is through your pain, not round it. (Here we talk of emotional pain, because physical pain indicates malfunction of a part of the body and may require the attention of the healer or a doctor or at least rest of the painful part.) Be grateful for your pain, it is a stimulus for growth."

Fear is just another form of emotional pain and is best dealt with accordingly.

B. "Fear paralyses thought and action. Fear therefore must be overcome and the best way to do that is to walk towards the fear and confront it. Constructive thought about the thing feared will help to alleviate the feeling. Once you know what you would do if the worst happened, you are better able to handle whatever does. Remember that you are not alone in any of this and ask for help whenever you need it. It is important to learn to overcome fears as far as is possible, because it will make helping other fearful people so much easier. You know how this is done – you just have to remember to do it. You are perfectly safe. Whatever happens to your body, your soul is safe with us."

B. "Fear will be the reason for the downfall of your planet. Fear cannot be overcome by force, but only by love. The way to combat personal fear is to go deeply into the feeling with your heart and solar plexus centres open. So also with the fears of humankind. The fears must be faced and the love must be felt before they can be overcome. The most important thing is openness of heart, without which the connectedness to other souls and to the universe cannot be felt.

The giving of free will to mankind and his intention to master the physical universe has separated him so far from his feelings of connection that he is afraid, except when surrounded by his own group of humans. This will be difficult for him to understand; but you must, by example, show that the feeling of fear is unhelpful. Look at the panic that occurs with the prospect of an epidemic of bird flu and you will see how fear distorts reality. They may slaughter every chicken in the land, but the epidemic will still arrive, for it is in the pattern of the planet for this to happen. The protective measures put in place by the politicians and the veterinary experts only serve to reinforce this fear."

A. *What would be the alternative way of handling the bird flu then?*
T. Isolate the chickens, kill the very sick ones and allow the rest to recover. Keep the flock isolated until all birds have regained health. This would provide useful immunity. The restrictions on travel are sensible, but the wellbeing of the birds has not been considered, only the wellbeing of man's livelihood. It would not be kind to allow the birds to suffer, but this wholesale slaughter, which was undertaken in your country with the cattle also, is a true manifestation of man's

fear and, in both these cases, fear of losing his livelihood.

We cannot tell you too strongly about the avoidance of fear in the face of adversity. Openness to the circumstances is necessary at all times, if possible, so that the fear can flow through you and can dissipate. If you close yourself off, it is like hugging the fear to you. This is the most important lesson that man has to learn as he makes his way back to love.

Separation

The separation of our conscious minds from the Source seems to be responsible for most of these problems. We are the only species living in this fear of extinction and it is our task now to deal with our internal fears and conflicts and connect with "All That Is," so that fear becomes a thing of the past. This is already happening all over the planet. Currently, humans have the innate capability to access planetary consciousness, the process we call intuition. We have to develop further for all of us to be able to reach to universal consciousness, and that is the journey we are all on. Then we will be in conscious communication with the whole universe and our feeling of isolation will be past.

B. "The separation of humans from the Source induces a fear that is not felt elsewhere in the universe. Humans are fearful because of their apparent aloneness and because they cannot see the reasons for what is happening around them. Knowing the reason for something makes it easier to understand and thus you have much less need to be fearful of it. The time for fear is almost over, but before that time comes, there will be an explosion of fear induced by the changes that are happening to the Earth. When this time comes, humans will have need of explanations – the reasons for the turbulence and upheaval. This will help to calm their fears. The fear inherent in man is responsible for most of the cruelty and the intolerances in the world that you know. It is time for humans to arise out of this fear and take their place as fully conscious members of the universe. It is time for men to realise that they are entirely responsible for their own actions and the consequences thereof."

ℬ. "Each human has a sense of right and wrong and an intuition of the way he is to go. This intuitive sense is built in and is to be consulted at all times. Humans tend to adhere to the morality of the group, rather than listening to their own. Their sense of aloneness leads them to cling to like-minded groups. This does not absolve them from being responsible for their own actions. The rise in consciousness will change all this, and the morality of the human will become his own, and he will be able to perceive the bigger picture that will make sense of his life. This will change everything."

A. There is a difference between imagination and intuition. Imagination is where I make a picture.
T. Where does that come from?
A. *Imagination would come from my brain, but intuition just comes without the intention.*
T. Yes, intuition is what you are being given and imagination is what you are creating, and when imagination and intuition work together in harmony, that is when a soul is creative, and nothing, but nothing, is impossible for that soul. Only the limitation they put upon themselves stops them.

Our soul growth is entirely our individual responsibility. Everything we need is within us, although some may need a bit of help to find inner stillness and to access what we need for our own healing. It is a wonderful and precious discovery to find that we are the source of our own healing.

"In your soul are infinitely precious things that cannot be taken from you."
Wilde

ℬ. "Today we will talk of light, of the spiritual rather than the physical wavelengths. Illumination in the physical is of objects, but here in the spiritual, it is of the mind and soul. Without spiritual illumination, which is another way of saying 'information,' then the soul cannot develop. The information necessary to a soul's development is always available and the soul takes it in when he is ready. The soul itself is always ready, but the person is not, and this is what has to be waited for.

The illumination, by information, of the soul is a fulfilling and even blissful experience. The surmounting of an unconscious pattern gives a sense both of peace and happiness. The evolved soul lives in peace, happiness and bliss. When humans have all evolved enough to live in bliss, then so can their world. This is what you are aiming for. Remember, as you struggle, what awaits you. Bliss and fulfilment are available to all. There is no need to suffer any more. Throw off the shackles of your childhood patterns and become the soul you truly are. There is no time to lose. Awake!"

B. "The ability to believe only what your eyes can see limits greatly your powers of perception. If you can break through what has been called 'The Cloud of Unknowing,' then the whole universe in all its brilliance and complexity is laid before you. This is the way that man is headed. This is what we over here can already see. When you can see, you will no longer require faith; you will know. You can already know whatever you wish to know, but not with physical eyes. It is this preoccupation with the physical that delays man's development.

All this will change when the consciousness rises to the point that there is no longer a barrier between Earth and heaven. When this happens, man will see that he is not separate from the rest of creation, and then the age of harmony can begin. When man can see that he is not separate from the whole of creation, surely he must recognise his connection to his planet and the other beings on it. If he sees himself as part of them, surely he cannot continue to treat them so cruelly and unthinkingly. Once he understands that, then he will realise that neither can he treat his human brothers with the callous disregard for their wellbeing that has characterised his actions so far. When he understands that, he will be taking the first steps on the way to living in harmony with himself and his neighbours. These events are eagerly awaited by the rest of the universe and their time is nearly here."

B. "The force that drives the universe is yet soft and nurturing and immensely peaceful. This great force of love permeates everything in all the universes and is readily available to all who have learnt how to use it. When humans have learned how to keep their hearts and solar plexus centres open, they can use it too. The Earth itself is full of this force of love and it provides limitless energy, more than you can ever use. The lesson is how to use this peacefully and in harmony with the planet and the other species living on its surface. Harmony requires that all viewpoints are taken into consideration and that harm comes to none by your actions. This is the lesson to be learnt by man before the age of harmony can be achieved."

B. "The ability of fire to change physical matter has been a powerful factor in the development of Earth, and of the life upon the Earth. The breaking down of matter by fire, and then the aggregation into different forms of the molecules thus produced, is the way that life in all its forms was produced. Complex organic molecules have risen from the burning and allowed life to appear on this planet.

As you know, all life has a soul, which has many aeons of development to undertake for its own learning and purification before its soular journey is complete. It is the purification of souls that allow a planet to reach up to its own next level of evolution. Every soul has to evolve to its own perfection. The souls of planets and stars are no exception.

Fire provides physical purification and change. The soul itself must provide emotional purification and change. The changes wrought by fire and the changes made by rigorous self-examination and intention are the same in essence. The evolution of a soul to a state of perfection produces such change that the perfect soul does not recognise as self its imperfect predecessors. There is no judgment in this; the soul literally is no longer the same. The matters with which a soul concerns itself change also and become more altruistic and loving with increasing perfection.

Each soul is where it is, and it is not to be judged as better or worse, but just as where it is. Souls of a similar level will congregate to work or to play, but that is because of their common preoccupations, not because one is better than the other. The judgment of humans is misplaced, as all are loved by the Divine at whatever level they have reached. From those who have achieved a high level, much is asked, because they can work for the good of the universe once their personal struggles are over. They are also privileged, in that they have access to a greater level of love, understanding and knowledge by virtue of their own growth. The information for soul growth is contained within each individual soul and any soul need not look to another except for encouragement.

The evolved soul lives in peace and harmony, in as far as a human can, a forerunner to the state of bliss that exists when all negative emotions are jettisoned on entry back to their home in the world of spirit. The fear that humans have of this transition is also misplaced. The souls are returning to love and safety, and what is there to fear in that?

It is the fear that the spirit world does not exist that is responsible for much of this fear of what humans call death and we call birth."

There are many spirits from many worlds helping us with our transformation, and each of them has evolved through our current difficulties. They are anxious that we do not just see them as critical. In the spirit worlds, they tell it as it is and they have not heard of euphemism!

B. "The purpose of our messages is to inform and help the human race find a peaceful way through its difficulties. We speak not to condemn, merely to inform and encourage. From where we are, we can see that life is beautiful and ecstatic and we wish humans to be able to participate in this vision. As the consciousness rises, more and more will find their way to this experience, but first they must understand what they are looking for and comprehend the benefits of the way of life of which we speak. We are not sitting in judgment. We have no right to do that, but we are hoping to help the human race to its own salvation. This means that humans will have to understand and transcend some of the unpalatable truths about their nature. Negativity is to be learnt from and overcome, and a human must do that for himself. Only then can he come out into the sunlit uplands of peace and tranquillity. There is no other way."

Until I was taken to other worlds to meet the inhabitants, I had no idea that most of the universe lives in harmony, peace and tranquillity, resolving differences by negotiation rather than fighting. Part of our difficulty stems from our inability to recognise infallibly when someone is being, in that most elegant phrase, "economical with the truth." On most worlds, they have complete telepathic communication, one with another, which makes lying an impossible option. I would really like to attend a human meeting where everyone spoke his truth. Imagine it, and imagine also what would happen to our politicians! What an extraordinary thought!

War and Peace

B. "The Earth is a very warlike planet and much of the human population has not yet discovered that wars do not provide solutions to the planetary problems. There are a number of current wars that illustrate the point perfectly. Wars are conducted in fear and with the heart and solar plexus closed; it is not really necessary to say more.

With the heart and solar plexus open, it is not possible to drop a bomb on another being.

Short of war, disputes between neighbours occupy a good deal of human time and effort, and the same solution applies. For the Earth to be at peace, and for man to live in peace and harmony with his neighbours at all levels of being, he must be ruled by his heart, not his head. The rules are very simple.

Keep the heart and solar plexus centres open, and consider how you would feel if somebody treated you in the way you are proposing to treat others.

This is the recipe for peace, but there is a very great deal of fear to be allayed first. The combination of the rising consciousness, the coming Earth changes and the reduction of the population will do a lot to alter men's views of what is important in life. The survivors will begin to understand and will begin to know. They will begin to understand that they are safe, after they have come through the turbulence. They will begin to understand how to treat each other, the planet and the other beings. This will bring the peace."

B. "Most of the inhabitants of the universe live in peace and harmony. This is one of the many benefits of conscious connection to the Source and one's fellows. If nothing can be hidden, then all difficulties can be understood and surmounted in negotiation rather than argument. If there is no separation, then peaceful cooperation is easy. It is the separation that causes problems. At the times when you feel at one with everything, would you be able to argue? Feeling the connection increases the understanding to a point where argument is unnecessary. If everything can be seen from everyone's point of view, what value has sticking to your own? Harmony is joyful in itself and the accompanying peace transcends individualism. This is how peace will come on your Earth. It will be born through the turbulence that is to come and will make humans glad to be there at this time."

The spirits point out that it is not only the individual that is limited and damaged by our internal conflicts. Our leaders start wars and kill millions, because they have not attained their own peace. The limited nature of our responses leads us into some very terrible acts. Look at all the wars that have been fought in the name of people's gods!

B. "The peace and harmony of the Earth will arrive when humans find peace in their own hearts. Peace comes from within and can only temporarily be imposed from without. 'The peace that all over all the Earth the blessed angels sing' comes when humans have resolved their own internal conflicts. When this has happened, then humans will no longer wish to argue with each other. It is all dependent on an increasing understanding, especially an understanding of the emotional forces that shape human responses. Once it becomes natural for everyone to resolve their inner conflicts, then the incidence of outer conflicts will decline rapidly.

Wars have been fought as a result of the unconscious patterning of the leaders involved. Is that not silly? The resolution of these conflicts is what humans came here to deal with. The unconscious patterning must be replaced by thoughts that serve the human rather than those that hinder him. The entire universe is longing for men to understand this, so that they can create their own peace. Peace is an internal state of being."

B. "Peace works from the inside out and cannot be imposed from the outside in. From the outside, all that can be done is to provide the conditions in which peace can occur. Peace occurs within, with the resolution of internal conflict and the clearing of unconscious patterning, so that there is nothing left to fight about. It is not within humans' power to clear all their negativity, as some must remain to create the balance necessary for life on Earth. However, the most troublesome problems can be cleared. The principles are the same when applied to healing of ourselves or the planet. When we work to raise and harmonise the energies of a sick person, we are providing optimum conditions for the person to heal themselves. When we learn to nurture our planet also, we will again be providing suitable conditions for it to heal itself."

B. "Peace and harmony are necessary conditions for health in a mind, a body or a planet. It is the being that needs the healing that actually does the job. The same principle applies to education and government also. Coercion is purely a short-term solution. In the longer run, it provides the opposite to what it intended. Oppression and resentment are not good conditions for peace and harmony within.

It is time for peace and harmony to come to the Earth. As the consciousness rises, humans will understand better how to live, and when they have all reached their own peace, so can the world on which they live. When the human race can reach its own perfection, so then can the planet."

B. "Peace of the world can only follow peace of the heart. It is for each soul to find peace within himself, so that he is not inclined to war with anyone. This is the purpose of the rising consciousness. When humans can see clearly the effect of their warring and self-interest, they will become dissatisfied with their actions. This in the end will lead to peace. The resolution of conflicts in human hearts is the necessary precursor to their making peace with others.

They must also make peace with the planet and its other inhabitants and learn to live in a way that supports their world, rather than destroying it. The speed and completeness with which they do this will determine the extent and severity of the turbulence to come. The Earth must take her ease, but the severity is up to the human race on your planet at this time. Lip-service will not be enough. Humans must hear and, having heard, take action."

Love

The spirit world does not think much of our interpretation of love, which they understand as the basic force underpinning everything and everyone.

B. "Each man must work through his emotional patterning until he is freely capable of giving love. Love is not the sentimental emotion beloved of teenagers and magazines, but a deep heart connection with another which desires only the good for that person. Mother love, when properly expressed, probably comes nearer to the true expression of love than any other human form. Love is without judgment, but is also clear sighted. Love will refuse to accept the fiction that a person has set up around himself, but will express this refusal with kindness and compassion as well as honesty.

Love, as we have discussed, is the energy of the universe and is therefore all powerful. The 'warring planet' has a long way to go to express love truthfully, but this is what must be done to avoid the planet's extinction. Love is helping with clear vision, as we over here are helping humans to find new technologies that will not harm the planet.

Love is not rescuing another person. They must find their own way. (This is not to say that you must not put out a hand to save a neighbour from drowning; in emergency situations, the instincts take over.) Love is allowing people to die when their journey is over. Love is selfless, altruistic and honest. Love is very difficult for a human ego to express continually.

Self-love is the essential component of love. If you love yourself truly, you will behave honestly, and thus you cannot mistreat any other being. There is nothing blind or ignorant about love."

ℬ. "Love is a powerful force, not a feeling. The feelings of love must be considered separately from the force. The force that powers the universe is incredibly strong, but acts gently in order not to destroy what it empowers. Man equates love merely with the feeling, and that has been responsible for some very great misunderstandings, particularly the equation of love and lust.

Lust is a primeval urge to insure the continuity of the species and has little to do with love. Lust is a 'me' force, love is altruistic. A large part of Western civilisation is based on this misunderstanding, as is much of their literature. The condition of being 'in love' is a temporary form of madness which facilitates the reproduction of the species. A true level of bonding with another person can only come about when the madness, which is truly blind, has worn off and each can accept the other as they are. This is rare in human terms and certainly not what most relationships are based on.

Love must be openhearted. It is not possible to be angry with an open heart and solar plexus. The force that runs the universe is properly expressed in non-physical life, as you have experienced. There is no isolation in the spiritual world, so the feelings of fear and aloneness and self-protection do not occur. That is why there are no 'wars in heaven.' The opposite of love is fear, not hate."

ℬ. "In your language, the feeling between man and woman is given the same name as the one used for the force that drives the universe. Is not this a pity, as it obscures the reality. The feeling between the sexes is of a much lower vibration than the love that creates the universe. This lower feeling is a matter of attraction between the sexes for the purpose of creating children and has very little to do with love. In some partnerships, a feeling that can properly be called love may grow, but it is by no means universal.

The force of attraction is temporary; the force of love is not. There is much misunderstanding of this matter in your culture. The force of love in the universe transcends time, space and generations. Humans have to be taught how to love, which is strange, since the instructions are so simple:

'Keep your heart centre open and do as you would be done by.'

The understanding of this will increase as the level of consciousness rises, but in the meantime, it must be taught, most importantly by example. The love you have felt while travelling the universe from the beings you met is much closer to the love of the universe than what is meant by the word in human terms. Remember that."

B. "Love, may we remind you, has little to do with lust and is more properly thought of as the force that drives the universe. Each soul has an equal share of this impersonal force. There is rejoicing with those that are finding their way, and sadness for those that are lost, but the love for each is equal.

Spiritual development of a soul depends on him understanding what he has to give, as well as what he can receive. This is made easier, though the way itself is sometimes hard if there are tough lessons to be learned, by the joy that each soul feels when it is on its true path to fulfil its destiny. This is what each soul must do, but it has unlimited time and innumerable incarnations to do it. Each soul finds its own level among similar beings. The level you occupy will inform what you see, feel and understand of the principle of the Creator God.

We tell you repeatedly to keep your heart and solar plexus centres open. This is how we are over here and this is how we can be in a constant state of bliss. There is always more to learn and higher levels to aspire to, until the individual soul can truly merge again with the Source, with its job done. This is so far into the future as to be unimaginable. The development of the spiritual connection is of paramount importance and is the basic journey of the human soul. Prepare your life so that you are ready to feel the bliss when you come home with your task well fulfilled."

This message from the beings of Antares is typical of many I have received from other worlds.

"We are from Antares. We would like to talk to you of love. Love, not as a human sees it, but love as an eternal, supernal, all-powerful force, which, as you have been told, runs the universe and everything in it. Everything, whether it be spirit or form, is created of the energy of love, because everything is created from the Source, the 'All That Is,' and the essence of the Source is love. This is why the only thing that separates you from the Source is closing your energy centre of love.

Out here in the spirit world, we cannot, and would not wish to, close ourselves off from the Source, so we are always aware of the energy of love and of the feeling of bliss in which we live. We feel sorry for you poor humans, who cannot feel their connection all the time. We are working, as are many others, in this universe and the rest, to help your people become aware of the energy of love, so that they can perceive that their behaviour is wrong. In bliss, it is impossible to be cruel or predatory, and we would have you feel as we do.

The turbulence of your Earth threatens to disrupt our harmony and stability at many levels; like a painful stomach upset, it interferes with everything. We are all using our energy to calm and reorder, so that the love can emerge as the primary force on your planet also. We know why you lost the sense of connection, but it is time now to reclaim it and to join us of the spirit world.

Keep your love energy centre open at all times, together with the centre for the will. This way, you will become able to feel your connection to 'All That Is' and your loneliness and fear will cease. We will help you."

25

Change

There is nothing in the universe that is static. The whole is a dynamic, pulsating, everchanging series of patterns, most of which are too large in scale for us to be able to perceive from Earth. Everything in the universe flows constantly, including the circumstances of our human lives. If we cannot respond to the changing patterns of life, we can become very rigid and stuck, and life becomes most uncomfortable.

B. "Water is the life force that sustains many inhabitants of your planet, and it is subject to the same energy principles as everything else. Water is driven by the force of love, just like everything else. We cannot tell you too strongly how important it is to absorb fully, and act on at all times, the principles of love. Love is what will save your planet and much about the love still needs to be taught.

Examine yourself when you are in difficult circumstances. Are you able to keep your centres open and to flow like the water? This is what will make the harmony. We are not asking you to do anything that seems to you to be wrong, but to act in a fluid way to changing circumstances. Digging in your heels will not help; it merely causes obstruction to the harmonious flow of others, and as you have already discovered, nothing in the universe is static if it is healthy. There is always a way around the problem, and the example of water flowing in the easiest way, of finding little openings, will serve you well.

The stubbornness of humans, and their unwillingness to negotiate a solution to their problems, has always caused misery on your planet. The weaker the human, the more he digs in his heels – it is fear. The strong feel confident enough to discuss alternatives. There will be much need for negotiation in the coming times. The task is to see all sides of the problem, and this demands openness; fear closes.

Fear must be faced and dealt with wherever it arises. You must do this for yourself before you can expect it of others. Everyone has a right to his own ideas and, if a person cannot be persuaded, then he must be allowed to live the consequences of his decision. As the consciousness rises, so the need for harmony will increase."

B. "The waves of the sea carry information and power and are a seemingly eternal force driven by the winds. If the winds did not drive the water and the moon did not affect the tides, the sea would be inert, static and dead. It is the movement that keeps the water alive. This movement is essential to everything alive – a continuous flow and change, a dynamic force for life. When living forces become static, there is death and dissolution.

The energy of movement is necessary to maintain the dynamism of life. This principle is true at every level. It works in human life also. How often do frightened humans stick to the status quo and die emotional death because they are unable to flow with the life process?

Out here in the universe, nothing ever stays the same and the possibilities are, of course, infinite. Learn to flow with the changing patterns and your life will evolve effortlessly. Clinging to the past causes pain and stops development. Allow the changes as they arrive in your life to flow harmoniously.

You are never alone. The spirits that take care of each soul are with you constantly. They can help you fulfil your destiny, but first you must allow them to help you. No spirit can interfere with another's life except at their request. Allow your spirits to help you and see how wonderful your life can be."

One of the pitfalls of self-development is thinking that you know what is best for others, and this the spirits describe as arrogance. Each soul has his own intuitive sources of information and his own guidance and is responsible for his own decisions. All any of us can do is to provide fuller information to allow the soul to make those decisions. I found this next passage very liberating from the "oughts" and "shoulds" of our lives.

B. "The pitfalls of wishful thinking will persist, so it is important for you to become completely certain where your information is coming from. Truth in these matters is essential to avoid manipulation of people for one's own ends. Remember, you are not responsible for other people. Once the true information is given, it is for them to decide what to do with it. It is a form of arrogance to make yourself responsible for other people's destinies. You are far from the only one that can help them. To help another out of the feeling of duty, rather than a genuine wish to help, lessens the gift. Only give when you want to, not when you feel that you should. Allow others to know where their souls are going. Remember to rely on your instincts in these matters, as in all others."

A human life is peppered with mistakes, because we feel cut off from our Source. It is designed to be so for our learning, but that does not make it comfortable. One of the most comforting things they told me was

"Understand of yourself, the mistakes you have made are human mistakes, not soul mistakes. The road is meant to be riddled with questions and what would seem like mistakes."

One of the difficult parts of dealing with our mistakes is forgiving ourselves for our parts in their consequences. Eventually it occurred to me that, if the Creator could forgive me, it was silly of **me** *to refuse to forgive myself! Here is what they said on this subject:*

B. "Today we will talk of penance. It is not required that you should cover yourself in sackcloth and ashes, but it is required that you put right what was wrong. It is necessary to apologise, not necessarily in person, to anyone to whom you have acted badly. It is necessary to learn what this action of yours feels like from the side of the receiver. It is necessary to give help to other souls who have received the same treatment from another. And that is all.

Everything can be forgiven by the Creator. It is man who does not forgive himself and, with continued self-criticism and hatred, holds up further soul development. Self-forgiveness is necessary. Forgiveness from another is not. Many souls are harder on themselves than anyone else. It is necessary for you to forgive your own mistakes, learn from them and go forward. Without mistakes, you would learn very little – they are necessary for a soul's development.

Everything can be forgiven by God and must be by man on his own account. Resentment for another's wrong is hardening to the soul who feels it – just as damaging as hardening of the arteries. Open your heart and solar plexus centres as wide as you can and allow the resentment to flow through you until it is no longer important. Resentment implies that you expect to be treated correctly at all times. This is most unlikely to happen, especially in the prevailing mindset.

All you are expected to do is the best you can. The energy of love is without judgement, which is not yours to use. A soul may judge himself, but only himself, and after that, he must learn to forgive himself. There is no condemnation in the cosmos. Some of our work here is to help souls understand and forgive themselves."

If everyone is responsible for his own soul, then it follows that we cannot live by the principles of another. There surely must be a way of living on this planet so that most of us are not in some way subject to another's rules. Each of the worlds I have visited abide by universal laws and the laws of their own world, but beyond that they seem to be free. Our power is so often surrendered to a parent, partner, peer or organisation, including the formalised religions. If we can live by the truth in our own hearts, we can take back this power. If we are to live as fully conscious adults, this is what must be done.

> *"Truth is within ourselves: it takes no rise*
> *From outward things, whate'er you may believe.*
> *There is an inmost centre in us all*
> *Where truth abides in fullness."*
>
> *Browning*

Power

I still find the limitless nature of our soul's capabilities frightening, but the rules for exercising power are the same as those for dealing with pain and fear:

"Keep your centres open and do as you would be done by."

B. "The power in the universe is limitless, as you know, and the power enclosed in each atom of matter is nearly so. The power is of the Source and, like the water on your planet, can never run out. The spark of the Source at the centre of the Earth has limitless power, and the spark of the Source which is contained within your body at this time has the same. You have the power to do whatever you really believe you can. It is the doubt and fear that holds humans back from exercising their full power.

There are rules, of course, there are rules. Your power should never be exercised to damage another soul. Your power should be used to create rather than destroy, and your power is for the benefit of yourself, your companions, your planet and your universe. Your power is given you by the all-powerful Source and is to be exercised for the glory of the Source and the good of the universe.

Bearing these laws in mind, you can do whatever you will and create whatever seems good to you to create. There are no limits to this, there are only limits imposed by your fearful minds. Creation has been an explosion of beauty, harmony and intricate, exquisite design. Let your lives on Earth mirror this and create something worthy of this principle. Do not take away another's power. Exercise your own wisely and for good. Create, create."

B. "In order to understand power, one must first be powerless. Power has enormous benefits, but also considerable and matching responsibilities. Power cannot be exercised in a vacuum. The proper exercise of power needs the exercise of wisdom to temper its effects. The judicious use of power requires that just enough to achieve the desired effect is exercised. No need to 'use a sledgehammer to crack a nut,' and it is not good to show off with power or to exercise it irresponsibly 'pour encourager les autres.' You have seen aspects of the Source and felt the sleeping power that lay within it. Power can be perfectly peaceful, as you have observed. The power that is given you in your abilities must be used responsibly. Throughout your world, the misuse of power is widespread, and it is easy to understand its corrupting force, because you can see so many examples.

In the exercise of your own power, it is important to check repeatedly with yourself that you are being honest with yourself and acting for another's highest good. Then you will not fall into the traps that you have seen so many do. Power brings confidence and abolishes fear. Exercise your power wisely and ask for help when you do not know what is best to do. Humility is a necessary accompaniment to power. Without that, it is possible to fall into the spiritual trap of omnipotence.

Remember that the power is given to you in order to achieve your goals and fulfil your destiny. It is not for personal misuse. If you remember that your power is part of the universal force of love, it will help you not to misuse it. Each soul has their own power and it is their own responsibility to use it wisely for good. So many souls give away their personal power to partners, corporations, armies and more powerful individuals. Without one's own power, one cannot achieve one's destiny. Remember this."

> "The most powerful weapon on earth is the human soul on fire."
> Marshall Foch

Wisdom is merely a matter of taking all the available evidence into consideration, which is why we become wiser as our experience becomes greater. I was always relieved, when working with the many intelligent young doctors I met along the way, that there was no short cut to experience!

Here is what the spirits had to say:

B. "The quality of wisdom can only be gained through experience and is the ability to keep personal emotion away from decisions and actions. This is not to underestimate the power of intuition, but that is not properly considered to be an emotion, although it is described and presents as a feeling. Wisdom is far seeing and tends to be altruistic, although intuition is a condition of the moment. Wisdom can take many factors into account and depends on a good knowledge of the subject in question. Wisdom is wise!

If man fully understands what he is doing to his planet, he would become wise enough to act more sensibly. Wisdom cannot be found in a vacuum. When man is wise enough to order his own life harmoniously and for his fulfilment, he would do the same for his planet.

Wisdom allows, it does not drive, and it is flexible with changing circumstances. To become wise, man must first study his inner knowing and then test his thoughts against all the circumstances, leaving aside his fears and patterning. Wisdom comes from within."

Once our consciousness rises to the point that we are in conscious communication with every other soul on the planet, then we will also be able to be in conscious communication with the Source. Experience of the "All That Is," which some men call God, is freely available to all who can still their minds enough to find their inner connection. No religious practices or gurus are necessary. No travel is necessary, although there are peaceful places on Earth which make it easier. All this is found within your own heart, and all that is required is the stillness and solitude to allow the submergence of the "me" in the peaceful being and knowing of the Divine and the whole universe. Separation ceases to be. It was always an illusion anyway. The mystics of all religions understand this. The central experience is the same from wherever you start. One of my most profound experiences of the Source felt physically as if I was enveloped in blackberry-coloured velvet of infinite depth and softness, but the feelings of bliss were as the mystics describe.

From what I have been told, it seems that the experience of bliss becomes stronger and stronger as the soul approaches perfection. If that is the case, then perhaps it becomes easier to understand how the high beings, such as Jesus, are able to incarnate and endure all the cruelties and misunderstandings of the human race without faltering. Christ consciousness I understand to be the continuing conscious connection to the Source during Earthly incarnation, enabling the messages from that Source to be made available to this world.

B. "Life is a continuum and not extinguished by death of the body. The soul, once born, is eternal and has its destiny to fulfil. Each and every soul works through its own given pattern towards its merging with 'All That Is.' In many things, a soul has choice, but this path is given.

'There is a destiny that shapes our ends, rough hew them how we will.'

The path of the soul is from God to God, and the learning achieved on the journey is shared with every soul. The final merging is more glorious and exquisite than can be imagined. There are not words to describe the fullness of the bliss. This is the journey of life that we take and this is our inheritance."

There have been many human attempts to capture this journey in poetry. This is what Clifford Bax, better known as a composer than a poet, made of it:

"Earth and moon and sun.
All that is, that has been, or that ever time shall reap
Is but moving home again, with mighty labours done.
The many to the everlasting One.
And this is the meaning of man,
For the spark of the spirit imprisoned within it,
The task of the soul.
In all things one and the same,
The labour of worlds, and the plan
Aeon by aeon and minute by minute,
That is set for the whole,
Is longing to leap into flame
To shatter the limits of life and be lost in a glory intense and profound
As the soul with a cry goes out into music and seeks to be one with the sound."

Faith and Limitlessness

The exercising of our power and limitlessness require us first to believe that we can, and this is a matter that still needs faith. In the following passages, I was amused that they advised me that actually moving mountains might not be the best outlet for my limited physical energy!

B. You have been told that faith can move mountains. Let me show you how. If you truly believe that something is so and act as if that is the truth, you will create the reality of it in the physical.

A. *What about wishful thinking?*

B. Wishful thinking means something that you wish to be so, not something you believe to be so. That is a different mechanism. If you believe in your heart that it is possible for you to write a book, for instance, then you will do it. If you do not believe it is possible, then it will not happen.

A. *But I can only write this book with your help. I couldn't attempt it alone.*

B. Who asked you to do it alone? You are not expected to do anything alone. Nothing worthwhile can be achieved without help. It takes many on the earthly side to create a published book, and it takes many on the spiritual side to inspire, inform and teach you, so that you have something worthwhile to say. Everything in the universe is created by teamwork.

The process of creation is initiated by the Source, but the development of creation is influenced and moulded by many sources. So the Creator and his creation are all part of the same thing, but the diversity of creation changes the form and expression of each unit of creation, be it man or mouse, tree or rock. So, if you want to create something, you must first believe it to be true. Mountains are made of energy like everything else, so if you did want to move one, it is perfectly possible; but with the time you have left, you are better to confine your efforts to something you really think is important for you to achieve!

B. "Faith is the ability to believe in what one cannot see. Now, you know that what you cannot see makes up most of creation, but at the beginning of this journey, you did not know that, you just had to believe.

Should you wish to move a mountain, it can be done, but today I am talking about the mountains of non-belief and entrenched positions. The way to change minds is not to dig at them with the shovel of persuasion – that is very hard work. The way to help people to change their minds, for you cannot change them for them, is to illuminate the dark corners with new information and the light of truth. If you speak the truth, you will illuminate a few dark cobwebby corners. This is all you can do.

If the souls are willing to clear out this corner, then the clean wind of change could start to blow through some of their beliefs. In this way, you can gradually help souls to move their own mountains. If this happens, you would have achieved the movement of the mountain without effort or striving! You will have moved the mountain the easy way! If you could move the mountain without explosives, you will do much less damage to the souls who are trying to help. The easy way, my dear, the easy way!

Remember your truth may not be another's truth. Allow every soul the freedom to go through his own process. Creation is big enough to hold everyone's truth. It is greater than you can possibly imagine."

B. "There is no limit to what can be achieved by simple belief that it is possible. For everything that man has made, there has to be the original idea and then the belief to carry it through to manifestation. You know this to be true, and you also know how unlikely are some of the inventions that have enabled man to master the physical world. On his way home to perfection, there is no reason why he should not continue to use his capabilities, but first he must believe that they are possible.

You see how easy it can be to move mountains. Anything is possible in the universe. The universe is made of energy, which is easy to change and influence with intention. If it is easy to change, then anything can be changed. Intention and love is all that is required to start the process, and the energy is fuel to carry it out. If you underestimate what you can do, you will never achieve your potential."

> *"From this hour I ordain myself loos'd of limits and imaginary lines*
> *Going where I list, my own master total and absolute......*
> *Gently but with undeniable will, divesting myself of the bonds that*
> *would hold me"*
>
> Whitman

26

The Lessons of Life

We have been given advice by many souls from many worlds as to how we best should live in order to fulfil our potential. Their understanding is deep because we are not the only world that got it wrong. On many worlds, the inhabitants have brought their planet to destruction, as we are likely to do.

On our own world, there have been many more advanced civilisations that have destroyed themselves. It is in the Earth's plan for this civilisation to be the one that enables the consciousness to rise far enough to prevent it happening again. There is a great deal of help available to us from many souls in the universe, as I discovered as I travelled around it.

> *"A thousand unseen hands*
> *Reach down to help you to their peace crowned heights,*
> *And all the forces of the firmament*
> *Shall fortify your strength."*
>
> Trine

B. "**Do not fear for how you will live. All is taken care of. Those of you who are staying on this planet are helping to bring in the age of harmony. How then would we not help you?**

    If your physical needs are not met, then you cannot do the work that you have come to do. To do so, your physical needs will be met and you will be safe until you are ready to go. Concern yourself with the work that you have to do, and trust that your physical needs will be taken care of.

When you feel fear, open your solar plexus and your heart centres, look into the fear and see what it is really about, and then see how things change. Be openhearted; this is the key to maintaining a loving attitude to life. If your heart remains open, you cannot be unkind. It is the closure of the heart by fear that causes the misery in the world.

Practise keeping your heart open in adverse circumstances, instead of closing off, and see how the circumstances change in their effect on you. They may not change, but the effect will. Kindness is love in action and is worth many high-flown sentiments. Kindness is altruistic and will return to you with interest. Kindness returns to the kind. 'Kindness in another's trouble, comfort in your own.'"

Life Plans

Each incarnation is preplanned by the soul undertaking it and designed to provide the lessons that the soul has chosen to learn on this journey into matter. The soul chooses everything about that life, including how he will die, although he cannot choose by whose hand. Sometimes there are alternative paths, dependent on the choices made by the soul experiencing the life. These life plans are available for us to study, and the spirits commented that

ℬ. "It would be good if humans looked at their own lives and saw their causes and effects. Looking at their life plans would help them."

They do not have a very high opinion of our grasp of cause and effect, although they admit that our scientists understand it well enough.

This is the life plan of one incarnation of a soul. It is necessary to obtain permission from the soul before looking at these lines. Any information that it is not right for the seeker to have will be withheld, and if there is knowledge that should not be passed to the subject, then the spirits will say so.

B. At this time, we would like to work on your understanding of the life pattern, the blueprint. It would be good for you to understand how illness will appear in a life pattern. We are able also to identify these illnesses. The purpose of this is that, even though the event is drawn upon the life pattern, not necessarily the specifics of the illness would be drawn at this stage. There are times when avoidance is not possible, when it is the lesson to be learnt. There are times when avoidance is most probable. We will take you through the pattern of a person – not someone that you know. We will give you a picture that we will create together. Go to the beginning of the life pattern; we would suggest birth rather than conception. Let the colour become more intense for you.

A. *It is dark blue. And I need to ask for the point of birth. There is a baby in an incubator... It has exomphalos – the abdominal wall has not closed over the contents. It is waiting to be strong enough to have an operation.*

B. This is good. Now look at the blue life pattern. See how it presents to you at the time of the illness the child came in with.

A. *It has a lot of little bends in it.*

B. When you look at those bends and look at the rest of the line that you can see at this time, what does it tell you about the bends?

A. *Hiccups, things not flowing smoothly.*

B. This is correct. Are they all at the same age?

A. *There are quite a lot at the beginning and I haven't seen any further yet.*

B. We will deal with the beginning. These cannot be avoided.

A. *The child came in with them and has to go through them?*

B. This is correct. You can heal this, but not avoid it. Go further forward along the line. Be very aware of the formation and substance of this energy line.

A. *It went along a little way and then it fell down a hole.*

B. Is there a gap?

A. *No, it is hanging down.*

B. Ah, there is a weakness. It could be an event that is creating a weakness. We would ask you now to go to that. Either an image will come, or a feeling.

A. *There was no image, but a feeling in my gut. He has an intestinal obstruction.*

B. This is good. This is, when the line falls in such a dramatic way, life threatening. The flow of life has lost its strength.

A. *So the line falling down a hole indicates that something really serious is happening?*

B. This is correct. So it is possible and essential to heal this part, because the life has not reached this point yet. You are looking ahead, although perhaps only hours or days. The timing we will teach you. You will get a feeling as you go along this path. We would ask that you would gather up the line, so that it looks as good as the rest. It will have a scar in it, but will be otherwise strong.

A. *So I am not healing the baby now, I am healing the line?*

B. You are healing the lifeline now, to avoid what can be avoided.

A. *And I do that as usual, with my intention?*

B. This is correct.

A. *It just has wriggles in it, but it is horizontal again.*

B. Straighten out those wriggles as much as possible. You can use your intention or a crystal.

A. *I am putting in an Indigo crystal. I am seeing a lot more energy detail and it looks chaotic.*

B. Chaos is the energy of the future knitting back together.

A. *So I can leave it to do that?*

B. You can. The outcome of that would be that the child would go through another blip with its health, but not life threatening. Now we would ask that you move forwards while looking at the line.

A. *I feel that the child recovers from all that. I'm still in childhood. There is another dip, not as violent as the previous one.*

B. Is this caused of an accident or illness in the body?

A. *I think it broke something.*

B. How do you know there is a broken bone?

A. *I don't know how, I just knew it was accident rather than illness.*

B. This is correct. This is what we are asking you to trust, that knowledge, that understanding.

A. *The dent on the line is a completely different shape.*

B. It could have been life threatening. Look at it and describe it.

A. *The line has stopped being horizontal and there is a circular dent in it. There is plenty of flow; it is not like an illness, not depleted.*

B. That is right. Can this be avoided?

A. *No.*

B. Then there is nothing for you to do. How old is this child?

A. *About ten.*

B. Understand, a child of this age, even when they are warned not to do something. This child at this time needed to break a bone. It is just part of this child's learning, about themselves and a little about authority.

A. *Coming up against one of the unpleasant happenings of childhood.*

B. We are glad you understand this also. Go to the next point on the line.

A. *Now there is something different. There is a place here where the energy is all over the place, like a skein of wool in a muddle, lines going in all directions. The muddle is illness, isn't it? It is not the decision one – that is jagged. It looks quite different from the previous two.*

B. Why would you say this?

A. *Because in the first one, the energy took a directional dive and, in this one, the energy lines are going in all directions.*

B. How old would you say this person is at this time?

A. *About fifteen.*

B. What would you feel this illness is?

A. *I have at least three or four illnesses. Let me pull back a bit. He is having nosebleeds – now is it just a low platelet count? No, this is something quite serious. He seems to be very sad, I can feel that.*

B. Is what is wrong with him life threatening? Would he know it is life threatening?

A. *Yes, he is fearful, but then he would be anyway. I am sorry, I am having a lot of trouble with my mind.*

B. Understand sometimes the mind gets in because the mind knows, and then you misinterpret. The mind is to be listened to also. Sometimes the mind repeats something and, because it is what you already have great knowledge of, you dismiss. You have a feel of it.

A. *Yes, I can feel it. He has some sort of bleeding disorder, but perhaps this is secondary. The nosebleeds are secondary to what is wrong with him. I don't think he has leukemia. I am having trouble with this.*

B. We will help you. This soul does have a problem with blood that is not leukemia, but is akin to it.

A. *Does he have lymphoma?*

B. This is correct. He was not born with this. Do your senses tell you this is avoidable? Could he avoid this or is it one he needs to go through?

A. *No, I don't think he can.*

B. Good, we agree. Can he recover?

A. *I can see the line with a frayed end.*

B. He will not recover.

A. *He is anguished.*

B. Can you see the outcome?

A. *I can't feel anything except the anguish.*

B. This child has not died yet. He has yet to enter the womb.

A. *So this is planned, but not lived yet.*

B. The purpose of showing you this line was to show you a part that could be healed. The first will have surgery and healing hands. The other will have healing only, but just to ease the passage. It is sad to know that there is a child coming into your world for such a short time. This will be a very special child.

A. *He is a teacher. Is that his only purpose or does he have things of his own to learn?*

B. He does. It is not necessary for you to understand all of the lessons, only the lessons as you hit upon an illness, for the understanding of an illness.

That soul left his human incarnation at a young age, and his life pattern showed no alternative outcome. But this is not always so. They also showed me the pattern of a young girl who died at age fourteen, because she chose not to learn the lesson that she came to learn. They showed me that, if she had, her life would have continued and she would have grown up to be a nurse. It was her choice to leave. The soul is always ready to learn, but the person not always so. They told me about the decision points in all lives, at which the soul can choose to leave the body. A point is a misnomer in human terms, though not in theirs. One point can last for several years.

A. *The soul whose life path I have looked at – she had a decision point at which she could stay or go. Do we have many of those?*

B. There are two.

A. *Two times in a single life?*

B. That is correct. There are times when the human may come very close to extinction, but it is not that human's time. They may think it was their time. There is a time that that decision is made for you, and that will be the end one of this particular incarnation.

A. *So when it is time to go, it is not our choice?*

B. In part it is, but it is a calling; you are called home.

A. *And that is for everyone?*

B. This is so, even if it be an accident. If they have not completed a particular task, it is maybe because they have started on the wrong foot and have delayed getting on to their true path.

A. *Do people ever leave because they have got it so wrong they can't find their way back?*

B. They do, they make that decision.

There is a world that the Eohm described to me, probably not in this dimension, where the infant souls who have not yet started their development live.

The Nursery World

Ɛ. "There is, in the universe, a giant sphere of gases. It is bigger than any of the other worlds and its purpose is to hold the new souls that have not started their development yet. They wait their turn until they are needed in new worlds. There are whole civilisations of new human souls waiting until it is their time to become the next civilisation for a temporarily barren planet. These we oversee as part of our task. There are no plans to end the universe, so there must be a constant supply of souls as the older ones reach their perfection and finish their incarnations. These souls are innocents but programmed with the information their civilisations will need. There are more wonders in the universe than you can imagine."

I went into the ball of gas and it was full with beings of light with no physical development. There was a feeling of joy and innocence, as if they were very small children. The ball of gas appeared white with the lights of all the infant souls. I was told that one of their lessons was patience.

The Planning Planet

There is a fascinating world where souls who are young in experience go, to plan their incarnations. The whole of the soul's development is preordained, in that the lessons to be learnt are all the same, but the soul can choose how and in what order it is to be done. It is a world of great wisdom and, as usual, it is perfectly easy to see past, present or future. They showed me one of my own future lives as an example.

T. We are taking you to a place where souls go at an early stage in their development. It is not the beginning of their time, but an early stage in their development, and we are going to take you through the progression. Let us take you there and you will understand. Can you see us all around? This is some distance, but we will do it in our time, it is quicker. We are going to the outer edges of your universe. What is around you, what is the sense you have as you travel?

A. *I've got a sense of space with planets in it, and moving forward quite rapidly, and I feel as if I am "all part of everything."*

T. Yes. You are travelling to a place you have once been on. We are not far now. Look ahead and you will see something bright.

A. *I saw a bright moonlit globe and it has got a lot bigger and very bright and I am landing on it.*

T. There are souls ready to meet you – young souls, but good souls. You will only find good souls here.

A. *I am surrounded by dancing children!*

T. That is how they choose to present themselves. Look closer.

A. *Their heads are not like children's – in fact, I don't know what they are like.*

T. You need to join in with the movement. They will communicate.

A. *We all danced round in a circle and it was very joyful, and suddenly they all wrapped themselves round me in a hug.*

T. They are welcoming you. To them, you are seen as an elder, for here you present as a Basidian. That is how they see you, they do not see the human, but they see you as a being of knowledge that has come to them. Let them lead you to the places they will lead you. They have something to show you.

A. *They have grabbed me by the hand and we are all rushing off. We* *have come to some sort of structure, which is not a building, but something like a statue, something big. It looks like stone, coloured grey.*

T. Look into the greyness.

A. *Inside the greyness it has got colours. It feels like stone, but warm. It feels hard. I'm not used to things feeling hard.*

T. There is a purpose for this. You need to go around it and see if there is an entrance.

A. *There is a door in the bottom and I have gone inside, and I have come into one of these great big crystal chambers. Is it their place of knowledge?*

T. It is.

A. *There are a lot of projections to this chamber, which it didn't have on the outside.*

T. Each one of these has a purpose. Look at the young souls that are in here and look at what they do.

A. *They all ran off and found a ladder, and they are climbing up to one of these projections, and they all go inside, and they are receiving something from it just by being there.*

T. Exactly so. They will communicate with you.

A. *It is information about the universe. It is like school – school for souls!*

T. Yes.

A. *They are all very happy there.*

T. They know nothing other than happiness. This is where the soul prepares itself for great happiness, for the soul needs to complete his cycle with this great happiness. That is the only way a soul can complete itself – as the beginning, so the end. It is not an end, it is a completion. That is the basis of all souls. We know and understand happiness, but through each lifetime, we have to experience another emotion; but happiness will be at the core somewhere. We may not be able to access it in that lifetime.

A. *But once you leave the body, you will go back to it.*

T. Yes. That is why you sense love when souls are out of body. It is not just happiness, it is about the journey. In this particular place, the souls are able to view the journey they have chosen. We will take you to one of the chambers higher up. You need to make a request, as you go there, to be shown. Everything is honoured here. Where are you now?

A. *In another of these projections, higher up, and I'm just sitting there.*

T. Information will come to you pictorially or through knowledge. You may just hear it.

A. *Is this my mind talking, or this is a picture of life on Oriaton?*

T. It is not your mind.

A. *Because that was a bit I've seen before.*

T. So it is just familiar. You will also be shown your emotions through lifetimes.

A. *Pretty nice ones on Oriaton. That feels like loving and giving.*

T. Ask them to show you a negative lifetime for balance.

A. *There is a very poor woman sitting on the earth, quite old I think.*

T. What is the negative emotion with it?

A. *Want, I think.*

T. What does it feel like?

A. *"I who have nothing." Is that a life that I've had?*

T. It is. Look around and see what she does not have and what she does have.

A. *She is living in a hut that is in the forest. There must be things there to eat and so on, but I think she is on her own.*

T. Yes. Would it be an attitude of mind or...?

A. *Yes, I am wondering about that. Is she starving in the midst of plenty?*

T. Yes.

A. *So it is a very negative life – "nobody cares about me" stuff.*

T. Yes. Does she care about anyone else?

A. *No, she is so lost in her own misery, she has no room for that.*

T. Exactly so, exactly so. You have the point of that life.

A. *Yes. It's really easy, isn't it, to look forward and back like that?*

T. It is not difficult. When you go to a place such as this, it is a not the beginning, but a very early stage you can see ahead.

A. *And this is before souls have been human? This is when they are choosing some of their future lives?*

T. Correct. There is a place within here where they would choose the soul line.

A. *So this is where they're doing the planning stage of the life of the soul?*

T. Yes. It is an important place. Understand and feel that it is done with pure love and happiness.

A. *Yes, and although the image is of children, they are young in experience* *but they are not children?*

T. They are not. It will be difficult for you to understand that they see you as you see us. But remember, you left your body behind in that chair.

A. *Is it a place in space or in another dimension?*

T. Another dimension. There are also animal souls here. If you like, we will show you some. You will see the difference in the size of the soul.

A. *I thought a soul was a soul?*

T. It is, but where animal souls are concerned, the light of their soul is different, because they are choosing an animal's life. As you have many cats with you, we wanted you to see what their souls looked like.

A. *Small and pearly, beautiful, but not as big as ours. Is that because* they have chosen a different soul pattern?

T. Yes, they will get larger. You see, you are looking at the human soul that starts off fairly large and can grow enormously.

A. *If the cat soul chose to go down a human line?*

T. Its soul would grow.

A. *So it could if it wanted to?*

T. Oh yes, in between lives it could easily.

A. *And so they are choosing a line where the emotional lessons are simpler, aren't they?*

T. Yes, and they are choosing a line that is mostly animal and therefore the emotions are less complex and the lives are shorter. They have many more lives. They evolve quickly to perfection, animals do.

A. *And when they reach perfection, they are indistinguishable from any other soul?*

T. Exactly so. But remember, you are looking at young souls and that is why you see the different size, just as forms of beings on different planets are different sizes. It does not mean that the soul is any less evolved. It is just that, when they are young, they start off at this light, and the light gets brighter, it becomes bluer, still white, but bluer. This is a whole world of young souls, and what they are collecting is a future memory of the bodies they will have. The soul is choosing the body.

A. *They are putting together a collection of lives.*

T. Each its own portfolio. There is much detail in their lives. That is why there is much work to do on this particular world. And yet they do not have the free will that humans have yet. Always souls have free will, but humans have it in greater measure.

A. *These are more likely to go along a prearranged pattern before they get to the point where they are evolved enough to try out a bit of free will?*

T. Yes. For many of your lifetimes, you will have already done that. When free will is involved with the evolution of the soul, then you get the opposite factions of happiness and unhappiness. You get the negative emotions. Your planet is not the only one with opposite emotions.

A. *And do the souls choose which emotions? Are they going as far as the human, at this stage?*

T. They will. They will map out the whole of the soul's journey to perfection, and they will know what they will get from one lifetime to the next. We say "Creator" as if it were a single being, but there is a collective energy that is the Creator that has the information that all souls need to learn, and this is fed into the souls as they leave that energy, as they become the new creation. As they leave that body of the collective to become the individual soul, to go to the first few planets, to go to their worlds, they have the knowledge within them of the path they need to take.

A. *So it really is preordained, right from the very start?*

T. It is, but they are then viewing "I prefer that one to that one," so to speak. It is not choosing what they will learn, only how they will learn. Some will choose all the negatives first, and some will choose the positives. Every soul goes through the same emotions at some stage.

A. *Each soul has to have the same experiences, but they can choose how they do it?*

T. Exactly so. That helps you to understand the evolution of the soul, but with much more simplicity. We are concerned with your energy.

A. *Goodbye, thank you to these souls, they are playful!*

T. They can see that you are too. They see that you are prepared to dance and skip with them.

A. *I enjoyed that. I haven't got enough breath to do that with a body now! The souls that have gone down the animal line — how do they get to learn the very complex negative emotions?*

T. They will have lives that they learn the negative emotion, where perhaps they are the attacker or have been the victim.

A. *So then all their emotional stuff is likely to be just as raw, but simpler?*

T. Yes, animals are much more direct.

It is also possible to look at the path of the developing soul, although this can only be a partial exercise. The first life on this particular path startled me, as I was not expecting to begin at the very beginning.

A Soul Journey

A. *Is it possible to look at a soul journey? Is there a way of tapping into relevant bits?*

B. This can be done. A lot of the information that is coming through human beings at this time identifies part of their soul journey. Some mistakenly think they know the whole of their soul's journey. That is wrong. The soul is given its journey at the beginning of its time. It is not chosen, it is given.

Think of a person that you know. Now we are going to take you back to the beginning of this soul's journey and jump forwards to lives where this soul progressed greatly. There are many lives that souls have, where they do not progress a great deal.

A. *Are the ones where they progress the harder ones?*

B. This is correct. Though there are times when a soul has an easy life and learns a great deal from that easiness. They needed to learn that particular lesson. We are going back to the beginning of this soul's journey Go through the vortex in front of you. Use the diamond to take you through, use it as a pointer.

A. *I can see dark red. It is a very long time ago.*

B. Good. We need you to go to the colours. They are colour shadows, at the beginning of creation.

A. *I can see something that looks like what you see through the Hubble space telescope. Clouds of yellow, red, orange and black. A cloud of colour in a sea of darkness.*

B. Good. Now watch as the soul emerges from the cloud, and see this creation begin.

A. *A tiny piece of rock!*

B. Go forwards with this till it has the form of a human. Put your intention so that you go forward till there is a lifetime as a human in this soul's journey that is important.

A. *I can see a man with very long arms, somewhat ape-like. A very long time ago. He is upright. I wonder what this is about.*

B. Go into the life and ask the question you have just asked. The answers come quite quickly.

A. *It is a transition – when they came out from the forest and went into the grassland.*

B. Now the human had free will at this stage.

A. *So he had made the decision to leave the forest. I think he is looking for a group.*

B. What will this soul learn from a group?

A. *Cooperation.*

B. Good. This is one of the early lessons that humans have to learn. Some never do. Now move forward and ask the question again, "Take me to a significant life in this soul's journey."

A. *Now I can see a woman standing and pounding something. She is flattening something. I don't know whether she is pounding the washing or cracking seeds.*

B. Look around her; from her eyes, look around.

A. *She is in some sort of compound of huts.*

B. What colour is her skin?

A. *Brown.*

B. What did she learn from this lifetime? What would be a good lesson for her to learn in this lifetime?

A. *The word "love" keeps coming in.*

B. Good, and did she?

A. *Yes. It was family, tribal love.*

B. Yes. Did she learn to give or receive love? They do not always go together. The first answer will be correct.

A. *I don't think she learnt how to give love as well as she learnt to receive. There is something not very giving about her. Maybe that is because of the amount of work she had to do.*

B. Was she able to speak at this time – was there language?

A. *She had clothes on, fabric clothes, not skin, so I guess so.*

B. To guess is wrong. She may have been without tongue.

A. *In fact, now I look more at her, it would not surprise me if she could not speak.*

B. What makes you say that? Observe what you are feeling.

A. *Frustration and a little bit of tension. Was this person dumb?*

B. This is correct. Words were used at that time, but she had to learn her lesson of love and receiving. She wasn't able to give it as much. You do not need to look at the rest of the life in each lifetime.

A. *You mean, once you have learnt the purpose of the life, that is enough?*

B. This is correct. Now go forward and ask for the next significant life.

A. *This is much later and she is rich. She is wearing a long silken robe with a medieval pointed hat and furs. A very privileged person. A court life.*

B. You are correct. What has she come to learn?

A. *How to handle wealth well.*

B. Wealth or position?

A. *Position, I think. Something that comes with privilege.*

B. This is correct. There is a responsibility and it is part of the life lesson to use that responsibility in a responsible way. Did she achieve it?

A. *No. The glamour got to her. She was not sufficiently mature a soul to learn that yet.*

B. She enjoyed her comforts.

A. *Yes. She lived the life of a court lady. So how is that of significance then?*

B. As you move forwards, you will start to understand the pattern.

A. *I will go on. This time she is wearing white and in an enclosure. I think she is a nun in some sort of order. She is picking apples in a courtyard. White robes and a veil head-dress covering the hair, not the face.*

B. In your feeling, is this a religious life?

A. *Yes, there is a feeling of reverence.*

B. Good. What did she hope to learn in an order such as this?

A. *Obedience.*

B. And obedience to whom?

A. *The words "to the will of God" came, but what she actually had to be obedient to was the reverend mother!*

B. Correct. Did she achieve this?

A. *Not completely. She still responded to her own will.*

B. Good. You have some lives where the lesson is not completed. Recognise what she has not completed. As you come forwards, they will become intertwined to create what may seem as chaos to you. Move forwards.

A. *Now this is a very young man, in a court again, in velvet short breeks and a floppy velvet hat. Now what has he to learn? Aha, obedience again, to the master. He is apprenticed to a titled man.*

B. What is this one's position?

A. *He is a young princeling, who has to be taught the ways of the family by a much older man, an uncle.*

B. Good. There is more than one major lesson to be learnt here.

A. *It is something about the use of power.*

B. Good. How did he use his power? Did he waste it?

A. *I think he possibly did. I have no impression of development into a mature wise man.*

B. This is correct. It is but a small jump to the next one.

A. *This time he is in red velvet, but a different style. He is still a member of the upper classes, so what has he come to learn here? This is completely different, in that he belongs to the professional classes and will be wielding a different sort of power, maybe the head of a school or some sort of academic institution.*

B. Part of this lesson is respect, both to be earned and to be given. Look at respect, the feeling, and it will show you the answer. Go by the feeling of respect.

A. *This time he learnt it. I don't know what at.*

B. Good. This matters not at this stage. Now take yourself forward.

A. *Here we are on a battlefield. The soul is a soldier in clanking armour, a foot soldier.*

B. Yes. And what would be his lesson?

A. *The words that came immediately were "to die."*

B. To die is part of the lesson. But the humility to give of his life for a cause is the underlying purpose.

A. *To give it up willingly.*

B. And did he?

A. *He died, but he wasn't very keen on the idea. I received a poem that might have been relevant:*

"Life to be sure is nothing much to lose,
But young men think it is.
And we were young"

A. *So I imagine he didn't die very willingly. The poem was written very much later than these events.*

B. That is understandable. It is just a way of explaining them. Now come forwards again.

A. *Now this is female and dressed in white and gold. There is a group of girls dancing in the open air. Another privileged life, but I have the sensation that this is where the understanding and wisdom began to kick in. I don't know when or where this was.*

B. That matters not.

A. *The soul I know now has a great deal of wisdom, understanding and beauty of soul. This is where some of it is beginning to happen.*

B. This is correct, it is her evolvement. Go forwards They may seem like small lessons each time, but they are very significant in the soul's growth. There are certain lessons that always need to be learned, and others that are individual for that soul.

A. *This looks like a circus and there is a boy marching round the ring.*

B. What could be learned in a life such as this?

A. *Something about living in a group of people that are your equals – trust.*

B. You were almost right before with the equals, but then you tried to work it out.

A. *First among equals?*

B. This is correct, and it is a two-way equality? And what would be the other lesson that this soul learned at this time?

A. *There is something about love and group support.*

B. Teamwork?

A. *That's it! It was a closed group of people who depended on one another.*

B. Yes, this is correct. Were they a happy group?

A. *Yes.*

B. Jump forwards now.

A. *This is much more recent, it is the First World War. There is a soldier in a dugout in the trenches, with a tin hat on, playing cards with a big* *smile on his face.*

B. This is similar to a previous soldier, would you not agree? What is the lesson this time?

A. *He is learning in some way to be content with his lot. How you can be content in the trenches, I've no idea, but he is learning to allow that what happens to him is what happens to him.*

B. Now you have hold of it.

A. *So, this is the lesson that the other soldier didn't manage. This one is going to die, but he manages to accept it's "thy will not mine." That made me cry, so that must be true.*

B. And to die without fear, a great lesson. Now you can jump forward to the present day, unless there is one more before.

A. *There is a baby here.*

B. Who does the baby belong to, and who is the baby? What is this baby's purpose?

A. *The baby didn't stay very long. I can't get it without my mind, but this baby must be a teacher, but to teach what? This baby is quite happy to die and it is happy being alive.*

B. It is prepared for death?

A. *Yes, and it has died of croup or one of those infant infections.*

B. Is the baby the one you work with, or does it belong to her?

A. *No, it belongs to her.*

B. Yes. Always look at the larger picture.

A. *So the baby is happy to die and I suppose she has to learn to let go of it?*

B. This is correct.

A. *This lesson was repeated much more often in the days before antibiotics. Did she learn her lesson? This is really difficult, because I can't help feeling that she must have, because there isn't time for another life before the current one.*

B. We understand totally, but you are assuming. Go back, ask the question and take what comes first.

A. *Oh yes, she did, painfully!*

B. Now step forwards into the present life. From the viewpoint you have here, look forwards now. Follow the blue-white light that is her soul line and you will know how long she has to go before she completes her learning. There will be what would look like notches or knots or lumps on the line. These are more lifetimes. Understand that, when a soul has completed its learning, that soul does not directly leave your world. That soul may elect to impart what they have learned. She is highly evolved, this soul. Understand your feeling when you looked ahead at her life purpose path. What was your instant feeling – were they good lives, difficult?

A. *At least one of them was difficult.*

B. This would be right. Once a soul has evolved, they do not necessarily choose easy lives, but perhaps they might choose an easier life that will point them in the direction of their greatest teaching. They will already have had the learning – it is now to share. This soul whose path that we have looked at together will be given added energy by you looking through the life path, the soul's journey.

The soul stays true to itself when it is in touch with itself. No matter about the human's free will, the soul will always return to itself, to its path (This is the same in animals.) It is when your life has that sense of balance, not in what you have around you, but in who you are, you will have a sense of peace descend upon you. It is from the internal that memory is born.

Your memory, your soul's memory, stays on the internal; you use the other, this lifetime's memory, externally. Even though your memory is inside your brain, it comes from your soul. Your thinking memory from this lifetime we see as surface. You will discard most of that memory and only hold onto the important. This is the way that you make space for what is important to you. A lot of humans worry greatly about memory loss. The memory loss that we see is like a clearing out, so that your important memory has space. Humans have a certain capacity.

A. *But the soul remains true to itself.*

B. That is all that is asked of you. In each lifetime, your guidance is there to help you to understand how to be true to yourself. It is not always heard and, if it is heard, it is not always heeded. We cannot interfere, as you know, in your will. These are the choices humans make.

B. There is one more thing we need to do before you leave, and that is for you to understand this soul's soul purpose.

A. *It is to love. Love and heal the people around her.*

B. And what about herself?

A. *Well, we always have to heal ourselves.*

B. Not necessarily. A lot of you in this lifetime do.

A. *So it is love and healing for herself and the people around her.*

B. This is the full picture, for until you can love and heal yourself, you cannot love and heal any other soul.

27

Life After Life

Bodily death is another part of life that is viewed very differently by the spirit and human worlds. The fear of death seems to be endemic in humans and, in many, to persist until very near the physical end, although I have only once seen a person die who appeared to be still frightened. This is, again, because of our separation and our fear of extinction. The animal world does not have this fear of death and, I am told, does not distinguish so much between incarnate and spirit life. The albatross with which I flew had no sense of ending as it jettisoned its body like an unneeded overcoat. If soul life is a conscious continuum, then this is perhaps what you might expect.

The Basidian view the process of bodily death as entry into life – coming home, an occasion for rejoicing. They said to me once,
    "What do you need with a body? Come home!"

This is their view of the matter:

T. It is just so beautiful. "Why would I want to stay here?" was the feeling I got. I was so happy to go.
A. *Does anyone know that until they leave their bodies?*
T. I don't think so really. We may say the words, but until we have actually seen and felt that feeling... Because it is the feeling more than anything you are told. Once you have felt that, the fear goes,

there is no place for fear. It is just the evolution of the soul. That is what matters. Humans speak of it as the evolution of humans, but it is not, it is of the soul. Humans cannot see the soul; they speak of it, they say they understand it, but they do not. The soul is a library of memories. Everything that happens in each and every lifetime is stored within the soul. When the body dies, the soul lives on, of course, and will then cleanse itself of the unnecessary baggage and just retain what is necessary for the future.

This is what my father told me of his journey. His account seems fairly typical of others I have read (for example, see The Awakening Letters by C. Sandys).

P. When I first came over, it was an enormous relief. I was looked after by my Grandmama – she collected me. I went to a place of healing my soul, clearing the pain, and feeling replenished. I do not know how long that took me. Then I was shown the most beautiful places. I was shown the beauty in the world we are in. The only way to describe this would be "awestruck at its beauty" and it is a beauty that touches you, you can feel the beauty. Using our senses is one of the most important things that humans learn to do. Over here, our senses become much heightened, for we do not have the physical body, but we still have the spiritual shape. We can take on physical form if we wish. Then I went to a place of more learning – my choice. I went to the place of learning about my strengths and weaknesses. I reviewed my life. I also previewed the future. Because I love you so much – I loved my children – I needed to look forward, to see that you would be safe and well, and it gave me great pleasure to see that we would be together again.

A. *What did you do once you were comfortable about all that?*

P. I needed to learn more, I wished to learn more. I also needed to put in energy that I had taken out, and so part of my input was to you, to help and support you. The life I live now is very different to what you would expect where you are, but the life I have now is fulfilled. I feel fulfilled in so many areas.

A. *Can you tell me what sort of things you are doing?*

P. I offer guidance, I am a guide to three souls. I also work a great deal with souls who are taking their own lives. I help them over. It is not only me, it is part of my choice. The fact that I took my life, that I chose to end my life young, was just something that I chose. Every human being does this. Often those that haven't experienced it in one of their lifetimes are much more condemning. Those who have already experienced it have an understanding, they know not from where. I have been particularly busy, our group has been particularly busy, in the recent past, with many choosing to come over here at quite a young age. Once they come here, we teach them, we show them the ropes so to speak.

My evolvement here is concerned of higher knowledge. The more knowledge I get from the higher realms, the greater my speed of evolvement. I am a teacher. I was chosen to teach spiritual matters and so I do. I have human beings that I teach and there is a group of us, a body of us, that monitor souls' progress. We work with those who have chosen the healing professions on Earth. We give them guidance. Unfortunately they do not always choose to receive our message, but we nevertheless continue to try to contact them. It gives us great pleasure to do this, and sometimes sadness when our message is not heard. Working with the medical professions is also a way for us to be able to exonerate mistakes we made. Before we go to the Highest, we need to get everything right.

A. *There are a number of people that I have spoken to who still believe that this review of one's life is a desperately painful hell-like experience?*

P. It is not so. We do not feel that pain as such. We assess it from the outside, so to speak. We do not have those emotions. We have a different emotion that seems impassive, or would to a human being. It is not, we are not impassive, but we are softer. We do not judge either ourselves or others, but we do understand that it was again part of our evolution and what others deemed to be wrong was perfectly right. The only wrong that is not seen to be right is the taking of another's life.

A. *All the other wrongs could be said to be right if you looked at them from a different point of view?*

P. Yes, and understand there is more than one way of taking a life. Taking innocence from a child is what we see as wrong, and taking the life breath from a soul. Those souls go to a different place and review what they had done. The difference for them is that they feel the pain.

A. *Oh, I see, so there is in effect a hell in their minds...*

P. Hell is not a place we consider to be, it is a purgatory within themselves that they put themselves through. They choose to do that and they choose to undo it by working with those who are left behind, and they have to do it without any recognition.

A. *So how are you now?*

P. My feeling is bliss. All of us feel this. The only word that you would understand in your language would be "bliss," that "all is everything."

Life seems to continue very busily once we enter the world of spirit. As we leave our bodies, our souls travel to the highest realms that we have reached, accompanied by the souls who are dear to us. First we go back to the world that we call home, for healing, rest and regeneration. Many humans have been ill for long periods before they go over and, although it is not possible for a soul to be ill, their energies may be considerably depleted. Many also have to adjust to the fact that they have died, especially if their going over was a sudden event. Once we have recovered, we review our recent incarnation and find out what we have learnt and what still needs work. As my father has said, this is not a painful process, unless we have taken life. Any wrongs we have done must be righted, and we can look at what happened to us and the choices we made in the light of much greater comprehension.

In the world of spirit, all can be known, and there is no judgment in the face of complete understanding. The negative emotions are no longer felt, and the doubt and fear have been replaced with bliss, so it does not seem to be a traumatic process. When the healing and reviewing process are complete, we rejoin our soul group and consider our interests and occupations for the future in spirit. Much soul development continues between incarnations, which are only undertaken for specific purposes. When I have been able to be with the Basidian at home, so to speak, it has been joyous and sparkling, and I am conscious of complete love and support and safety.

Imagine life without a body! The spirits say that they do not get tired and, since there is no time, they can follow what interests them for as long as they choose to. There is no illness, and it is only necessary to replenish their energy levels at intervals. The universe is beautiful and friendly, and travel across it is almost instantaneous. Add to this that they live in a constant state of bliss – I do wonder why we are so frightened of dying, when all this awaits us!

The souls who I know personally in the Basidian have described some of their current activities to me, but some I will not be able to comprehend until I arrive there. The soul I call Uncle Theo has continued his professorial lecture tours, only now he is invited to visit worlds all over the universe! All the ones I know by name are members of the intergalactic medical council and oversee medicine on many worlds. All souls continue to evolve towards their own perfection and, as they rise, their tasks change.

Angels

Once souls have completed their learning and evolution, they join the ranks of Angels. Angels are beings of light. Light is pure energy, so the purification process must be complete, but they can come from many worlds. They are completed purified beings who are helping others. They all have tasks to help not only Earth, but other worlds, depending on the level of angelhood they have reached. There is a "trainee" level, who oversee a flower, a tree, an animal, and sometimes a human. There is no soul that does not have its guidance. The lowest rank of "qualified" Angels oversee humans and beings from other worlds. These are referred to by humans as Archangels. The next level have much wider influences and are guardians of whole worlds. The final layer are "beings who are purity itself."

A. *The highest rank of Angels are purity and they are not "doing" anything I would recognise?*
T. They are not. There are not words in your language to describe them adequately. How would you describe the Source – they are as one?
A. *They are too close to the Source to separate?*
T. Exactly so. They are not what you would describe as doing, but they are the beings of the universes. They oversee all of the universes.

The highest rank of Angels who have come to talk to me are the Eohm (ℰ.), whose world and purpose is described in the previous section. They are very awe-inspiring and stern. This is how they described their work:

E. "Our role in the universes is second only to the Creator. We do not create, but we order what the Source creates. We have many tasks within this, of ordering the stars in their courses, of ordering the beings on the stars, of ordering the flow of information in the universes between the worlds and beings, so that all events occur at the proper time for the most harmonious outcome.

We have enormous power, but that power was created of love and we act with love at all times. There is no longer negativity within us. We control the flow of souls from their infancy to their perfection, so that there are always the right beings to populate the worlds. Because our minds are so closely connected to each other and to our Source, our mental capacity is also enormous and our understanding is complete. Thus, we can carry out the will of the Creator over vast spaces, dimensions and intentions without difficulty or mistakes. We have no limits. Above this layer, it is not possible to distinguish individual beings from the Source. They have returned from whence they came, which is our journey and our wish."

Black Light

This level is the one at which the Angels live. The journey to the level of "black light" was astonishing. The light is only black to human eyes, which cannot see the wavelength, and once I was in it, contained more colours than I had names for. It was also illuminating about what happened to souls at the moment of death. The Basidian live here, although they travel all over the cosmos. It is not a level that a soul can aspire to until after human incarnations are completed. But we can use the energy from this level in our healing work and are able to visit it, if the spirits take us there.

> *"You will never enjoy the world aright till the sea floweth in your veins, till you are clothed with the heavens and crowned with the stars, and perceive yourself to be the sole heir of the whole world, and more so because men are in it who are every one sole heir as well as you."*
>
> *Traherne*

Journey to the "Black Layer"

T. You are going to the edge of your own universe; the black energy surrounds the outer edges of your universe.

A. *So it is an energy that is in a physical space, as well as being a spiritual level.*

T. It is, and you are coming towards it. Look ahead of you.

A. *It is getting darker, but the dark I'm coming towards has got little bits of gold and purple in it.*

T. It has all colours. As you come into it, we need you to sense its energy, feeling, and describe as you come in. We will take you deeper. You now require us to take you further.

A. *I am going into this now. It stopped being black and is lots of colours and little bits of gold, a little bit of all sorts of colours and just little dots of... I can't describe it.*

T. Intend to touch one of them, just touch one.

A. *I just touched a purple bit and it is very soft.*

T. Yes, and how does it make you feel?

A. *I felt love and support and comfort and "everything is all right."*

T. Look around you, touch into the energy, feel the power you are within. What is the power?

A. *It is limitless and it is gentle, but infinitely powerful.*

T. Exactly so. What would it contain that would affect you on your planet. How would it help you? While you are in this space, the knowledge would be within you.

A. *Well if everybody felt like this, they would not have to do most of the things that they do.*

T. Correct. More than that, how can it help you? How can you as a physical being use this energy, tap into this energy? What use is the knowledge of this energy to your work and to you?

A. *For my work, it is the healing energy, the highest level of healing energy that I can attain to. For me, can I tap into this energy for my purposes, so can the inhabitants of my world tap into it for whatever they want to do?*

T. Exactly so. They do need to be able to journey here, not necessarily journey as you have today, but they do need to be able to put their intention to it. They need to reach a certain level, before they realise they can do this. Those who are not evolved sufficiently in this particular life will not be able to access this. Those who are not sufficiently developed would bounce off it, the energy is so strong. Now, the energy also has a benefit to the physical surface of your world.

A. *If I can use it for my healing, presumably so can the planet?*

T. Correct. The more of you that would tap into this energy would be able to heal your planet. So, to answer the previous question, they need to be of a certain level in understanding that the planet can be healed, in order to enter into this healing. This can never be drained, this energy; its ability to heal is also limitless. It is to be used wisely, this energy, for the power level that it is could heal but drain a human being, if they take too much of this energy at one time. You yourself have experienced draining from the healing, when we have put a higher level of energy into you. You feel well, you feel great benefit, but then you drain. This will do it tenfold.

A. *So you have to step it down to use it on humans?*

T. We do, we dilute it down.

A. *But this is where you live, and when you want some more energy, you just take some?*

T. We do, we just absorb. We would like you to come into it and come through it. You will see the vastness of it. All spirits come here when they die. Some are able to linger, some are not. We will show you spirits arriving. You will see the spirits that are, not rejected, but unable to stay. Look at the colour particles. You are now looking at the energy that is between matter, you are in it.

A. *So what I am looking at is magnified thousands and thousands of times for my eyes.*

T. Yes. We will take you a little further, where you are able to observe beings that are dying a physical death and coming for renewed life here. This is where a soul will come to be replenished, some staying for a while, others would go on. Many go to different places. This is a level of the highest communication.

A. *I have an impression of beings bouncing into this area and immediately dropping out again.*

T. Exactly so.

A. *So, is that souls arriving and finding it a bit too strong and dropping back again?*

T. They have made contact.

A. That is all that is necessary?

T. For some. Others will wish to stay and are unable to do so, but those that can, do. It makes no difference how old the soul is; it is just progression of the soul that matters. Not all old souls have progressed so far as they could, just as it is on your land. The age is not a precursor for knowledge or wisdom.

A. Is there any chance I could see you – how you are while you're at home?

T. We will present ourselves – coming now.

A. I've got an impression of floating veils of mist.

T. Look at them – they have substance.

A. They are full of little whizzles of energy and they are not quite as formless as I thought. They have got very definite edges.

T. We are not like mist. We are very substantial, but we would appear insubstantial in a physical sense. We are not solid and we change our shape, our emotions change our shapes. Look around, you will see some of us here, many.

A. I have a sense of that. I would really like to feel how you are energetically. Is that possible?

T. Yes it is, we will come to you as you come to us. Come into what you call the mist. We will envelop you.

A. Well that made me cry, which I expected, but it also made me feel as if I was completely separate from, and had nothing to do with, my body, in that I was up here with you, at home and protected.

T. That is how we feel and, when you are with us, you are able to feel it also for short bursts. But for the most part, you are not journeying for your pleasure, you are journeying for your advancement of knowledge, and so you have not fully allowed yourself to feel. Now you know how we feel, it can become stronger for you.

A. I'm feeling part of this group of wafting beings and nothing to do with Earth whatsoever.

T. Exactly so. While you are here with us, you have nothing to do with Earth and you are experiencing your own spirit, your own soul.

A. I'm sure I'm not getting anywhere near the intensity of love and bliss that is available, but there is a complete absence of negative stuff, which is nice.

T. It is. When you have this feeling, you are able to do anything for anyone and anything, for there is no judgment. Judgment holds humans back. They make many judgments during their waking day. We just are.

The next part of this most exquisite journey was a horrible surprise. I found it very difficult to describe what I saw, but some months later, there was a picture, on the front page of The Times, of a volcanic eruption with a simultaneous lightning storm. It looked like that.

T. We are going to take you through, so that you can view another universe. We are at the outside.
A. *We must be going into another dimension?*
T. Correct.
A. *Is the black energy in our dimension?*
T. It is. It joins dimensions. Remember it is the pure energy that supports. It creates an edge to your solar system in the universe, in as much that everything is in the place it is meant to be.
A. *Is it spatial, this edge, as well? We can't see it because of the different dimension, but it is next door?*
T. It is, you are correct. What are you viewing? It will be different to anything you have seen before and yet it is a universe. Speak of the colours you see.
A. *I'm seeing fiery colours, almost as if this was a universe of volcanic fires.*
T. Now look at this, look closely. We are with you, we are protecting you. You do need protection here.
A. *When I look at it more closely, it changed colour. I don't know what I'm looking at.*
T. No. It is not in your human mind.
A. *It looks like fire, and clouds of fire, as much as anything else.*
T. What are you feeling, observing this? Would you feel they have the same feeling as your own universe or is it different? What is their predominant feeling?
A. *It is different. It is more like lightning than anything else.*
T. How would you describe looking at this by the emotion, from a human point of view, which is the only way you can?
A. *It is quite violent. Although there is a sense of love, whatever is happening in there is happening very violently and suddenly all the time. Presumably the beings in here are comfortable in it, but I have to say, I would not be.*

T. You would not be, and nor would we. That is why we have banded together very closely, for protect you we must.

A. *Thank you. It's like being inside one of those nuclear explosions that make stars.*

T. This is a place that souls come to. But there are souls in here and on their planets that are warring. They have an aggression here. (All souls will have visited; some will have been destroyed in it, for wanting to stay longer.)

A. *Our universe is a universe of intention. What is this one, can I know that?*

T. This universe also has intention, but it is negative. It is trying to turn itself around. It has been trying for many many ages. It has too much anger, too much fire in it, and so souls that have committed the taking of life come here. They come through to this universe, to this dimension.

A. *To stay?*

T. Unless they learn.

A. *So there is a hell! The Pope was right after all!*

T. You would know it as that, yes. We would not call it as such. It is another dimension.

T. When you look at this universe, you will perhaps understand they are not self-destructive, because there are planets of growth and learning there. They have to work their way through, to come back through this energy, to come back into your universe, and this energy will not admit someone from that universe, a soul from that universe that is not clearly ready to move on. It would be known as a place of great learning and also a place where baser feelings are observed. It is, we feel, sometimes abusive.

A. *Is it the universe of learning how to deal with anger – the universe of learning how to overcome anger?*

T. To understand anger and to understand the energy of anger, and in understanding the energy of the emotion will be the first step into full understanding and healing and stepping out. Some souls that come through to here... there is a place where they come to. Those souls that you saw rejected – often they would come here. The ones that only touched and left will come here. The ones that stayed even for a short time (it is longer than it would appear – you are looking at our time, not yours), they would not be coming here. Those that have committed atrocities upon other beings on your planet go to this place and they have to earn their way out. It can take many lifetimes perhaps, and each lifetime, they would go to a progressive planet. You have planets you can progress on. They have to go to other planets. They do not revisit.

A. *You mean that everything on one planet is at about the same level, and they have to go to another one to get to the next level?*

T. As you would understand, steps, and perhaps you can understand the intelligence of Earth when you look at this. How the Earth is a place of growth, of renewal, in our universe. Earth is an important planet and that is why humans in the physical human body want to stay on Earth. There is a feeling of wanting to stay. Those of us who have lived many lives on Earth have a longing to return to safety and love.

A. *Can we go back now? This is very nasty.*

T. Yes, come through back into it and feel the positivity, it is softer…..

A. *That was frightening.*

T. That is because you were there once.

A. *You can't be frightened if you don't have a memory?*

T. You cannot. Those that are visiting for the first time are eager, they have no memory. It is not necessarily souls that choose to extinguish their lives at the first opportunity that go there; it is souls who have extinguished lives that have not wanted to go; and not necessarily, from your understanding, those that have killed by accident; it would be by intention.

A. *"Hitlers" and terrorists, for instance.*

T. It is correct. We smile at those who say they are doing this in the name of their gods.

A. *There are an awful lot of awful things done in the name of people's gods.*

T. Correct. We wish you to be here to absorb this beautiful energy, this power, to take on this power as your own. Remember this power has no limitation. You may feel a sense of awe with this power. This is part of the Divine. It is a large part of the Divine. It is as if holding a child in the womb.

A. *This is for souls that have got past Earthly lessons?*

T. It is. We all have a purpose when we are here.

A. *Yes, the afterlife seems to be rather busy.*

T. It is. It is just as well we have no time.

A. *Yes, and that you don't get tired.*

T. We do not. We rest. We do not sleep, we do rest.

A. *Sleep is for the physical, but why do you need rest if you don't get tired?*

T. It is not tiredness that you would understand.

A. *There is something of you that needs replenishment apart from the energy?*

T. Correct. Look at the particles – how big are they really?

A. *In whose terms?*

T. In yours.

A. *I think what I am seeing is the energy particles, so they are very small.*

T. Yes they are, but they can magnify. Understand, you are looking at energy. Each part of the energy has its own intention, it is collective intention. Every particle has its own intention and every particle supports the other particle, but also supports what is not identical. This is pure energy. It is not something you have on Earth. Now perhaps you can understand what the energy is like within a human body – it is between matter. On the outside of the human body, the energy that keeps that human body in that shape (because that will be intentioned for that human body), it would form a field around that human body.

A. *The field of energy throughout and round the human body is what keeps it where it is?*

T. Correct, and if that field is broken in any way, the shape of the human body would start to alter, either from the inside or outside. That is why sometimes humans damage their limbs, lose limbs, it is because their energy field is damaged.

A. *And if an internal organ becomes deformed, it presumably becomes ill, so it is the basic cause of physical breakdown of whatever sort?*

T. It is, and when you look at the breakdown of the human form, the energy that is lacking there is love, and it is then replaced with fear.

A. *And then illness happens.*

T. It does, even in an infant. They would have brought the fear in with them and they would use the previous memory to create illness.

A. *So that is how you get neonatal illnesses.*

T. Correct, it is. We understand humans being saddened by this, but it is of course that journey which they themselves have chosen.

A. *If it is somebody that is close to you, then that is difficult. A child, for instance.*

T. Very difficult, and we understand that. We often support those that are afflicted in this way.

A. *Which presumably, like everything else, every soul must experience.*

T. It is. You will have experienced this yourself.

A. *Yes, I know how it feels, so I must have.*

T. Yes, every time there is recognition, you have already done that.

A. *I think you said that everything in the universe had a pattern and it was just that much of it was so big you could not see it, so there isn't any chaos except where there is meant to be chaos temporarily.*

T. It is, correct. That was a place you would need to be escorted to and we needed to take you through to the other side to let you know not to go there without being assisted. We would not like you to put your energy into that field.

A. *I have no wish to. Is it the only negative universe?*

T. There are others. That was the worst. There are other positive universes. You do know of the others. We do not know all of all, we know all of what we know. There are universes that we have not visited. It is infinity you are in; you are experiencing infinity. A difficult thing for a human being to understand. To understand, yes, but experiencing is difficult. We are aware of your energy. We will bring you back now.

A. *I have been right out to the edges of the universe! Goodness gracious me!*

T. There is a journey for you!

This is the only unpleasant part of the multiverse that I have been to, and it is not in the same universe as ours. For the rest of this gorgeous, vibrant, colourful, friendly, living organism called the universe, the journeys have been pure pleasure.

The development of the soul is profoundly complex, as it must be if each soul needs to have every possible experience, and there is very much more that I have not learnt yet. I am so grateful for the privilege of being shown all these wonders. I can truly say that I am having more fun than I ever had in my life!

28

Last Thoughts

B. "It is your way preordained that you shall speak the words that we give you."

The spirits tell me that the words I have been given come from the Source. It has been my destiny to write of them and I am fulfilled that this book is now complete. There is nothing that I do, to enable the Basidian to speak with me, that you cannot do also if you want to. It is a wonderful experience to talk with them and travel with them and to be able to "put out your hand and touch the feet of God."

By the time this six-year conversation started, I had learned to follow my intuitive sense about what feels good and right and allow it to override my left-brain rationalisations. They tell me that this allows you to follow your soul's path. Some call this "being away with the pixies" and I would agree, so long as you are prepared to substitute Angels for pixies!

There are many who are now able to access the non-human worlds, and every one of us has the capability. All that is required is the wish to do so and a little work. Much of the necessary development is a condition of being rather than doing, and the only essentials are stillness and of course intention. Everyone who wishes to do so can communicate with their own guides and helpers. There is no magic about it. The techniques are not difficult to learn. For people like me, the most difficult bit is stilling the mind and allowing what will come to come, without striving for it. Those who would prefer to be formally introduced will need to find a medium who can channel them clearly. Not all can.

The rewards of learning about this included making me feel lighter, happier and less troubled by fear and doubt than ever before. I think it is what we call inner peace. Inner peace is the goal sought by the soul to clothe its personality. The peace brings wisdom, which is "a pearl of great price." Inner peace leads to outer peace and the end of restless searching, whether this be for "All That Is" or a new hat. Humans bother themselves more with the hats than the divine, and it is only when they are brought to a stop by illness or disability that they give themselves space to reflect on who they are and what they truly want.

This is the gift of illness, that nothing is expected and the burdens of man's outer life can be laid down for awhile. Inner peace can only be attained by putting down one's busyness and turning within. The joy of this discovery transcends all Earthly methods of achieving happiness and one does not have to strive for it; it is. The gift within you must be sought, but when it is found, it is yours by right.

B. "We have been telling you of inner peace and grace and love. All the spiritual development of a soul in human form is directed to uncovering the central love and truth of who he really is. This truth is overlaid by the conditioning of the psyche, so that the human forgets who he is and where he is going. The truth and love are always within his soul and when uncovered will lead a soul to behave, while in human form, with the love and integrity that are his soul's nature. Expressing his love, integrity and truth will lead a soul to his true path in his incarnation and finally to his destiny. This is the task of the human incarnation."

As the vibrational level rises, this will all become easier and easier until it is a normal form of communication. But until then, a little work is necessary. The spirit world use all our senses to communicate with us and I often find it difficult to decide which sense they have used, or if it was just an inner knowing that provided the information. Our guides are part of the universal consciousness and say that there is nothing that can't be known. We should remember that we are the only beings in the universe who are not able to access all this knowledge at all times. There is nothing strange or unusual about it.

A. *I have been getting an inkling about the things within things.*
T. We teach you much when you sleep.
A. *Yes, there are many things I don't know anything about yet, but less of what you talk about is completely strange.*
T. This we understand and it pleases us. As you grow into your own in doing this work, growing into who you truly are, you begin to remember who you are. Remembering is of course from memory and we are awakening your soul memory. It is what if humans could allow themselves, they would be communicating from the soul and that is why you recognise certain people, you resonate with certain people. It is at soul level, because they were speaking from the heart. The heart is the voice of the soul.
A. *'And your soul is my friend.' That's what you said when we first met.*
T. Yes, and when you resonate with souls like that, they feel familiar, as you are familiar to them. There is a familiarity, a knowing, and it's an ancient knowing. With those that you form friendships with, for whatever reason, there is a deeper connection. Your world, it can be such a wonderful place. It is a beautiful world. There are other worlds that you have seen different beauty, and the inhabitants appreciate the beauty. Not enough humans appreciate the beauty of it.

The spirits are firm that all souls are loved equally and that the love is completely inclusive. They are not very impressed by the various religions, because they tend to be exclusive. Their teachings are very pure. They do not wish them to be adulterated by a human religion, be it Eastern or Western, because they say religions are created by man. Uncle Theo is particularly disparaging on the subject of religion.

"Religion is based on guilt and so a hell would have to be invented; it was never in the original writings."

ℬ. "It is important that the readers are quite sure that it is they who are loved and that there is enough love, and to spare, for all of them. There is no exclusion in the universe, except by any soul who rejects the love. It is freely offered to all without judgment and without consideration of race or creed. There is enough love for every soul, whatever he may have done. There is enough love for every soul of every race whatever his beliefs may be. Religions are fashioned by man and are against love in their exclusivity. The universal love is for every single soul, whatever type of physical body he is experiencing. The energy of the universe is the energy of love and it must act according to its nature.

Oh man, know how much you are loved. There is nothing whatsoever to fear. This love is without limitation."

We are limitless beings. The limitations that are upon us are put there by ourselves. The beings on Oriaton teach how to access one's limitlessness to a wide variety of beings from many worlds, but I think that we have to believe we are limitless before we can make progress. I would really like to be able to create a sofa out of a piece of energy, without having to go through the physical processes. The inhabitants of many worlds do not have to construct things; they just create them whenever they need them.

The true expansion of which we are capable is available to us if we can avoid negativity. Not only that, this is the best way that an individual human could help his world. The coming of peace and harmony comes through the turbulence and arises from the ashes of conflict and disaster. There is no need to fear. What happens is what happens and whatever does happen, the soul will be safe.

ℬ. "The souls who inflict great wrong will have to put right the damage that they do. It is not for humans to judge. From here, where we can see the bigger patterns, we remind you of what we said before: 'What is right in whose eyes?' It is for each human with awareness to keep himself centred and keep his heart and will centres open. This way, he will not be tempted to join the war-mongers and he will act as a steadying light upon others.

This is what you must do. Keep steadily on your path and you are doing the most good that you can. Do not allow the turbulence, either man-made or of the Earth, to distract you. This is your path, keep to it.

When the peace arrives in the heart of man, all this will be over and the age of peace and harmony can begin. Thinking with the heart is the key to this transformation and will arise when man can see the greed and wish for power of your leaders as they truly are. This time will come, that we can promise you, but it is not quite yet. There are emotions to be released first, both from humans and from the Earth that they have damaged. The releasing can be violent and this is what you are experiencing now on your planet. Once the poison and the pressure are released, the healing can begin. This we have told you many times.

There is nothing you can do except to be the most harmonious being you can be. If all beings not directly involved in the turmoil were peaceful within themselves, then this would aid the recovery of the whole.

Nation is not going to speak peace unto nation at this stage. There are too many vested interests. But man can speak peace unto man and this will have a great effect. The energy of the islands of peace will join together and affect the whole, in time. There is beauty and harmony awaiting you. Do not let the poison corrupt the peaceful. From where we are, we see the lights of the peaceful shining and we rejoice in them.

It takes a good heart just to be steady in the midst of turbulence, but that is what will make the difference. Let your light shine and be peaceful. This is what you could do."

This next transmission came shortly before the 2008 US presidential election, when the spirits were concerned that another war-monger would be elected. They told us to put out the intention for a peaceful president, and the more of us who intended this, the more likely it was to happen. It is a technique that is not restricted to choosing presidents!

B. "In the calm after conflict, there is the opportunity for reaching true peace, which is the peace within the self. This is the only lasting peace and it is infinitely worth going to war with one's human nature to achieve it. This is the peace that 'passeth all understanding' and, once it has been attained, a man cannot make war. Take care in the times that are coming to choose leaders that have achieved their peace. Not weak men, but peaceful men. The stronger the peace a man can radiate, the more beings he can reach."

Negativity turns out to be really pernicious. Whatever you send out, you get back, but multiplied!

I have read in the past a number of channelled works from various sources. Some of their message is beautiful and resonates with what I have been told, but there runs through them a strong theme of paranoia. They describe takeover bids for Earth by alien forces for their own purposes, and the mind control of humans by a small ruling group who are intent on keeping us subservient and unable to think for ourselves. These beings are also systematically poisoning our minds and our bodies. These writings have puzzled me, because they are quite unlike anything I have received, although they are all rather similar to each other. When I asked the Basidian about them, this is what they said.

A. *One of the theories on this planet is that we are being controlled by an overseeing group of alien souls. I wonder if it isn't our own innate humanity that hasn't developed far enough, rather than somebody controlling us?*
B. The latter is correct.
A. *It is not a conspiracy?*
B. It is not. That is made of men's minds.
A. *So, despite the fact that some beings from Sirius, Arcturus and the Pleiades have channelled this, the conspiracy theories have come from the minds of the people who wrote it down?*
B. Correct. What humans need to understand is that we are not warring planets.
A. *These books have beautiful things in them, but the rest are full of conspiracy theory.*
B. This is not correct.
A. *So the authors have been deluded?*
B. Correct.

A. *So why were they allowed to publish?*

B. It did need to be out for debate. Part of it we needed to be heard.

A. *Part of it resonates with things that you and Uncle Theo have told me, but the rest is horrid. The other interesting thing is that there is nothing about the Earth changes in them.*

B. This is because the souls that were being connected to did not progress further to understand about this. Communication was ceased. The complete works of this were not given by us. The increased awareness of some souls, of many souls, some have used and abused the information they had been given in order to gain recognition for self, and that is how it has become misused and misunderstood. It saddens us and yet we expected this of some humans. That is the people, not the spirits.

A. *A lot of the people would prefer it to be a conspiracy, because then it is not our fault.*

B. Correct. It means that, if the changes do not happen, it means they were correct and they have been thwarted.

A. *Did Sirius try to take over the Earth?*

B. No, it didn't. We would have no purpose. We do not wish to control anywhere.

As far as I can tell, the only thing wrong with man's mind is his unwillingness to use it. After every disaster, however caused, there is a media outcry for someone to blame. If everything is seen to be somebody else's fault, then we do not have to be responsible for anything. Almost every lesson I have learned in life has shown me that this is not true. We alone are responsible for ourselves, our actions and their consequences, our health and the course of our own lives. My laboratory technicians used to tell me that they weren't paid to think! I, who was, thought that they were mistaken then, and I am certain of it now. So many others give up their power to the boss, to corporations, to the government, the Army, the church, the list is long. This does not absolve us of our personal responsibility; it just makes it seem so. Each soul is equal to another, even if each human appears not to be.

I suggest that the conspiracy theorists are trying to avoid anything being their fault. The idea of other civilisations trying to damage us and take over our world is very far from the picture that the Basidian have been showing me. They have told me about and shown me many of the peoples who are trying to help our turbulent planet. However, if that is what you believe, that is what you will find. The Basidian are suggesting another explanation.

I have also read much about the instantaneous change of the level of vibration of this Earth so that we all achieve higher consciousness in a twinkling . This may possibly just be a difficulty with interpretation of time. The time differences between a year on Earth and a year in the spirit world are very large. One of our years is only a couple of hours from the spirits' perspective, or put another way, a month in the spirit world is roughly equivalent to 330 years on Earth. One needs to know whose time they are talking of!

The spirits have of course told me of forces who think differently and who are prepared to break the universal law of non-interference with other worlds.

A. *Is it safe for me to state that dark forces can only successfully attack negative planets or souls?*
T. Correct.
A. *So these entities that attach themselves to people can only do this if the people allow it?*
T. This is so.
A. *And the lost souls that come back, they can't take over people, but they can interfere with their lives if they are allowed to.*
T. Yes, it is driven by the person themselves, the human themselves, it is about their free will. The ones who come back, come back to complete something that they did not complete. They would come back to help the human understand something about themselves, not necessarily just the trouble they are causing. Those that cause humans the greatest grief throughout their lives are often their greatest teachers.
A. *And these are all damaged and negative souls that are getting this sort of trouble, so we are quite safe from all this if we are a being or a planet of light?*

T. Yes. It does not stop the beings from having negative patches in their lives, but they would not normally attract dark forces.

A. *As far as I can see, there are plenty of you to overcome the dark forces?*

T. Far more. When souls fear dark forces, they attract them.

A. *So it is all ourselves that do this?*

T. It is. Humans need to remember about their energy fields.

A. *I don't think humans have a very good understanding of energy fields, even the ones that probably think they do.*

T. Yes, it is so.

A. *And I can safely tell everybody that they don't need to worry about dark forces?*

T. Exactly so. They need to understand that it is there, but there is not as much dark as there is light in the whole of all the universes.

So if we are filled with light, the protective fields are too strong, just as a light-filled human cannot be poisoned by the acid pollution dropping from our atmosphere. In adverse conditions, when the protective fields are weaker, it may be possible for invasion by other beings. But it is our own actions that weaken these fields, so once again it is of our own doing. When the world of Ohnm was invaded by other beings, the Eohm were not allowed to prevent it, because it was in the plan for this world that this should happen. They undoubtedly had the power.

The cosmos that the Basidian have shown me is just gorgeous. It is full of beauty, wisdom and more love than you could imagine. In the absence of fear and doubt, the love just flows. Here is what they said:

B. "Have no fear for your lives, all is taken care of. Your future is assured, whatever the Earth may do. There is no need to be fearful about how you will live and what you will eat and how you will warm yourselves. There are plans and arrangements already made that you will be able to live comfortably on the Earth. For you are the future of this beautiful planet, and there are many helpers from many worlds working to ensure your survival and comfort. We are excited by the change that will come upon the Earth once it has undergone its turbulence. We can see the peace and harmony of the future and we are longing for it to arrive. There are so many of us here ready to help you through your turbulent times that you could not believe it.

Many worlds have gone through this stage of development, some of them many times. We understand what is needed. We will always help you. Ask us to help at any time and we will respond. We cannot interfere with your chosen life path, but we can help you with your life along it. You are our brothers and sisters on the Earth and we are connected to you, as everyone and everything in the whole universe is connected. We look forward to the time when you can feel your own connection to the very Source and so to all other beings. This time is soon. It depends on you. We love and care for you. You are not and never have been alone. Blessings to all of you."

Even when I thought this book was finished, more messages kept coming.

"We want you to say in your book..."

Here are the final ones. First, from the Basidian:

ℬ. "The energy of love, being `All of Everything,' transcends every other energy and power. There is nothing more powerful than the energy of love. With enough love, all the ills that humans have inflicted on their world can be healed and all the damage undone. When the level of consciousness of humans rises enough, they will know this to be true and then they will know how to live. **This message will not be received by everyone; not all minds are ready. But this does not mean that it is not true. 'Those that have ears to hear, let them hear.'**"

And the last one, from the Eohm:

ℰ. "We have one more passage for your book. We wish you to say that the future of Earth depends on the human understanding of love becoming more illuminated. Love, the energy, is 'All of Everything' and nothing else was necessary to create the universes and all that is in them. This being so, it is all that humans need to heal their world. Blessings to you all."

The spirits asked me to make sure the love shows through. I hope I have.

They described it as:

ℬ. "A book of truths to awaken men's minds to who they truly are."

I offer it to you as they offered it to me. With love.

"All shall be well and all shall be well.
And all manner of thing shall be well."
                                        TS Eliot

Annie Paxton
Birchwood